FAULKNER

F A U L K N E R
The Transfiguration of Biography

JUDITH BRYANT WITTENBERG

University of Nebraska Press • Lincoln and London

The publication of this book was assisted by a grant from The Andrew W. Mellon Foundation.

Library of Congress Cataloging in Publication Data

Wittenberg, Judith Bryant, 1938-
  Faulkner: the transfiguration of biography.

  Includes bibliographical references and index.
    1. Faulkner, William, 1897-1962—Criticism and interpretation. 2. Psychology and litera-
ture. 3. Fiction, Autobiographic—History and criticism.
PS3511.A86Z9858   813'.5'2   79–9230
ISBN 0–8032–4707–9

Manufactured in the United States of America

Contents

Acknowledgments

I AM HAPPY TO ACKNOWLEDGE a large indebtedness, both general and specific, to those who have written about Faulkner's life, whether in personal or formally biographical terms. Chief among them is Joseph Blotner, whose *Faulkner: A Biography* has been an indispensable resource.

I also wish to thank the following:

Jill Faulkner Summers, for her permission to quote from "Elmer," an unpublished typscript by William Faulkner;

The University Press of Virginia, for permission to quote from *Faulkner in the University*, edited by Frederick L. Gwynn and Joseph L. Blotner, Copyright 1959 by University of Virginia Press;

The Liveright Publishing Corporation, the author's estate, and Chatto & Windus, for permission to quote from *Mosquitoes,* A Novel, by William Faulkner. Liveright Publishing Corporation, New York, N.Y. Quotations used by permission of the publishers. Copyright 1927 by Boni & Liveright, Inc. Copyright renewed by William Faulkner;

Random House, whose editions of William Faulkner's works I have used throughout my study, for kindly granting permission to quote extensively from:

Sartoris, by William Faulkner, Copyright 1929 by William Faulkner; Renewed 1957 by William Faulkner;

Light in August, by William Faulkner, Copyright 1932, by William Faulkner; Copyright 1950, by Random House, Inc.;

Absalom, Absalom!, by William Faulkner, Copyright 1936, by William Faulkner; Copyright 1951, by Random House, Inc.;

The Marble Faun and A Green Bough, by William Faulkner, *The Marble Faun*, Copyright 1924, by The Four Seas Company, Renewed 1952, by William Faulkner; *A Green Bough*, Copyright 1933 and Renewed 1960, by William Faulkner;

Faulkner: A Biography, by Joseph Blotner, Copyright © 1974, by Joseph Blotner;

Selected Letters of William Faulkner, edited by Joseph Blotner, Copyright © 1977 by Joseph Blotner;

Lion in the Garden: Interviews with William Faulkner 1926–1962, edited by James B. Meriwether and Michael Millgate, Copyright © 1968 by Random House, Inc.

I am grateful to the staff of the Alderman Library at the University of Virginia for their courtesy in making available the extensive collection of Faulkner materials in their possession.

Finally, my warmest thanks to those friends and mentors whose assistance was crucial at various stages in the preparation of this study: Dorothy Scura and Arthur Blair, whose comments when we discussed the idea were quite helpful; Mark Spilka and Michael Millgate, who were kind enough to read the manuscript and who offered valuable suggestions; and Hyatt Waggoner, whose guidance and support throughout the project were invaluable in every way.

FAULKNER

List of Abbreviations

B   Blotner, Joseph. *Faulkner: A Biography*. New York: Random House, 1974.

FIU   *Faulkner in the University*. Edited by Frederick L. Gwynn and Joseph L. Blotner. Charlottesville: University Press of Virginia, 1959.

L   *Selected Letters of William Faulkner*. Edited by Joseph Blotner. New York: Random House, 1977.

LIG   *Lion in the Garden: Interviews with William Faulkner, 1926–1962*. Edited by James B. Meriwether and Michael Millgate. New York: Random House, 1968.

Wells   Wells, Dean Faulkner. "Dean Swift Faulkner: A Biographical Study." Master's thesis, University of Mississippi, 1975.

Introduction
The Man and His Art

NEAR THE END OF HIS LIFE, William Faulkner contemplated with awe the impressive array of his fiction. His literary powers seemed miraculously to have come to him from some mysterious source. "I realise for the first time what an amazing gift I had: uneducated in every formal sense, without even very literate, let alone literary, companions, yet to have made the things I made. I dont know where it came from. I dont know why God or gods or whoever it was, selected me to be the vessel. Believe me, this is not humility, false modesty: it is simply amazement" (*L*, p. 348).[1] On another occasion, Faulkner expressed this same view of himself as a "vessel," a receptacle for ideas that virtually erupted from an unknown origin. "I listen to the voices and when I put down what the voices say, it's right," he told Malcolm Cowley. "Sometimes I don't like what they say, but I don't change it."[2]

Faulkner's reference to "voices," though couched in the usual disingenuous phraseology of his public statements, raises the crucial, yet thorny, issue of psychogenesis. Those voices, the promptings of the individual's subconscious, are of great importance in the creative process. But Faulkner, like most writers and their critics, was unwilling to attempt to examine them closely. The writer's disinclination to do so is understandable, for much of his material comes in some way from the half-understood and turbulent regions of his psyche and is better used than analyzed. Critics are often equally disinclined to analyze, because the exploration of matters psychogenetic involves speculation (though often no more than that involved in assessing literary influence) and, more crucially, a distasteful intrusion into the writer's private life. Yet the marvelous mystery of the creative mind, especially that of a major artist like Faulkner, as it mines and refines the ore of the subconscious, merits such explorations. The writer's psychology ultimately has aesthetic ramifications; it is revealed in patterns of characterization or motif and in modulations of mood and theme over periods of time. Though we may never be able to account for the splendor of what his "voices" told him, an understanding of Faulkner's inner life as a living force in his art does much to illuminate major recurrent psychological patterns in the fiction. It also helps to explain his motives for becoming a writer and for altering the thematic focus and emotional mood of his work at various points in his forty-year career.

For the writer's work is the reflection, however shadowy, of his essential self. "A book is the writer's secret life, the dark twin of a man: you can't reconcile them," says a character in Faulkner's early novel *Mosquitoes*.[3] Although the statement appears to insist on the disjunction between a man's life and his art, its second part contradicts the first. Because twinship is the most intimate form of kinship, as Faulkner himself, who filled his fiction with sets of twins, well knew, if the artist's fiction is the dark twin of his life, the two can be reconciled in crucial ways—morally and philosophically as well as psychologically. Even when the art, the mirror image of the self, is reversed or deep in shadow, it still reflects its creator in some fashion.

Nonetheless, Faulkner firmly rejected the idea of biography and seemed determined to perpetuate the idea that his life and art were discontinuous. He disliked any sort of probing, even for the ostensibly unimportant data of his "outer life." In response to a 1930 request, Faulkner instructed his agent, "Dont tell the bastards anything. It cant matter to them. Tell them I was born of an alligator and a nigger slave at the Geneva peace conference two years ago" (*L*, p. 48). Some years later, his answer to Malcolm Cowley's query about information for a "profile" was more eloquent but equally adamant. He told him that "it is my ambition to be, as a private individual, abolished and voided from history, leaving it markless, no refuse save the printed books." He wanted recorded "nothing at all prior to the instant I began to write, as though Faulkner and Typewriter were concomitant, coadjutant and without past on the moment they first faced each other."[4]

Unlike many major novelists, Faulkner left no autobiographical writings, save for one or two unused prefaces and the semifictionalized essay,

"Mississippi," which he wrote in 1953. Most of his letters deal with matters financial and technical; many of the more personal letters are still unpublished and inaccessible. Because of his distaste for biography and because his fiction is in no obvious way confessional, Faulkner has generally been treated as an "objective" writer, one who writes from a "negative capability," responding in infinitely various ways to the needs of theme and subject, and whose work shows, as Wellek and Warren put it, "the obliteration of his concrete personality."[5]

Yet Faulkner's work proves to be, upon closer examination, extremely "subjective," capable of being read in its chronological totality as an autobiographical document. And, however opposed he might have been to biography per se, Faulkner revealed at times that he accepted the essential concept of art-as-biography. He admitted to Malcolm Cowley that "I am telling the same story over and over, which is myself and the world."[6] Later he told students at the University of Virginia, "That's all any [writer] ever does, he tells his own biography, talking about himself, in a thousand different terms, but himself" (*FIU*, p. 275).[7] Faulkner knew that his fiction was all about Faulkner. Like so many other writers, he "was," in one way or another, many of his characters, from Julian Lowe to Bayard Sartoris, Quentin Compson, and Lucius Priest. Their narratives told the continuing story of his life, providing, as it were, a sounding board for his official biography, and even a kind of supplement to it.

Faulkner knew that his work was often directly autobiographical. He also conceded on one occasion that it was always indirectly psycho-biographical: "The writer unconsciously writes into every line and phrase his violent despairs and rages and frustrations or his violent prophesies [*sic*] of still more violent hopes."[8] If many of his characters were based on the "outer Faulkner," their dramas and the other characters in those dramas emerged from the "inner Faulkner," from his fears and fantasies and from motives that ranged from self-castigation to wish fulfillment. Falkner's deep-rooted personal struggles were transmuted into and pervaded his fiction. Thus his inner life "became" his art in the intensest possible fashion.

Writing was for Faulkner from the first all-involving, necessary, demon-haunted. He later recalled the moment he began. "It was 1923 and I wrote a book and discovered that my doom, fate, was to keep on writing books: not for any exterior or ulterior purpose: just writing the books for the sake of writing the books."[9] He repeatedly called the artist "a creature driven by demons," adding: "He don't know why they choose him, and he's usually too busy to wonder why" (*LIG*, p. 239).[10] Faulkner described the process as working "in a kind of an insane fury" (*FIU*, p. 194). He wrote desperately, to achieve some form of catharsis, to find peace: "It worries me so much I've got to get rid of it, and so I put it on paper" (*FIU*, p. 14). Faulkner admitted that his compulsion to write developed from an urgent sense of lack. He once spoke of Shakespeare as one who "probably would have liked to be a prince and take part in tragic love, but, since he never got to, he wrote about it,"[11] and thus obliquely revealed much about the psychic foundations of his own art. "Maybe [I wrote] because I wasn't as tall or as strong as I wanted to be" (*B,* p. 1442),[12] he said wryly, suggesting how art offered him a nonphysical means of ordering and controlling the world. Writing was also for Faulkner a means of coping with traumatic emotional situations even as they occurred. "You don't commit suicide when you are disappointed in love. You write a book," says one of his characters,[13] describing a motive which seems often to have impelled the novelist to begin a new work. Throughout his life, Faulkner's past and present anxieties gave rise to some of his most effective fiction, and his personal vulnerabilities and his artistic strengths thus became intimately intertwined. As Edmund Wilson pointed out in an essay some years back, for the artist as for Philoctetes, his "wounds" and his "bow" are close allies.[14] This explanation of the creative process certainly holds true for Faulkner. His wounds were perhaps less severe than those of a predecessor like Charles Dickens, with whom he has often been compared, but his imaginative response to them, as realized in his fiction, was persistent and pervasive.

The most important resource for a writer, said someone only half-facetiously, is an unhappy childhood. Undoubtedly Faulkner's emotional reaction to his early years was far from happy, for his fiction is full of males, young and old, who are beleaguered by the past and by memories of difficult formative experiences. Faulkner's childhood was superficially stable but fraught with minor disruptions and underlying tensions that deeply disturbed the sensitive boy who experienced them. Consequently, Faulkner's later life reveals, as does his fiction, the conflict between stability and disorder. Much of that fiction also embodies his inner struggle with the troubling figures and relationships of his childhood and young manhood. These often appear in the form of reiterated motifs, such as tension between father and son, fraternal hostility, and the failure of love, and in recurrent character types, like the powerless child, the absent mother, the destructive father, and the young man who is impotent or doomed. Faulkner's wish fulfillment fantasies, terrors, and exorcistic impulses were also produced by personal situations he lived through or anticipated as an adult. His war experiences, both thwarted and actual, his unusual marital history, and the changing structure of his family all reemerged in his work, both as they occurred and as his subconscious perceptions of their nature altered.

Faulkner's demon-driven compulsion to write and his obsessive return to images from his personal past were the basis for his "inspiration." Psychoanalytically, this has been called regression in the service of art.[15] But in the process of creating a coherent work of art, "inspiration" must be accompanied by "elaboration," in which the artist's critical faculties work to solve aesthetic problems and to objectify his psychic impulses in an effective manner. By the end of his life, Faulkner showed a clear understanding of how this process operated in the genesis of his own works. He spoke of the author as having "a sort of lumber room in his subconscious that all this [his experience] goes into," and from which an element might emerge to inspire him, "an anecdote or a sentence or an expression"—or, in the case of *The Sound and the Fury,* a visual image, a little girl with muddy drawers climbing a tree. Only later does the conscious artist take control: "Then when I have got a lot of it down, the policeman has got to come in and say, 'Now look here, you've got to give this some sort of unity and coherence and emphasis.' "[16]

Faulkner's conscious artistry, the "policeman," operated in many different ways, some of them so closely related to the unconscious content that the psychological unity of matter and manner is quite striking. His rhetoric is by turns lyrical and forceful, but often oxymoronic and always engulfing.[17] At the dramatic level, he learned to render the conflicting currents of his own mental life in terms of pairs or even trios of close but contrasted and often warring characters. It was a measure of the adaptive function of his art that he was able to recognize his contradictory urges, to embody them in separate characters, and to show them either functioning comparatively in a hierarchy of morality or psychic health or conflicting overtly for dominion and even survival. These groups of paired or tripled characters occur in nearly all of the novels. They are fictional objectifications of contrary impulses in the author himself, impulses that he in some sense mastered by his very ability to perceive and portray them. Because the characters were projective fragments of Faulkner's psyche, the predominance of one type or another in a novel or series of novels tells us much about what was going on in his inner life at the time.

Many of Faulkner's most impressive experiments in form had the same psychic origins as did his paired characters. Although they were in part conscious, craftsmanlike explorations of the new frontiers of technique opened up by influential predecessors like Joyce and Conrad, such experiments were also products of his intense compulsion to tell and retell the same story, as in *The Sound and the Fury,* to circle desperately in a quest for the ever-elusive central truth, as in *Absalom, Absalom!,* or to balance a tragic, romantic vision of love with a comic and cynical repudiation of it, as in *The Wild Palms.* The tensions created by these contrapuntal or fuguelike forms and the unresolved search for meaning which they reveal may be traced back to Faulkner's own inner restlessness.

Faulkner himself came to realize what he was attempting to do in his fiction: "I discovered that my own little postage stamp of native soil was worth writing about and that I would never live long enough to exhaust it, and by sublimating the actual into apocryphal I would have complete liberty to use whatever talent I might have to its absolute top" (*LIG,* p. 255). That "native soil" of which he spoke was northern Mississippi, but it was also himself. Whatever Faulkner felt about the unimportance of his life as a life, it was, as he recognized, a vivid and ineradicable presence in his work. Faulkner the man, often unhappy and always filled with contradictory impulses, estranged from his town and family, wrote and rewrote his own story. He objectified and amplified it to create finally a mythic land, but one populated with the demons he found in his own psyche. Faulkner's *oeuvre* delineates regional geography, history, and culture, but it offers at the same time a topography of the writer's inner being. His creativity depended upon his willingness to confront the darkest promptings of his psyche, his capacity to observe and portray what he saw there, and his consummate ability to "sublimate" the actual into the "apocryphal." His art, in its psychological vitality, exhibits the complex and persistent transfiguration of his own biography.

1

Family Portraits and the Early Years

IN A PHRASE WHICH REVEALS MUCH about his notion of personal history, Faulkner said, "No man is himself, he is the sum of his past." He added: "There is no such thing really as was because the past is" (*FIU,* p. 84). Since Faulkner also envisioned his art as a special sort of biography, in which he was "telling the same story over and over, which is myself and the world,"[1] the links between the man, the past, and the fiction were at once intimate and persistent.

The past of which William Faulkner and his novels were the "sum" was a complex and weighty one, extending deep into his family history. Rarely does a figure as removed from a writer's daily life as a long-dead great-grandfather exert a powerful psychological influence over the young mind, but such is the case with William Faulkner. Faulkner's sense of the Old Colonel, William Clark Falkner (the writer added a *u* to the family name),[2] who was murdered eight years before the birth of his great-grandson and near namesake (Faulkner's parents exchanged Clark for Cuthbert) in 1897, had early psychic effects that ultimately emerged in his art. These effects were partly attributable to the ineffectuality of Falkner's own father as both a parent and a male exemplar, but they were also engendered by the glamorous legend of William Clark Falkner, with its dark substrata of violence and moral ambiguity.

The legend was a vivid presence in the household into which the boy was born, for his great-grandfather had become a semimythic personage in the region of north central Mississippi near the Tennessee border. The Old

9

Colonel was remembered as a romantic, reckless figure of heroic proportions, a dashing cavalry officer in the Civil War who later ran a railroad, wrote several books, and killed two men before being murdered by a third. His life offered a dramatic contrast to that of Faulkner's own father, Murry, which seemed pallid by comparison. Murry, moreover, was remote from, and often hostile to, his eldest son. All these things led the boy to seize upon the Old Colonel as a fantasized surrogate-parent figure, whose influence upon his great-grandson and his fiction went beyond the schoolboy's announced ambition, "I want to be a writer like my great-granddaddy." Echoes of his life and the glamorous legend which surrounded him appear numerous times in the novels, from *Sartoris* (or *Flags in the Dust*) onward. Faulkner eventually perceived, however, that the spiritual inheritance passed on by his great-grandfather had morally equivocal aspects. As a result, he also criticized his code in *The Unvanquished* and caricatured him in *Absalom, Absalom!* as Sutpen, paradigm of all that was flawed and ruthless in the nineteenth-century southern way of life.

William Clark Falkner early evinced a stubborn independence and a daring that was occasionally self-destructive. These qualities reappeared in various forms in every one of his male progeny. In addition, there are striking parallels between the Old Colonel's life and that of his great-grandson. At some points the experiences of the first William seem almost to prophesy those of the second. In 1847, for instance, he went eagerly to the Mexican War with the Second Mississippi Regiment and was deeply frustrated by the fact that he never participated in the actual fighting, later using his imaginative concept of the battle as the basis of his long poem, *The Siege of Monterey*.[3] The experience was much like that of his great-grandson, who was also thwarted in his effort to participate in a war but superseded frustration with creation in the form of his first novel, *Soldiers' Pay*. In addition, both men had a sense of irony which existed simultaneously with their desire for glorious heroics and allowed them to caricature their own missed apotheosis. William Clark received his only "war wound" of 1847 when he left his camp without permission, possibly in search of amorous dalliance, and was shot in the foot by Mexican guerrillas. He mocked his own ignominy in a stanza of his poem:

> Full well I know the feeling of lead—
> I have never fought, but freely bled.
> Mexican soil hath drank my gore
> But I disgrace, instead of glory bore.[4]

Similarly, William Cuthbert trenchantly satirized his own appetite for vainglory in the character of Julian Lowe, whose grief over his lost opportunity for heroic death Faulkner shows to be comic and ludicrous. Though numerous other parallels between the two lives can be adduced, there are differences, too. These are equally important in that they help to account for Faulkner's sense of what he was not, of where his own life was flawed, just as the similarities fostered a certain sense of destiny.

The Old Colonel was born in 1825 to a poor family which had recently migrated to Tennessee from South Carolina. He left home when he was seventeen in the ultimate act of revolt against his father, who had whipped him severely after he bloodied his brother's head with a hoe. The situation is rather extreme, with its overtones of Cain and Oedipus, but suggestive of those gestures of rebellion and removal most males find psychologically necessary in order to become "men." The younger William also revolted against his father, although in more passive fashion, and the two lived in uneasy and uncomprehending propinquity until the older man died. As the family legend goes, William Clark encountered, en route to his uncle's home in Mississippi, a young woman whom he promised to return and marry. He did so, long years later. This tale of delayed fulfillment has its counterpart in the life of William Cuthbert, who met his wife twenty-six years before he finally married her. In each case, the woman's family raised strong objections because of the low esteem in which the man was generally held.

When he was twenty, William Clark earned his first money from the pen in a manner unlikely to please the morally fastidious, for it combined violence and notoriety. He wrote up in pamphlet form the life story of an ax murderer whom he had helped capture as a member of a posse and sold it to onlookers at a good profit on the day of the execution. Falkner subsequently came to local notice as a murderer himself. In 1849 he killed Robert Hindman of Ripley after an argument concerning, ironically enough, membership in the Knights of Temperance. Hindman's enraged family and followers erected a gravestone for the dead man which read "Murdered at Ripley, Miss. by Wm. C. Falkner," and continued hostilities until Falkner had shot and killed a friend of Hindman's and narrowly averted a duel with his brother.[5] Despite such moments of turbulence, Falkner was acquiring wealth and status as a lawyer and slave-holding planter in Ripley and was also beginning to write in his spare time.

With the outbreak of the Civil War, Falkner found a more publicly acceptable sphere in which to act on his willingness to confront danger and possible death. As the colonel in charge of the Second Mississippi Infantry Regiment, he was soon commended for his bravery and daring at the Battle of Bull Run, and called by some "the Knight of the Black Plume" (B, p. 23), though others charged him with recklessness. He was a severe disciplinarian to his troops, who accused him of being a martinet and eventually deposed him from command. Back home in Ripley, Falkner began writing a series of letters to the Confederate government that were at once angry and pleading and revealed a sense of persecution. He insisted that he was being treated unfairly and asked not only for reinstatement but for promotion to general, telling President Jefferson Davis, "I was cast aside simply because I done my whole duty."[6]

Falkner was almost captured by Federal troops when they invaded Ripley, and he soon thereafter resumed active duty as the head of an irregular regiment which he had raised, the Partisan Rangers. With them he undertook an exploit for which he would long be remembered in the area, his bizarre and foolhardy attack on Sheridan's troops at Rienzi against overwhelming numbers, during which he led a thundering charge down the main street of the town.[7] The often reckless and violent deeds of this part of his life are recordered in *Sartoris* in heroic terms and given more complex treatment in *The Unvanquished,* where they are filtered through the sensibility of a young man much like Faulkner himself in his early years, who at first perceives only the bright side of the legend and only gradually apprehends its dark elements.

Family legend has it that the Old Colonel rode with General Nathan Bedford Forrest for the rest of the war and in the following decade single-handedly built up a local railroad. In actuality he left the war in 1863 for reasons of illness, in the inglorious guise of "indigestion and internal hemorrhoids," according to the surgeon's report, and he had only a brief period as president of the Ripley Railroad before it failed. He later re-entered the enterprise as vice-president and a major stockholder. Falkner nonetheless continued to be a vital force in his town of Ripley and his region of northern Mississippi. He helped found a college, worked at law and on the railroad, and, midway through his sixth decade, began to write novels which were popular, if not critical, successes. *The White Rose of Memphis,* a sentimental melodrama published in 1881, uses a masked ball as a framing device for the narrative, which contains autobiographical elements such as the averted duel. The puzzling use of an incestuous brother-sister relationship in both this novel and the one which appeared the following year, *The Little Brick Church,* would find its counterpart in his great-grandson's fiction of the next century. Incest is relatively uncommon in American fiction, and one is tempted, in both these instances, to speculate about its psychological origins. Despite this unusual thematic element,

Falkner's work bears throughout the impress of the romances of Sir Walter Scott and the comedy of Mark Twain, and the last book he published, *Rapid Ramblings in Europe,* was a humorous travelogue patterned after *Innocents Abroad.*[8]

In the 1880s, apart from his writing, the building of a pretentious and somewhat grotesque new house, and the commissioning of an enormous marble statue of himself, Falkner was deeply engrossed in his railroad. This he was expanding by means not unusual in the South during Reconstruction—the exploitation of laboring convicts, leased like animals from the state penal system, and the coercion of towns along the railroad's path into making "contributions" (B, p. 44). He had gained control of the railroad from his partner, Richard Thurmond, after a feud which they supposedly resolved by drawing lots to see who would buy out the other. The feud was apparently not settled to Thurmond's satisfaction, and in November 1889, on the very day the increasingly prosperous Falkner was elected to a seat in the state legislature, Thurmond shot him in the mouth. Falkner had known of the threat to his life, but feeling he had already shed enough blood, he chose to go out on the street unarmed, like John Sartoris of *The Unvanquished.* The injury killed Falkner within twenty-four hours. He was sixty-four, the exact age at which his great-grandson would die in 1962, and while the Old Colonel's death was the almost inevitable culmination of a lifetime of violent encounters with other men, his namesake's would be the ultimate result of years of scarcely less violent encounters with horses and alcohol.

Both men leave their observers perplexed. They were publicly colorful and privately complex, combining apparent egotism and arrogance with vitality and generosity, ambition with an ironic sense of its vanity, a felt sense of accomplishment with an unsatisfied restlessness that persisted to the end. Faulkner was haunted by his great-grandfather, fascinated by both the man and his deeds, and eventually became very much like him in certain essential ways, unconsciously patterning his life after the Old Colonel's. Yet he forever retained an ambivalence toward his ancestor. Near the end of his life, Faulkner revealed in an interview his immense admiration for that man who "rode through the country like a living force," but also his scorn for his arrogance and ambition[9]—a contradictory vision which, as already suggested, surfaces in his own fiction in a number of ways, with the Colonel John Sartoris of *Sartoris* as its most positive embodiment and Thomas Sutpen as its most negative.

The Old Colonel's killer was acquitted of murder charges, and his oldest son in some sense repudiated the code of violence by which his father had lived and decided not to seek revenge (B, p. 51). His decision, unlike that of Bayard Sartoris in *The Unvanquished,* may not have been entirely a matter of conscience, however. John Wesley Thompson Falkner, the author's grandfather, was born in 1848 to his father's first wife, who died soon thereafter. He was given to an uncle to raise, and his father subsequently remarried and had a second family, a situation inevitably troubling to a small child and likely to cause some hostility toward the parent who "abandoned" him. Throughout his life, John referred to his father as "Kunnel Falkner,"[10] which revealed respect, perhaps, but also a sense of distance.

The Young Colonel, as he came to be known around Oxford (to which he moved from Ripley in 1885), was physically a commanding figure, tall and dignified in his linen suits and Panama hats. His professional accomplishments were also impressive. He achieved success at various times as a criminal lawyer, railroad president, state senator, and banker. He used some of his substantial income from these ventures to build an imposing house known as "The Big Place," where he lived surrounded by children and, eventually, grandchildren. In some areas of his private life, however, the Young Colonel showed signs of underlying disturbance. For a period he was, one grandson said, "the loneliest man I've ever known," and also an extremely heavy drinker whose near-legendary bouts with alcohol sent him frequently off to the Keeley Institute for the "gold cure."[11] Moreover, the impulse to derring-do which the Young Colonel inherited from his father never found the proper arena for its expression. The daring that led the Old Colonel to an almost suicidal charge against a powerful enemy took in his son such forms as a drunken automobile ride around the town square that culminated in the throwing of a brick through the window of the bank of which he was president. Asked later about his motives, he announced alliteratively, if not very illuminatingly, "It was my Buick, my brick, and my bank."[12]

Like his father, John Wesley Thompson married twice, but in at least one respect he made unfortunate choices. His first wife, Faulkner's grandmother, was an ardent member of the WCTU who despised alcohol and spent a good deal of their married life packing her husband off to Memphis for the "cure" (B, pp. 52, 56). William Faulkner later vividly recalled those departures: "I recollect my grandfather taking his last drink of bourbon and cussin' 'cause grandmother was makin' him go off to take the waters" (*LIG,* p. 65). John's second wife was similarly negative about her husband's drinking and resorted to the brutal, though effective, strategy of putting ipecac in his whiskey (B, p. 153). This profound disparity in hus-band-and-wife attitudes toward alcohol repeated itself in the following gen-eration, when John's son, Faulkner's father, also an alcoholic, also mar-ried a woman who despised liquor. The situation in the Falkner family had some of its roots in southern culture of the period, for, as Faulkner's brother explained, "Liquor was an accepted way of life as far as many of the menfolk were concerned. Few women would touch it on pain of certain and universal condemnation by the community."[13] Whatever its origins, the disparity found an equally catastrophic "resolution" in the succeeding generation, when the heavy-drinking William took as wife a woman who herself became an alcoholic.

Alcoholism, equally with a propensity for self-destructive acts, was a chronic "disease" that plagued the Falkner male line. It led to incidents that created colorful and entertaining family lore, but also had graver con-sequences in the production of divided and emotionally chaotic house-holds. Alcoholism, of course, is a pervasive problem which researchers are still attempting to explain, but it is known to occur with particular fre-quency in the offspring of alcoholics and especially in cases where just one parent has been an alcoholic and the attitude in the home toward liquor is sharply divided.[14] Not surprisingly, William Faulkner suffered from the ailment as an adult, having been introduced to alcohol while still a young boy, when his paternal grandfather let the child drink the "heeltaps," or dregs, of his toddies when they were together (B, p. 125).

John Wesley Thompson Falkner was a less potent figure in the imagina-tion of his fiction-writing grandson than his father, the Old Colonel, and appeared only occasionally in the novels (as Old Bayard in *Sartoris* and as Boss Priest in *The Reivers*). Nonetheless, he had a strong influence during William's developing years, both directly, as when he taught the boy to drink, and indirectly, in the recurrence of his difficulties with his son Murry in the struggles between Murry and his own oldest son, William. Murry, born in 1870, grew to be a tall, strong-jawed, and rather handsome man, but remained very much dominated by his father. Having forced Murry to go to college, for which he had neither desire nor aptitude, the Young Colonel next "allowed" him to take the railroad job which had been his life's ambition, only, in effect, to sell the railroad out from under him. Murry made one inept and futile effort to buy the railroad himself, and then retreated into the role he would play for the rest of his life—that of the ineffectual man whose every move is controlled by his father and who can express his opposition only by failing at most of the jobs his father finds for him. William's rebellion against his father took a similarly passive form for several years, until he discovered his vocation as a writer and until fate, in the form of his father's death, ended his need for denial.

Murry's early years were marked by emotional turbulence. His strong-willed and heavy-drinking father was often at odds with his equally strong-willed mother, and the resulting domestic chaos undoubtedly contributed to his volatility and withdrawal. He became taciturn, exhibited a limited capacity to form warm human relationships, and tended to lose himself in hopeless romantic dreams. As one of his sons wrote, in a statement which spoke bitterly, if obliquely, about Murry's failings as a parent as well as about his thwarted hopes, "The only things Dad ever loved were [the] railroad and horses and dogs and the Ole Miss football and baseball teams."[15] Murry was an enthusiastic horseman and an avid reader of pulp Westerns, and long after the responsibility of a wife and rapidly growing family had effectively trapped him in Mississippi, he clung to a desire to go out West, start a ranch, and become a cowboy. It was a project to which his wife, not surprisingly, was fiercely opposed. According to one source, he "never forgave her" (B, p. 68).

Murry's passion for railroading was more realistically founded and more capable of fulfillment. There, too, he was thwarted, partly by his father's heedlessness, but also by his own temper. When the Young Colonel, ignoring the painfully obvious desire of his son to keep the railroad in family hands and to continue working on it, decided to sell the enterprise, Murry made one desperate attempt to salvage his future. He rushed into the Bank of Corinth and asked the president to lend him $100,000 to buy a railroad. The man laughed and the easily angered Murry turned on his heel and stalked out of the bank without another word. Later the president said that if he had known Murry was serious, he would gladly have loaned him the money, but by then it was too late (Wells, p. 1).[16] Murry never recovered from his yearning for the railroad, and one of his sons said, much later, "I can always remember how he used to listen when a train would pass and when it would blow its whistle."[17]

Murry's temper got him in trouble on an earlier occasion, when it led to a slightly more ludicrous version of his grandfather's homicidal encounters. Affected, perhaps, like the convict in "Old Man" by his reading of shoddy romantic fiction, and like Quentin Compson of *The Sound and the Fury* by an abstract idea of preserving a woman's "good name," Murry one day in 1891 volunteered himself as the chivalric protector of the reputation of a young woman about whom a local wag was making remarks.

Challenged to a fistfight, Murry's adversary ungallantly shot the would-be knight in the mouth, a wound uncannily similar to that sustained by his grandfather two years before. Murry's plight was serious, for the bullet lodged in his throat and the doctors despaired of saving his life. In a solution that was efficacious if not splendidly "romantic," his pragmatic mother administered a cathartic and the life-threatening bullet was quickly expelled (B, p. 54). Murry's father next decided to avenge his son's honor but succeeded only in misfiring his pistol six times and getting himself shot in the hand. With that incident and Murry's recovery the abortive heroics drew to a close.

One romantically impulsive gesture Murry carried off successfully, his 1896 elopement with Maud Butler. Although the union produced William Faulkner, Murry's personal triumph quickly proved a Pyrrhic one, for the marriage was fraught with difficulties. Even on her deathbed long years later, at a time when sentimental reminiscence might have been expected, Maud Butler Falkner looked back upon her marriage with a jaundiced eye, expressing horror at the prospect of being reunited with Murry for eternity and a willingness to do anything in order to attain eternal separation. She and William were talking about "heaven," and she asked, "Will I have to see your father there?" He answered no, and she said, "That's good. I never did like him" (B, p. 1762). Her comment reveals not only her marital disillusion, but also her peppery outspokenness, which was certainly an expression of her independent turn of mind but may also have had a defensive element, first developed by the family upheavals that occurred in her late adolescence.

Maud Butler's father, as the sheriff of Lafayette County, may have been effective in maintaining law and order around Oxford, but he had problems keeping peace at home. He was apparently unable to manage his money with any efficiency, and this created conflict with his wife, Lelia, a woman known for her stern Baptist piety and her capacity for being "difficult." When Maud was seventeen, her father abruptly abandoned his family, leaving them penniless. Butler reportedly went off with a beautiful octoroon (B, p. 57), much like the woman whom Charles Bon "morganatically" marries in Absalom, Absalom!. Thus began several rootless years for the mother and daughter (Maud's brother had already left home), as they moved from relative to relative while Maud worked as a secretary to support them. Lelia had artistic talent and at one point she was offered a scholarship to study sculpture in Rome. But with well-meant, if perhaps misguided, parental devotion, she gave up all such serious opportunity in order to care for her daughter—somewhat like the mother of Faulkner's

Miss Zilphia Gant—and found creative outlets during her remaining years only in desultory painting and such ephemeral exercises as molding butter into tiny ears of corn (Wells, p. 4).

Lelia, who came to be known to her grandchildren as "Damuddy" (the name by which the Compson children refer to their grandmother in *The Sound and the Fury*), combined her artistic gifts with imperiousness of manner. Both qualities were passed on to her daughter, in a cycle of repetition like that which marked the Falkner males. Thus Lelia was distraught when she discovered that Maud had married into "that family," because she knew that Murry was a heavy drinker, like his father before him, and for five years she refused to acknowledge the marriage, addressing letters to "Miss Maud Butler, care of Mr. Murry Falkner." It was an unpleasant gesture of repudiation which deeply troubled Murry and continued despite his countless pleas to Maud to "get your mother to stop this" (Wells, p. 5). It was an uncomfortable experience for both of them, bringing an unwelcome additional tension to the new and struggling marriage. Yet Maud in turn would do virtually the same thing, first to her brother, whom she "wrote off" when he married a woman of whom she did not approve, and subsequently to her own children, when she showed great reluctance to acknowledge her sons' wives (Wells, p. 4).

Although Maud was a tiny woman who never reached five feet in height, she was sufficiently large in impact, with a vivid and occasionally fierce personality which led one of her grandchildren to describe her as "indomitable" and as "having been born with characteristics enough like the Old Colonel's to have been his daughter" (Wells, p. 3). It may have been this quality which made her attractive to the relatively colorless Murry Falkner, who met her through his sister, of whom she was a close friend and occasional house guest. The couple courted for a time and then, during a ride through the countryside one day, impulsively went off and got married, thus starting a pattern of informal quasi elopement that would be repeated by every one of their four sons. They settled in New Albany, a small town not far from Oxford, where Murry was then working as a passenger agent for his father's railroad.

It was a far from ideal combination, and one fraught with the potential for family tensions. Murry was generally withdrawn, but given to outbursts of irrational anger. He was also characterized by a rigidity that demanded, for example, that the noon meal be on the table precisely at twelve o'clock, else he would do an actual about-face and leave the house (Wells, p. 38). Maud was more outgoing, but equally self-contained: a sign in her kitchen, "Don't Complain—Don't Explain," summed up her philosophy. She despised alcohol and criticized those who used it, including her heavy-drinking husband. She had, like her mother, a degree of innate artistic talent and late in life became an earnest painter in the primitive style. She also read a fair amount of serious literature, including the novels of Joseph Conrad, to which she introduced her oldest son, while Murry cared only for westerns, like those by Zane Grey.

The two were thus intellectually as well as temperamentally incompatible and would convey deeply conflicting attitudes to their children. As William published his novels, his mother gradually became a proud champion of her son's talent, while Murry refused to read the work, calling it "trash" and counselling his acquaintances to do likewise (Wells, p. 122). Yet Murry cared deeply for the outdoors, for dogs and horses and riding and hunting, and much of this fervor was communicated to his oldest son. William in turn embodied it in some of his finest writing, from "The Bear" to the horse-race sequences in *A Fable* and *The Reivers*—but not, significantly, until after his father had died. Perhaps because of the sharp division between his artistic mother and his sporting father, William had difficulty in publicly integrating his artist and sportsman "selves," tending to keep the two aspects of his life entirely separate and to play one role or the other at any given moment.

The inauspicious union of Murry Falkner and Maud Butler, likely to provide a troubling environment for any sensitive child, brought forth its first son on September 25, 1897. When it came time to name him, Murry deferred to his father's opinion, as he did in nearly every other area of his life, and allowed the boy to be called after the Old Colonel, changing the middle name from Clark to Cuthbert because the Colonel himself had disliked the former (B, p. 62). William, called Billy by intimates throughout his life, was a rather frail baby who suffered from infant colic, which kept him awake during the night for much of his first year, just as insomnia would in his adult years. He early showed physical qualities that identified him closely with his mother and barely at all with his strong-jawed and burly father. From Maud he inherited hooded, brownish black eyes and a small mouth and chin, and like her he would be unusually small as an adult, reaching an eventual height of about five feet, five inches. Since his father and his society valued strength and physical prowess, which were often equated with height, the petiteness was far more troubling to William than it had been to his mother. His size created for Faulkner psychic problems that emerged in his fiction in various ways, most strikingly in his early tendency to make his heroes tall, as if size were an index of masculinity, and in his depiction of threatening and lascivious young women—like

Cecily Saunders—as tall and long-legged. It also led to an actual defeat, when his desperate desire to join the American Army Air Force in the First World War went unfulfilled because he was too short.

The family moved from New Albany to Ripley in 1898, and in 1899, when William was two, his parents' next child, a boy, was born. The second son was always called Jack but was named Murry, after his father. Indeed, he came to look a great deal like his father, tall and heavy-jawed and somewhat saturnine. William became sick after the birth of this baby, and again after the birth of John in 1901, when he was seriously ill with scarlet fever. It is questionable whether one can go very far in diagnosing these illnesses as regressive responses to the threatening appearance of additional claimants on the limited parental affection, but the pattern is interesting. Faulkner did later prove to have a strongly regressive streak— he would drink until he had to be put to bed and nursed like a small sick child, requiring constant attention and having to be spoon-fed. Moreover, the brothers did prove to be very real emotional threats to the sensitive William. Jack soon received particular attention from his maternal grandmother, who cooked him special foods, and before very long he would surpass his older brother in height; John was a very handsome child, in contrast with the unprepossessing William, and would soon become easygoing and talkative, unlike the silent older child, and a fine athlete whose performances far exceeded William's. These early disparities between Faulkner and his brothers, along with his father's singular hostility toward his oldest son, caused the latter some anxieties, and his fiction strikingly reveals a need to compete with, to assimilate, and, in his fantasy world, to annihilate these troubling competitors. Several of Faulkner's most powerful works contain intense, rivalrous, and destructive sibling relationships, characteristically ending in the death or madness of one of the males.

When William was five, he witnessed several changes in his family's life, nearly all of which had an impact on him. It is perhaps not accidental that in "Elmer", an early unpublished work that seems intensely autobiographical in some respects, the most disturbing scene occurs when Elmer is just five years old: the family house burns down, and the vulnerable and frightened child, who is symbolically naked, watches in terror the destruction of his few treasures and the "disintegration" of that which he believes "stable and impervious to sudden change."[18] That year of 1902, at his father's behest and after his futile attempt to buy the railroad, Murry moved his family from Ripley to Oxford into his father's house in order to run the livery stable his father had procured for him. The unwelcome uprooting and the frustration at seeing his dreams of railroading and ranching forever thwarted plunged Murry into bouts of severe drunkenness, storms of rage, and even occasional violence. Not long after he arrived in Oxford, Murry got into a fistfight with a local constable and knocked his opponent through the plate glass window of a grocery store (B, p. 80). Maud had by now learned to greet these domestic outbursts with stoic silence and to cultivate a certain detachment. Unfortunately that detachment extended even toward her children, and although Faulkner ostensibly maintained a good relationship with his mother throughout his life, the portraits of mothers in his fiction reveal his sense that she had failed him in her way almost as badly as had his father.

That sense may have had its origins in the disrupive year of 1902, which also saw alterations in the composition of the Falkner household. Lelia Butler overcame her disdain for her son-in-law when she needed different living quarters and moved in with Murry's family in Oxford. Maud was devoted to her mother, and the two formed an alliance which excluded Murry. Ultimately they even shared a bedroom, while Murry slept alone (Wells, p. 6). Lelia's piety, coupled with her favoritism toward Jack, could well have given William his awareness that even a deeply religious person may be capable of moral injustices. At the same time, her interest in art, however amateur, may have had some more positive influence, and it is certainly true that William's early artistic efforts seem to have been as often visual as verbal. Also in 1902, Caroline Barr, the black nurse who was to be a member of the household for almost forty years and to whom *Go Down, Moses* is dedicated, joined the family. A tiny but willful woman, she quickly assumed authority and became a "second mother" to the Falkner children. She captivated William in particular with her endless storytelling. "Mammy Callie," as she was called, gave the children welcome additional affection, but she also had a disturbing tendency to disappear unannounced with a new man periodically and to be gone until she summoned someone to fetch her (B, p. 100), thus introducing an unstable element into her loving devotion. Her arrival in the family, like everything else that happened in 1902, had ambiguous effects on the children, especially William, who early revealed himself to be the most vulnerable and inward of the boys.

It would be both simplistic and incorrect, however, to depict those early years as an endless emotional maelstrom for William Faulkner. His nascent artistic genius was nurtured by many positive elements in his small world, and in certain respects Oxford and the Falkner household provided a stimulating environment for his particular artistic sensibility. There were his mother's books by Conrad, Shakespeare, Dickens, and Twain and his father's western romances to read; there were the folk tales told by Mammy Callie and the war stories told by the old Civil War Partisan Rangers at reunions sponsored by Faulkner's grandfather—narratives that were not only entertaining at the time but formed an important resource on which he would later draw. There were big yards and the freedom to invent the endless projects and mischief which develop a child's imaginative powers. William's ingenious goading of his brothers into painting a henhouse and some of its hapless denizens red or helping him to build a steam engine, or even, *mirabile dictu,* an almost full-sized airplane, showed a resourceful and creative mind at work. A friend remembered that William was always "the leader in these little projects. He had his grandmother's artistic talents for making things, and his imagination was obvious even then."[19] The boy also had sports like baseball and football to play, the big woods near Oxford in which to hike or hunt, and the family cabin on a nearby lake as a place for fishing—all activities which William pursued with periodic enthusiasm.

He occasionally turned to playmates outside his immediate family. Among the most important of these were Sallie Murry Wilkins and Estelle Oldham. Commentators have often been puzzled by the recurring presence of sisters and twins in the fictional creations of this writer who had neither, and it is important to realize that while such figures do play a symbolic role in the fiction and are related to William's unconscious psychic struggles with his mother and brothers, they also have an origin in biographical fact. His cousin Sallie Murry, the daughter of Murry's sister, was the closest to a biological "sister" William Faulkner had. Born in 1899, the same year as Jack, she was an energetic tomboy who followed the three older Falkner boys happily on many of their communal escapades and often spent time playing with William alone. Both of his brothers later described the affectionate sisterly relationship they enjoyed with her—Jack called her a "sister" and John said that "the four of us were together like we were one family."[20]—and the boys' father was equally fond of her, once jokingly offering her mother "any two of my boys for your girl" (B, p. 79).

If Sallie was William's "sister," Estelle Oldham was for a time his "twin"; she later became his wife, and his responses to her were, to say the least, complex. The Oldhams moved to a home in Oxford near the Falkners' in 1903, when William was six. Estelle was small like William but had other qualities which made her seem different and thus somehow alluring. Estelle's family stood out in the small town, for her father was anomalously Republican in an overwhelmingly Democratic region and earned what was regarded as a princely income. Estelle herself was a year older than William and quite ladylike, offering, with her demureness and her frills and bows, a marked contrast to the boyish Sallie. William was drawn to Estelle and began to be more like her than like his boisterous brothers; he gradually became fastidious, neat in appearance and attentive to his clothes. He also started to play a great deal indoors with Estelle, making up quiet games and, as he grew older, reading and listening to Estelle play the piano. He one day began to write for her, little stories and sketches and bits of poetry.[21] As the years went on, William spent increasing amounts of time at the Oldhams' house, although the precise moment when the relationship changed from that of fraternal childhood playmates to that of romantic "sweethearts" is difficult to pinpoint. In some ways, indeed, the transition was never fully accomplished, and the persistence of the incest motif in William's later fiction may have much to do with his having ultimately married his "twin sister."

Though there was much that was pleasant about William's first five years in Oxford, the family tensions never abated, and when he was ten, several climactic events occurred from which, psychologically, he never fully recovered. 1907 was a psychically pivotal year for William Faulkner, and it is suggestive that the second crucial period with which he deals in the autobiographical "Elmer" occurs when Elmer is eleven and beginning to feel rootless as the family moves from house to house, just as the Falkners were starting to do when William was ten. Elmer's mother is restless and querulous, marked by her "bright fretful energy," and his father is "bland" and ineffective as a parent, for "about all Elmer's father had ever given his children was lightish hair."[22] William, too, was beginning to feel unfairly treated by his parents. His mother always punished William more harshly than the other children for any misdemeanor, often forcing him to sit alone in the living room for an hour or more without speaking.[23] His father, too, was more severe in his chastisement of his oldest son than of the younger ones (Wells, p. 24). He also showed a mildly cruel streak in his treatment of William, calling him "Snake-Lips" (B, p. 187) and allowing the boy to believe he would learn how to read on his first day of school, then laughing uproariously and teasing him in front of the entire family when he could not read aloud from the newspaper that evening.[24] Neither occurrence was necessarily traumatic for William, but both are symptomatic of Murry's unawareness of, or indifference to, his son's sensitivity.

Tensions existed between William and his parents, and they became exacerbated by the events of 1907. The trauma of "Elmer" 's eleven-year-old protagonist focuses on a single event, the boy's loss of his beloved sister, who disappears mysteriously from home one night. For William Faulkner, as he completed his first decade, the losses were multiple, manifested both in actual deaths and in symbolic betrayal.

The deaths were those of both his grandmothers. Near the end of 1906, Granny, his father's mother, became terminally ill with stomach cancer and died just before Christmas. Her death and the family's grief cast a numbing pall over the holiday season. Soon thereafter, Damuddy, his mother's mother, who lived with the Falkners, showed symptoms of inoperable uterine cancer. Her decline was a grim and lengthy one, and she suffered terribly before dying in June of 1907. Faulkner memorialized her funeral and its impact on a group of bewildered children in *The Sound and the Fury*, and the event itself must have caused emotional upheaval in the Falkner boys. They watched her die painfully under their very roof and had then to face the dislocation of being sent from home while the house was fumigated to expunge any traces of her illness. "Death was our constant familiar," says the young Lucius Priest in *The Reivers*, and there is little question that Faulkner was harking back to childhood memories which had persisted to the end of his life.

Another event that year had more serious consequences for the sensitive and introspective child. His mother had been constantly attentive to the dying Lelia during the first half of the year, and her overwhelming grief at her mother's death preoccupied her during the ensuing two months. Then in August she gave birth to her fourth son, Dean Swift, upon whom she bestowed her dead mother's middle names. William had greeted the arrival of the previous two babies by falling ill, and although on this occasion he seems to have avoided sickness, he nonetheless responded to the event as an act of betrayal. The death of her own parent had made Maud all too aware of the fragility of life and accentuated her desire to nurture this new baby carefully. Moreover, Dean suffered from a severe case of cradle cap, and both Maud and Mammy Callie were constantly busy over a period of several months preparing unguents and special silk caps for the baby, with the result that the older children were left to their own devices, to wander through the town or to be sent off to their grandfather's.

Though this was a time when William needed maternal attention and reassurance to cope with his grandmothers' deaths, his brother's birth, and the approach of adolescence, he was in effect emotionally deserted by both his mother and his nurse. His yearning for, and sense of betrayal by, these two maternal figures were amplified by this event and emerge in both his later life and his fiction in terms of regressive behavior and problematic attitudes toward women. Psychoanalysts have commented extensively on the way in which a boy's experience of such maternal "treachery" at a vulnerable age results paradoxically in his feeling even stronger ties to his mother. He tends thereafter to divide women categorically into madonnas or prostitutes and, affectively, to separate tenderness from sexuality; he also acquires a certain fear of women which may eventually impair his potency. Faulkner's work clearly indicates that he had been deeply affected in just this way, for his female characters tend to be either decent and virginal or sullied and sexual, while his male protagonists are occasionally impotent and always feel betrayed by women. Faulkner's secret desire to annihilate the individual who had usurped his mother's affection also surfaced overtly in at least two novels in which a Dean-figure is destroyed.

The birth of Dean also magnified William's feelings of estrangement from his father, for Murry, who had long been hostile to his oldest son, greeted the baby with joyous acceptance. "He's the best birthday present I ever had," said Murry of the new child, who arrived two days before his own birthday (Wells, p. 7). From the outset he was loving and indulgent toward the boy, readily accepting from Dean the sort of behavior which he would not tolerate from William. This sort of parental favoritism inevitably involves a form of moral injustice which is deeply felt, if not understood, by a child, and there was an especially glaring disparity in Murry Falkner's attitudes toward his oldest and youngest sons. Dean thrived under the indulgent attention of his parents and became a happy and exuberant child who charmed his mother and pleased his father by excelling at sports and the outdoor pastimes that Murry loved. Meanwhile William, though kind and tolerant toward his baby brother, managing to repress his darker responses, became increasingly solitary and withdrawn. William's future attentiveness to all children and his sympathetic fictional portrayal of them revealed an empathy with youngsters and a desire to protect them from the world which may have derived from his own sense of having been insufficiently nurtured and all too quickly thrust into that world.

Within two years of Dean's birth, William reacted to his sense of having been betrayed by his parents by punishing the betrayers, by figuratively rejecting them and their values. His mother prized excellence at school-work and carefully set aside a study hour at home each evening for her boys, but William, who was obviously intelligent and had made the honor roll nearly every period at school since he started, now lost interest in academic subjects and began quite regularly to play truant from school (B, p. 122). Soon after rebelling against his mother, William struck out at his father, both as parent and as symbolic representative of the cultural mores, by refusing to "work" in any conventional sense. He started to dodge his chores in the livery stable and ever thereafter evinced a total lack of interest in the workaday world in which his father doggedly, if futilely, toiled. By the time he became a teenager, William would sit in a chair in the town square for hours, staring into space and provoking a peer to call him "almost inert, the laziest boy I ever saw" (B, p. 154). This echoed the judgment of his father, who eventually called his son "nuts" and completely disavowed his art (Wells, pp. 47–48). Although William continued to live under his father's roof until he was thirty-two and married, the two had little communication or mutual sympathy. Murry's occasional gestures of conciliation were feeble and doomed: once, when his son was nearing adulthood, he remarked, "I understand you smoke now"; giving him a cigar, he added, "Try a good smoke," whereupon William abruptly broke the cigar in two and stuffed half of it into his pipe (B, pp. 178–79)—an act of repudiation that succinctly expressed William's contemptuous judgment of his father's lifelong inadequacy as a parent.

When he was entering his teens and in need of adult male companionship, William turned for a period to his grandfather Falkner, spending time with the older man and even going so far as to imitate his dress and mannerisms (B, p. 125). In 1909 his grandfather bought a car, the first in town, and this glamorous vehicle, along with the drama and uncertainty of its propulsion, amused and engrossed the boy, giving him the material he would use fifty years later in his comic novel *The Reivers*. The alliance could have been destructive—as when John Wesley Thompson offered the boy the remainder of his toddies and thus encouraged his inherited tendency to alcoholism—but it soon petered out when the older man made a disastrous second marriage that gave him little peace until he persuaded his new wife to move away to California. When William was well into his teens, his grandfather lost the bank he had founded—a defeat which the grandson later avenged by turning the victor into the villainous Flem Snopes—and spent his few remaining years in solitude and silence.

Unable to find sustaining emotional relationships within his family or among his peers, who now for the most part found him "weird" or "queer," and with Estelle away at school in Virginia, William took increasing refuge in writing and drawing, which he had begun at an early age (B, p. 160). By the time he was sixteen, he had left school entirely and was spending much of his time writing, almost obsessively. His "demons," as Faulkner was later to refer to his compulsion to write, were already upon him, but he still lacked tutelage and some sort of satisfying relationship with an older male who could serve as a role model.

Both of these he found in Phil Stone: their meeting in 1914 at once filled an emotional void in his life and provided him with a mentor. Stone was four years older than Faulkner and had just received a B.A., his second, from Yale. Worldly and interested in literature, enthusiastic and voluble, Stone offered a striking contrast to Faulkner's father and a fitting complement to Faulkner himself. The latter, fascinated by this responsive and literate new acquaintance, produced some of his poems and received from Stone's immediate and excitedly positive response some badly needed encouragement. As Stone later recalled, "Anyone could have seen that he had a real talent. It was perfectly obvious" (B, p. 162).

Stone provided Faulkner not only with a necessary audience, but also with piles of books and endless words of advice. Before many years had passed, the friendship would become a burdensome one to Faulkner, as Stone's proprietary air toward his protégé eventually became oppressive and he continued to take credit for monitoring work long after the writer had stopped showing it to him, but for a crucial period the two were almost constantly together. Stone was a valuable influence in those early years, and Faulkner would be conscientiously grateful to him until the end of his life. He dedicated the Snopes trilogy to Stone, even though the older man's public comments about him had become denigratory, and revealed his resentment only in his somewhat uncomplimentary portrayal of Stone as Gavin Stevens. For more than three years, Stone supplied Faulkner with books, especially recent literary works, discussed his reading with him, and held forth not only on literature, but on topics like the Civil War and the rules of grammar. Stone also took Faulkner to meet the poet and dramatist Stark Young, who in turn introduced Faulkner to the future Mrs. Sherwood Anderson.

Apart from his friendship with Phil Stone, Faulkner was generally estranged from his family and friends and well on his way to becoming a town oddity. After leaving school, he worked for a while at his grandfather's bank as a bookkeeper—a job whose merit, apparently, lay in the access it afforded to a supply of whiskey of better quality than the "corn" he had hitherto been drinking: "Quit school after five years in seventh grade. Got job in grandfather's bank and learned medicinal value of his liquor. Grandfather thought the janitor did it. Hard on janitor," joked Faulkner later (LIG, p. 7). He is reported to have spent much of his free time on alcoholic benders with the town drunk, and nearly all of his salary on expensive clothes—fine shoes, a dress suit, and tight-fitting pegged pants. The combination of his drinking sprees and his often elegant appearance soon led him to be known around Oxford as "Count No

'Count,'' a sobriquet that followed him down the years until he became famous and rich, and hence less an object of scorn.

The "Count" was just one of a series of defensive masks which the vulnerable Faulkner adopted during his lifetime, either to make himself seem more glamorous or to protect himself from the judgments of his world. Yeats referred to the "mask" as the expression of the complementary antiself, and R. D. Laing has designated the "mask" as a necessary defensive tactic in a hostile and distorted world where the "real" self is thwarted.[25] These seem to be the functions of the various personas which Faulkner used over the years. He presented himself, through talk and costume, as an injured war hero or an English gentleman when he wished to win sympathy or acceptance. When he was feeling alienated and defiant, he became a barefoot Bohemian or an unshaven back-country farmer in dirty clothes. Growing up in a family and small town where he, like so many of his protagonists, could not find a niche, he turned naturally to various masks or personas as measures of self-protection, although, ironically, they often served only to dramatize and augment his alienation from his environment.

All through his teens and into his early twenties, Faulkner was frustrated and estranged from his milieu. These feelings were intensified by his experiences of 1918. That was another difficult year, the most traumatic of his young adulthood, just as 1907 had been a bitter landmark of his preadolescent period. Once again William was betrayed or defeated by both the male and female elements in his world: he was thwarted in his attempts to become a fighter pilot, and Estelle Oldham, the one woman in whom he had shown romantic interest, married someone else. Both were emotional experiences whose repercussions echoed throughout the fiction and poetry he wrote for the entire next decade.

At this stage of his life, Faulkner was physically quite unprepossessing. He was also troubled by what he described in an autobiographical story as a "feeling of defiant inferiority" toward women.[26] Though the oldest of the brothers, he was now the smallest; his face was narrow and immature, and until he was almost thirty, he looked like an adolescent. Problems of appearance and stature can often be overcome, but in Faulkner's case they were compounded by the difficult relationship he had had with his parents during the period of adolescence, when a boy needs healthy interchanges with both father and mother: the rigid and aloof Murry was inadequate as a male parent with whom either to identify or to compete in the classic Oedipal confrontation, and the perceived "betrayal" by his mother when he was ten left Faulkner alternating between yearning and anger. It is hardly surprising that Faulkner found difficulty in developing a mature attitude toward women or toward himself as a man. During his late teens he apparently paid almost no attention to girls his age,[27] and it was at about this time that he seems to have begun to visit prostitutes in Memphis (Wells, pp. 40–41).

Estelle Oldham was the one female companion he saw regularly, but even she began to be cut off from him by her slightly greater age and by the social gap between them, which widened as time passed. The vivacious and pretty Estelle went off to college when Faulkner was still floundering in the tenth grade. She became much like the conventional image of the southern belle, outgoing and popular, while he drew increasingly into himself. As Estelle reached marriageable age, her parents began their partisanship of the suit of a gregarious and successful young lawyer, Cornell Franklin. Faulkner, though in some ways a second son to the Oldhams, was unacceptable as a son-in-law, for he had no prospects and they, like their society, saw marriage as an institution that required stable economic underpinnings.

When Cornell Franklin sent Estelle a diamond engagement ring and talk of wedding dates began, she offered to run away with William. Unlike the Falkner men before him, who had willingly eloped, William chose to observe protocol and suggested that they discuss it with their parents. He was being uncharacteristically observant of convention, probably because he was reluctant to tie himself down in marriage, possibly because he had some fears about his adequacy as a husband. Predictably, both fathers were enraged by the idea; Murry cited William's youth and Mr. Oldham his joblessness. The situation had all the potential for a Pyramus-and-Thisbe-like dramatic escape, but William continued to respond passively, proffering no alternatives and simply letting the parents have their way. His later fiction would indict this sort of passivity, but at the time he clearly had neither the will nor the capacity to change things.

The date for the wedding of Estelle and Cornell Franklin was set for April, 1918. Even as preparations began, the rejected suitor continued almost masochistically to bring his poems to show Estelle. As the day drew nearer, he at last found the situation intolerable and left Oxford. On the day Estelle went to the altar with Franklin, driven there in what must have seemed Judas-fashion by Faulkner's own brother,[28] Faulkner himself was in New Haven, Connecticut, working as a clerk at Winchester Repeating Arms Company and staying with Phil Stone, who had returned to Yale for a law degree. It may well have been this loss of a sister-lover which Faulkner invoked in portraying Quentin Compson's desperate plight when confronted with the announcement of Caddy's wedding in *The Sound and the Fury*.

Faulkner's curious sense of powerlessness to stop the marriage probably grew out of self-doubts about his worth and masculinity. Such a problematic self-image certainly colors much of the poetry he wrote during the next few years. A good deal of this verse was collected in *The Marble Faun,* his first book, which was not published until 1924 but contains works written much earlier. The controlling figure is that of the faun himself, whose singularity and paralysis and responses thereto dominate the book. He has his origins in Faulkner's own emotional conception of himself, which led to, and was amplified by, his failure to prevent Estelle's wedding and to claim her for his own.

The Marble Faun is a loosely unified cycle of pastoral poems which follows the rhythms of the seasons from spring through winter and imagined death. The work merits discussion as Faulkner's first published volume, containing hints of his developing creative powers, and for its psychological interest. Artistically, its flaws—monotonous melancholy, self-consciousness, and an amateurish imitativeness—offset its merits, and it would scarcely be read now had it not proved the forerunner of some major fiction. It did, however, have a number of strengths, and one of its two reviewers commented on several of them: "Mr. Faulkner possesses to an exceptional degree imagination, emotion, a creative impulse in diction and a keen sense of rhythm and form—all attributes demanded of a fine poet."[29] *The Marble Faun* contains the precisely observed and emotionally heightened nature images that would appear in Faulkner's later work, and the central figure, who is simultaneously emotionally involved in—even obsessed by—and detached from the scene around him, is characteristically Faulknerian.

What the poems reveal about Faulkner's frame of mind is perhaps most significant. The very first poem, "Prologue," contrasts the feminine poplar trees, which recur in the work, with the faun himself. The trees are slim and elegant, as was Estelle, and are described as "slender girls" and "poised dancers." But they are heedless, apart, and their sap-filled life differentiates them from the cold marble stasis of the faun. He is helpless in thralldom:

> The sky
> Warms me and yet I cannot break
> My marble bonds. That quick keen snake
> Is free to come and go, while I
> Am prisoner to dream and sigh

> For things I know, yet cannot know.
> . . . The whole world breathes and calls to me
> Who marble bound must ever be.

A sense of impotence pervades this and all the following poems; the word itself is used several times, and the idea is implicit throughout in the specifically sexual images Faulkner uses to evoke that world of nature in which the faun cannot participate. There are "birches springing suddenly/Erect in silence" and a brook

> Flashing in white frothèd shocks
> About upstanding polished rocks;
> Slender shoots draw sharp and clear
> And white withes shake. . . .

The faun finds some slight consolation in winter, which mirrors his state of "enthrallèd impotence," his "chilled and marble woe"; in the thoughts of old age, when "nameless pain" will no longer haunt him nor send him "crying 'Hence!'/At my unseeking impotence"; and in the prospect of the ultimate surcease, death, when

> in the earth I shall sleep
> To never wake, to never weep
> For things I know, yet cannot know.

The faun's marble bondage is unwilled and therefore makes him a creature to be pitied for his inability to participate in the sexual vitality of the natural world. We also sense, however, that sex for him is associated with darkness and filth. The faun has a night vision during which wild "dancers in a blatant crowd" appear. Their sexual exuberance is an "unclean heated thing" that alarms him and the poplars and is exorcised only when "the clean face of the day/Drives them shrinkingly away." This dark view of sex will appear in much of Faulkner's fiction, especially in *Sanctuary,* where impotence and debauchery are closely linked.

With these 1919 poems that later went into *The Marble Faun,* Faulkner began the important process of recording and artistically objectifying the troubling phantoms which stalked his psyche and thereby, in some way, coming to terms with them. After Estelle had been married ten months, she gave birth to a child, an event Faulkner later treated in the unpublished "Elmer" in an apocryphal way, by having Elmer father the child upon the protagonist instead of the woman's husband. Ethel seems based on Estelle; she has told Elmer, "You are much younger than I am: like a brother,"[30] and revealed her intention to marry another man. They have a sexual encounter, but otherwise Elmer reacts passively to the crisis, learning only later that she has borne his child. That this portion of "Elmer" had many points in common with Faulkner's real and fantasized experiences of 1918 and 1919 is indicated by the protagonist's going off to war and incurring a serious wound.

Elmer's war wound links him in a wish fulfilling way with Faulkner's other psychically traumatic experience of 1918, his inability to get into action as a pilot in World War I. During Faulkner's lifetime more inaccuracies and partial truths were perpetrated about this phase of his life than about any other, and Faulkner himself was generally responsible for them. His desire to be a pilot seems to have dated from the beginning of the war. As he later wistfully recalled: "I had seen an aeroplane and my mind was filled with names: Ball, and Immelman and Boelcke, and Guynemer and Bishop, and I was waiting, biding, until I would be old enough or free enough or anyway could get to France and become glorious and beribboned too."[31] For this and other, deeper-rooted reasons, his rejection by the American army's pilot training program in 1918 was a grave affront. After several years of being obsessed with airplanes and nearly twenty-one years of being at odds with his own father, Faulkner turned to an impersonal and seemingly more appeasable masculine authority that would also allow him to fly, but found himself once again unable to please. Contrary to the sentiment of the poster, Uncle Sam did not want him. Aware of the physical requirements, Faulkner tried desperately to gain heft before attempting to enlist; he ate vast numbers of bananas, but was still rejected as being under the regulation height and weight. The blow was bitter, and afterwards Faulkner plaintively asked a friend whether she knew of "anything that would make me grow tall" (B, p. 196).

His sense of frustration was only intensified by the fact that his brother Jack had become a Marine and was fighting on the French front, and even sixteen-year-old John had managed to run away and enlist, a scheme foiled only by his father's call to the adjutant general of Mississippi to get him released. All of the brothers had been closely following the battles since the war began, in a twentieth-century and more adult version of Bayard's and Ringo's games in *The Unvanquished,* and Faulkner's library at the time of his death still contained the *Complete War Map of Western Europe* on which he had written his name in March, 1918.[32] For him as the oldest to be the only one thwarted in his effort to join the glamorous legions of the military was a psychic assault of the first order. He became, his brother said, "as restless as I had ever known him to be."[33]

Desperate to be a pilot, William finally managed to join the R.A.F. in Canada as an officer cadet and was sent to Toronto for his training.[34] His visions of glorious fatality, however, came to nothing. The war was over before he had finished his training, and it is doubtful whether he had even a brief ride in an airplane. Undaunted by the facts, he nonetheless created a personal myth of Faulkner the daring and wounded flier. He wrote to his mother of soloing and of frequent "joy rides" and told his brothers about recklessly crashing his plane upside down in the rafters of a hanger.[35] He was discharged as a cadet and would not receive his honorary commission for a year and a half, but before leaving Canada he obtained a complete officer's uniform of the finest quality, including a swagger stick, and returned to Oxford wearing a uniform which he was unauthorized to wear and which regulations in any case required be donned only on military occasions. He got off the train limping, having also acquired a mythical leg wound in conscious or unconscious emulation of that sustained by his great-grandfather in the Mexican War.

Faulkner soon acquired a second apocryphal "wound." His brother Jack had been hit in the head by shrapnel during a battle in the Argonne in November and badly wounded, and when Faulkner later left Mississippi for New Orleans, he took with him Jack's head wound. His New Orleans associates, including Sherwood Anderson, who depicted Faulkner and his "wounds" in "A Meeting South," believed he had a steel plate in his head and showed him appropriate sympathy and consideration.

The brave English pilot persona clearly satisfied a need in Faulkner for virile self-presentation, and it was almost three decades before he ventured any repudiation of the myth. In the letters Faulkner exchanged with Malcolm Cowley in 1946, when the latter was preparing the Viking *Portable Faulkner,* his discomfort with the old mask gradually brought him close to honesty. The biographical sketch which Cowley submitted said that Faulkner had seen combat as a pilot and had crashed. Initially, Faulkner did not dispute the statements, but in a subsequent letter he requested, "If you mention military experience at all . . . say 'belonged to RAF 1918.' " When the topic came up yet another time, Faulkner finally said, still without disclosing the actual facts, "The only point a war reference or anecdote could serve would be to reveal me a hero, or (2) to account for the whereabouts of a male of my age on Nov. 11, 1918."[36] and insisted on the brief statement he had formerly mentioned. This was apparently as close as Faulkner ever came to telling the truth about his experience in Canada. He did, however, with his almost infallible ability for artistic self-diagnosis and for ironic self-portrayal, come nearer to the facts in his fiction. *Soldiers' Pay,* his first novel, published in 1926, would contain a satiric repudiation of the pilot myth in the characterization of Julian Lowe, and a short story he wrote soon after his return to Oxford showed more willingness to be honest than did either his conversation or his letters.

"Landing in Luck," Faulkner's first published piece of fiction, appeared in a November, 1919, periodical at the University of Mississippi, where he had enrolled as a special student. The protagonist is a cadet pilot, a "barracks ace," or a "rockin' chair aviator," as his instructor derisively calls him, whose major anxiety is that "he would show himself up before his less fortunate friends to whom he had talked largely of spins and side slips and gliding angles." On the day of his first solo flight, his ineptness causes him to strip a wheel from the landing gear on takeoff so that he must make an ungainly belly landing, which stands the plane on its nose and leaves him hanging face down from the cockpit. His attempt to turn disgrace into glamor is jeered by his comrades, who hoot, "He's the 'f' out of flying. Biggest liar in the R.A.F.," but the approval of the instructor allows him to remain impervious to such scorn and "cheerfully condescending."[37] Thus Faulkner's very first fiction shows the psychologically equilibrating role played by his art, as his propensity for intense self-dramatization is balanced by a capacity to mock it. In "Landing in Luck," he employs part of the myth, the soloing and the crash, but also comments on the folly of his pretentiousness, even though he could not bring himself to undercut his own myth entirely. It is this quality of being both in and out of his fiction, of viewing his experiences with mingled anguish and humor, that gives his work its special "balance."

For nearly seven years after he returned from Canada, Faulkner stayed around Oxford. He lived with his parents and for the first two years went occasionally to classes at the University of Mississippi, where he pledged Sigma Alpha Epsilon fraternity and received a D in English one semester. He also worked at odd jobs and wrote quite regularly, mostly poems and essays, a number of which were published in student periodicals,[38] to which he also contributed elegant sketches. His life was, for the most part, completely aimless and displayed rebellious, occasionally regressive aspects, as he refused to assume the sort of adult role demanded by the town and by his male relatives. He went through a period of playing with a group of children ten years younger than himself and was a scout leader for his young brother Dean's troop until a minister disturbed by his heavy drinking had him discharged. He also spent a great deal of time at the university, long after he had stopped going to classes, until he was in his late twenties;

students later remembered him as staying frequently at the dormitory and waking in the morning only to drink a toddy and go back to sleep.[39]

During part of this period, however, Faulkner worked at some conventional salaried jobs of the sort that would become an increasing rarity in his life. In the fall of 1921, in quest of some sort of significant change in his environment, Faulkner went to New York City. There, through the intervention of Stark Young, he found a job in a bookstore managed by the woman who later became the wife of Sherwood Anderson. At first he slept on Young's sofa, which Faulkner described as "antique Italian" but Young insisted was "homely denim," and then moved to a dingy room in Greenwich Village. Although Faulkner was, according to his employer, a competent book clerk and particularly charming to old ladies, his own recollection was that he lasted on the job only "until I got fired. Think I was a little careless about making change or something."[40] During the time in New York, Faulkner refused a job as postmaster at the university post office back home which was urged on him by Phil Stone.

When the bookstore job ended and Stone's insistence began to mount, Faulkner finally capitulated and returned to Oxford in December. He remained as postmaster for nearly three years but was probably one of the least efficient employees in the entire United States Civil Service, for he had only contempt for the job and rebelled against its obligations in his usual passive-aggressive way. He wrote or played cards with his cronies during working hours, turned a deaf ear to patrons' requests for service, and often tossed magazines into a trash bin from which the disgruntled addressees had to retrieve them. The patrons complained to their senator, and Faulkner eventually received an official communication charging him with neglect of his duties. He was forced to resign in late 1924. Enormously relieved to be through with a job he had not wanted in the first place and had never enjoyed, he made his famous parting shot: "I reckon I'll be at the beck and call of folks with money all my life, but thank God I won't ever again have to be at the beck and call of every son of a bitch who's got two cents to buy a stamp" (B, p. 365).

2

The Anderson Period

BY THE END OF 1924, Faulkner's restlessness was extreme and he was clearly ready to burst the "marble bonds" he had written about with such feeling in his early poetry. Even his friendship with Phil Stone, though crucial to his early development, was itself becoming one of the problematical restraints that made his life in Oxford seem stultifying. Although the ties between the two men were still close and constant on the surface, there were also troubling and potentially abrasive undercurrents. Stone was beginning to be managerial, and his quasi-paternal concern, at first so welcome to the floundering youth, might well have begun to seem like domination. Stone had pressured Faulkner into taking the post office job despite his great reluctance, and Faulkner rebelled as he had against his father, by doing his job poorly. Stone was also responsible for getting *The Marble Faun* published, and while his intervention in that project was far more constructive, it still had its disturbing elements.

Writing to Yale, his alma mater, about the book, Stone said, "This poet is my personal property" (B, p. 373), and his proprietary attitude is revealed more subtly in the preface to *The Marble Faun,* where it is tinged with condescension. As in subsequent statements, Stone reveals an ambivalence toward his pupil by damning him with faint praise. Toward the end of the preface, Stone makes some acute and complimentary observations about Faulkner's talent, commenting on his "shrewdly and humorously honest" mind, his "unusual feeling for words and the music of words, a love of soft vowels, an instinct for color and rhythm, and—at times—a hint of coming muscularity of wrist and eye,'' and his strong roots in the soil of northern Mississippi, which is ''a part of this young man's very being.'' The early part of the preface, however, sounds more as though it had been written grudgingly by an eminent professor about a wayward student than by a close friend and partisan of the poet. ''These are primarily the poems of youth and a simple heart,'' begins Stone, going on to cite the ''defects of youth—youth's impatience, unsophistication and immaturity,'' and adding, ''one has to be at a certain age to write poems like these.'' He then comments on the work's amateurishness and outlines a program for his pupil: ''It is inevitable that traces of apprenticeship should appear in a first book but a man who has real talent will grow. . . . All that is needed . . . is work and unflinching honesty.''[1] This can, of course, be viewed as scrupulous objectivity—Stone had after all, paid the several hundred dollars needed to have the work printed by a vanity publisher in Boston—but the undertones of deprecation are there, and they would grow more explicit as time went on.

Uneasiness under Stone's mentorship, coupled with unemployment and general restlessness, led Faulkner to look for a new locale in which to live and write. He needed to be at least briefly with some fellow artists, with people, as he put it, ''that have the same problems and the same interests as [the artist], that won't laugh at what he's trying to do no matter how foolish it might sound to the Philistine'' (*FIU*, p. 231). Faulkner's employer during his brief stay in New York in 1921, Elizabeth Prall, had married Sherwood Anderson in 1924 and moved to New Orleans, and a friend of Faulkner's suggested that he go to Louisiana and be introduced. Faulkner much admired the older writer, whose finest works, *Winesburg, Ohio, Horses and Men,* and *The Triumph of the Egg,* had all been published by this time. He particularly liked Anderson's story, ''I'm a Fool,'' which is, significantly, about a young man who assumes an artifical persona to get himself through a moment of emotional crisis. Anderson's reputation was then at its peak, and he was regarded as a writer whose innovative style and honest probings of sexuality and the subconscious had opened new frontiers for young Americans then beginning to write. He was also known for his personal warmth and openness and his accessibility to younger writers. Although it was the mere chance of his numbering Elizabeth Prall among his handful of friends outside Oxford that brought Faulkner to Anderson's doorstep in 1925, the conjunction could not have been happier if Faulkner had chosen him from a *Who's Who of Literary America*.

Although Anderson was nearly as old as Faulkner's father, the lives of the two writers had been uncannily alike in a number of ways. Each was the son of a man who was ineffectual as both father and businessman, and neither had had much formal education. (Faulkner was ostensibly proud of being "the world's oldest living sixth-grader," but Anderson tended to be less than truthful about his lack of education.) Anderson had rushed eagerly off to the Spanish-American War in 1898, only to arrive in Cuba after a peace treaty had been signed, just as Faulkner later found himself still a cadet in Canada when World War I came to an end. For a time, Anderson's interest in the visual arts was, like Faulkner's, as strong as his interest in words, though Anderson's paintings were bold and primitive while Faulkner's drawings were elegant and Beardsleyesque. Anderson had been successful in advertising and the business world but had abruptly left his Elyria Paint Company in 1912 to join the artists of the "Chicago Renaissance." His gesture of renunciation was as well known as Faulkner's parting statement on leaving the post office to join the "Southern Renaissance" of the 1920s would be later. Both men also drank heavily and tended to have difficulties with women, though Anderson's arose from his being interested in too many (he married four times) and Faulkner's, in the early years, from being interested in too few. Even some of the experiences of the two writers after their brief time together had striking similarities. Anderson became a commercial success as his artistic power began to decline, as did Faulkner, and both subsequently became publicly outspoken on the subject of man's injustice to man, Anderson arguing against economic inequities and Faulkner against racial. Each, near the end of his life, took refuge in the rolling countryside of Virginia, Anderson at Ripshin Farm in Marion, Faulkner at a series of homes around Charlottesville.

These biographical parallels are interesting, and perhaps even significant, but it is the role Anderson played in Faulkner's artistic development that is of crucial importance. Even though the two men were together only for a period of a few months in 1925, Anderson's influence on the younger writer was pervasive, and Faulkner continued to pay tribute to his "literary father" until the very end of his career. At the time when they were actively friendly, the most important of Anderson's direct contributions were his reading of the early stages of the manuscript of Faulkner's first novel, his strong encouragement, and his assistance in getting his own publisher, Horace Liveright, to print it. But there are also resonances of Anderson in a large number of Faulkner's works, although the similarities between the experiences of the two men sometimes makes it difficult to separate "cause" from "accidental parallel."

Anderson's provincialism was integral to his sensibility and proclaimed as his literary credo. His raising of the experiences of a struggling "poor white'' or a maturing youth in a small Ohio town to the level of the universal anticipated what Faulkner would do on a much larger scale with his Yoknapatawpha County. Anderson's myth of the grotesque, his sympathetic portrayal of those "twisted apples" who lived obsessed by a single idea or fragment of the truth, [2] evolved in Faulkner's fiction into such monumental and monomaniacal figures as Sutpen, Mink Snopes, and Hightower. Anderson's dim view of "progress," his awareness of the conventional Christian's sporadic perversions, his occasionally adroit mixing of the ludicrous and the tragic, his view of the constrictions imposed by too strong a sense of the past, his concern for the results of sexual frustration and for the processes of the individual consciousness—all these elements would also appear in Faulkner's novels and stories. There are specific echoes of Anderson in Faulkner as well, particular characters or incidents which can be traced to their Andersonian antecedents, [3] and while Faulkner's art eventually far surpassed that of Anderson in its power and sweep, his debt to the older writer was substantial, and he conscientiously acknowledged it.

When Faulkner arrived in New Orleans, Anderson was a central figure in the city's newly thriving artistic and literary renascence, which was giving the lie to H. L. Mencken's acerbic dismissal of the South as the "Sahara of the Bozart." The magazine *The Double Dealer* was publishing work by writers like Hemingway, Ezra Pound, Hart Crane, Djuna Barnes, and Edmund Wilson, and there was a colony of painters and sculptors working in the French Quarter. Faulkner stayed at the Andersons' apartment for a short time before moving into a room in the Quarter on what is now known as Pirate's Alley in an apartment occupied by the artist William Spratling. During this period, Faulkner wrote a number of pieces for *The Double Dealer* and the *Times-Picayune* which were published during the first nine months of 1925. These works, despite their brevity and self-consciousness, contain a number of important portents of the great later fiction.

In the sketches, Faulkner began to treat grotesque characters, to use interior monologues, to mingle horror and humor, to invoke Christian belief and ritual, and to combine poetic description with realistic dialogue. He also introduced particular characters, images, and narrative lines which would reappear later, such as the idiot in "The Kingdom of God" who developed into Benjy Compson, the Magdalen of "New Orleans" who returned in *A Fable,* the "terrific arrested motion" of Jackson's statue in "Out of Nazareth" that became a dominant motif in *As I Lay Dying* and appears in many of his works, and the horse that charges into the house in

"The Liar" and does so again in *The Hamlet*. "Sunset," perhaps the most effective of these short pieces, vividly demonstrates both the Anderson influence and Faulkner's departure from it.[4] The protagonist of "Sunset," a naive Negro who desperately wishes to return to Africa, is Andersonian both in his simplicity and grotesqueness and in the sympathy with which he is portrayed. But the work is unmistakably Faulkner's, with its fine balance of comedy and pathos and its juxtaposition of poetic images like the "bloody light" with the realism of Negro dialect. Its hero is a Faulknerian victim become victimizer. The terrified Negro who unwittingly kills three men and is hunted down like an animal foreshadows other pathological, yet sympathetic, figures such as Joe Christmas, Mink Snopes, and Rider of "Pantaloon in Black." Its structure, too, is characteristically Faulknerian: the opening in the present with the report of the three murders and the gradual exploration of their origin in the past, motivated by the fear and disorientation of the hero, would be used again in *Light in August*.

Although the literary relationship between Anderson and Faulkner was extended and significant, their personal friendship was more chaotic and short-lived. Just what impression Anderson made on Faulkner at the time of their 1925 comradeship is unknown, for Faulkner's equivocal review of Anderson's work at the end of 1925, his parody of Anderson in his 1926 work *Sherwood Anderson and Other Famous Creoles,* and his uncomplimentary portrait of Anderson as Dawson Fairchild in *Mosquitoes,* published in 1927, all were written after the two men had broken off the relationship and Faulkner's view of Anderson had presumably become more negative than it was at first. Anderson, on the other hand, shortly after meeting Faulkner, was moved to portray him in his sketch, "A Meeting South," that was published in *The Dial* of April, 1925.[5] Faulkner had evidently presented himself in the guise of a wounded war hero, and Anderson had responded with credulity and a paternal protectiveness. David, the fictional Faulkner, is a cripple with a limp who had been a "first rate flyer" in a British squadron and had broken both legs and fractured his skull and several bones in his face. He now lives "always in the black house of pain," pain so continuous that he cannot sleep and feels compelled to drink constantly. As if pain alone were not enough to arouse the sympathy of the Andersonian narrator, David has also touched him with his pathetic story about the decline of his family's great plantations. David's physical and spiritual malaise, as well as his smallness and delicacy, finally cause the narrator to conclude that he needs a "mother," to which end he brings him to the house of Aunt Sally, a retired brothel keeper. There David at last falls asleep on the brick patio, "a small huddled figure of a man." How

much, if any, of this portrait of Faulkner is authorial hyperbole is unknown, but what is clear in the piece is Anderson's warmhearted response
to someone he perceived as frail and vulnerable. Anderson's wife attests to
Faulkner's efforts during this period to drink himself to sleep every night
and his attempts to arouse sympathy with exaggerated stories, some of
which were about injuries in love as well as in war. He told Mrs. Anderson
that the girl he loved had married someone else but had had his baby,[6] a
tale which reappeared in "Elmer" and was apparently based on the
fantasies created by the 1918–1919 crisis with Estelle.

The two men had many moments of satisfying camaraderie, drinking,
wandering through the French Quarter together, and telling each other fine
tall tales, but Faulkner often proved a difficult companion, either retreating
into taciturnity or emerging from his shell only to be extremely rude to one
of the Andersons' guests.[7] The beginnings of a serious personal breach apparently came when the two men quarreled about miscegenation after having consumed a great deal of liquor, Faulkner insisting that the union between the white man and the Negro woman always resulted, after the first
crossing, in sterility, and Anderson retorting that the idea was ridiculous.[8]
The estrangement had begun, and Faulkner drove in the final nails with his
publications during the forthcoming year.

Though Anderson's reactions to Faulkner at this time, as well as later,
even after Faulkner had satirized him, were evidently open and generous,
Faulkner was slow to acknowledge his debt to Anderson publicly. In late
1925 and 1926 he seemed to be aiming for a hasty, if figurative, "killing"
of his "literary father." A long review article of the Anderson corpus
which he did for the *Dallas Morning News* in the late spring of 1925 contains, along with a reasonably fair appraisal of the work, a cruel anecdote
and a cutting comparison.[9] Faulkner speaks of Anderson's simple narrative
style and finds his work strongest when it stays closest to the soil and de-
picts "the old refulgent earth and people who answer the compulsions of
food and labor and sleep, whose passions are uncerebral"; at the same time
he criticizes Anderson for his lack of humor, his tentativeness, and his
failure to have matured artistically. He then goes on to recount a dream of
Anderson's in which he agreed to swap a horse for a night's sleep, but was
left foolishly waiting all night; the dream, suggestive of the credulity that
made Anderson so vulnerable, was later to be paralleled by the anecdote in
Mosquitoes in which a character based on Anderson loses twenty-five dollars when he naively "buys" a fraternity membership. Faulkner concludes
his review with the biting observation that Anderson is "as typical of Ohio
in his way as Harding was in his. A field of corn with a story to tell and a

tongue to tell it in.'' President Harding's reputation had by then been tainted with the Teapot Dome scandal and ''field of corn'' is a phrase hardly calculated to please the artist it describes.

Some months after this, Faulkner collaborated with William Spratling on *Sherwood Anderson and Other Famous Creoles,* a collection of Spratling's caricatures of the denizens of the New Orleans art and literary world, prefaced by Faulkner's brief parodic imitation of Anderson. The parody is mild by comparison with Hemingway's savagely repudiatory work, *The Torrents of Spring,* directed at the same target, but it was certain to wound the sensitive Anderson by its disparagement of his trusting fellowship, his humorlessness, and his simple style. Faulkner's preface opens innocently enough, evoking the appeal of the French Quarter with its ''richness and soft laughter,'' but it soon has the narrator appraising the local artists ingenuously: ''Though I did not know their names nor the value of their paintings, they were my brothers.''[10] It continues in a monotonous, repetitive manner, characterizing Anderson as a ''wheel horse,'' a term which connotes plodding diligence and a capacity to be exploited, and is followed by the first of Spratling's caricatures, showing Anderson with a huge, bearlike head and a small body. Anderson's wife said that when he saw the book he looked at Faulkner's preface and stated flatly, ''It isn't very funny.''[11] The timing of *Creoles* was unfortunate, for Anderson's confidence and ability had begun to slip, and the parody must have added salt to a newly opened wound. Faulkner later admitted that he had made Anderson's ''style look ridiculous; and by that time, after *Dark Laughter,* when he had reached a point where he should have stopped writing, he had to defend that style at all costs because he too must have known by then in his heart that there was nothing else left.''[12]

Not long after he settled in New Orleans, Faulkner began work on his first novel, which he initially titled *Mayday* in evocation either of the international signal for an extreme emergency or of the joyous rites of spring so ironically out of place in a world where even hope seems dead. By May he had completed it. The apocryphal story is that Anderson said he would help Faulkner get it published if he didn't have to read it (*FIU,* p. 22). He did in truth intercede with Horace Liveright to get the novel into print, but he also read a good share of the manuscript in the early stages. His favorable reactions encouraged Faulkner, who still regarded himself chiefly as a poet, to keep working at the novel. The episodic quality of *Soldiers' Pay,* its concern with the sexual aspects of interaction, and the manner in which it systematically presents the responses of several characters make the novel seem rather Andersonian. At many points it evokes a specific work by

Faulkner's mentor, *Dark Laughter,* which was published soon after Faulkner began work on his first novel. Faulkner includes passages about the simple Negroes' "careless, ready laughter" which had "somehow beneath it something elemental and sorrowful and unresisting" (144),[13] in contrast with the generally superficial life of the white characters. This contrast was a fundamental theme in Anderson's 1925 novel, and Faulkner may well have consciously picked it up for use in his own work.

However Andersonian it might seem at points, *Soldiers' Pay* was also directly related to some personal problems with which Faulkner was struggling and revealed, wittingly or otherwise, much that was significant about his vision of his world in early 1925. The novel is a work of postwar disillusionment, like the "lost generation" novels and stories that Hemingway, Fitzgerald, and others were writing. Although the book is to some degree unified by a series of responses to Donald Mahon's fatal wound, the novel's metaphor for the destructive violence of the war, it has weaknesses which mark it as dating from Faulkner's apprentice period and as the work of a young man—the self-conscious *Weltschmerz,* the sophomoric humor, the occasional vapid editorializing, the unevenness of tone, and the problems raised by making a speechless and inert victim the center of the book.

Hints of Faulkner's powerful talent do nonetheless emerge, and at the time *Soldiers' Pay* was published, it received generally favorable reviews and readers praised the quality of this new authorial voice. The *New York Times* said that it was written with "hard intelligence as well as consummate pity." A New Orleans acquaintance of Faulkner's called it "the most noteworthy first novel of the year," unaware that Hemingway's more effective work, *The Sun Also Rises,* which had a number of elements in common with *Soldiers' Pay,* was soon to appear. After the work was published in England, Arnold Bennett made his famous comment: "Faulkner is the coming man. He has inexhaustible invention, powerful imagination, a wondrous gift of characterization, a finished skill in dialogue; and he writes, generally, like an angel."[14] The novel reveals in embryo a number of the qualities that give Faulkner's later work its strength—the use of an image like the falling church spire to suggest the mixture of denial and affirmation so central to his vision;[15] moments of sympathetic insight into the human condition, man's struggle with desire and despair; the effective portrayal of a small southern town as a physical entity; the depiction of a series of psychological responses to a central character; and the balance of compassion and detachment.

The equilibrium between irony and pity is one of the most striking aspects of the work, especially when it is considered from a psychobiographical vantage point. Faulkner, to be sure, integrated the two attitudes less well in *Soldiers' Pay* than he did in later works, but it was, after all, his first large-scale treatment of the basically conflicting attitudes that he held toward himself, the war, and his abortive effort to participate gloriously in the fighting. He embodies these almost polar attitudes in two of the male characters, Julian Lowe, the comic thwarted hero, and Donald Mahon, the tragic maimed hero, pouring great satiric energy into his depiction of the one and equally strong sympathy into his portrayal of the other, and thereby reveals his ambiguous concept of himself as he wavers between objective self-criticism and passionate, wish fulfilling statement.

The opening fragment of inane dialogue between Achilles and Mercury in the context of modern warfare creates the Eliotic mood of deflation and dislocation which colors the early part of the novel and especially the portrait of Julian Lowe, who is the first character to be introduced and the central consciousness of the first chapter. Lowe, like Faulkner, is an ex–flying cadet, filled with self-pitying disappointment because "they had stopped the war on him." He is bitter, regarding the world "with a yellow and disgruntled eye" (7). His sense of frustration is only intensified when he meets the wounded officer, Donald Mahon, to whom he reacts with jealousy and fascination. Though Mahon's scar is sickening, Lowe regards him as one "to whom Fate had been kinder than to himself" (29). He cannot tear his eyes from so tragically glamorous a figure, and when Mahon takes a nap, Lowe watches and wonders, "Had I wings, boots, would I sleep?" (30). Mahon's wings become an obsession for Lowe because he sees them as "a symbolized desire" (45), and he desperately chants to himself, "To have got wings on my breast, to have wings; and to have got his scar, too, I would take death tomorrow" (45).

The wings represent the pilothood which has eluded Lowe, as it eluded Faulkner. Flying is often linked with sexual accomplishment in the daydreams of young males, psychoanalysts have discovered, and the association in the psyches of Faulkner and his protagonist is made explicit in *Soldiers' Pay,* as it would later be in *Pylon.* Aviation is in Lowe's mind clearly emblematic of sexuality, a badge of masculine achievement, and wings and flying are embroiled in his sexual fantasies about Margaret. Lowe, however, cannot act. Helpless, he muses, "If I had wings and a scar," as if they would solve his sexual problems. He then moves into an extremely sensual vision of flying, more explicitly sexual than his thoughts of Margaret. Lowe is "conscious of lubricating oil and a slow gracious restraint of braced plane surfaces, feeling an air blast and feeling the stick in his hand, watching bobbing rocker arms on the horizon, laying her nose on the horizon like a sighted rifle'' (47). In both his life and his fantasy world Lowe yearns for maleness and sexual fulfillment but is perennially frustrated. He is neither a pilot nor a "man," and he tries to find consolation in grandiose visions of himself heroically dead, of "a tomb, open, and himself in boots and belt, and pilot's wings on his breast, a wound stripe. . . . What more could one ask of Fate?'' (52).

Thwarted and powerless to change things, to make himself a hero and a potent masculine force, Lowe retreats into drunkenness, and some of the most vivid passages in the early part of the novel deal with the cadet's ingestion of raw whiskey, his body's initial recoil, and his subsequent slide into the haziness of inebriation. The experience was obviously a familiar one to the author, for he writes about it colorfully, with amused sympathy. "Cadet Lowe's outraged stomach heaved at its muscular moorings like a captive balloon. He gaped and his vitals coiled coldly in a passionate ecstasy'' (11). Lowe becomes quite drunk, with eyes "like two oysters," and earnestly, but futilely, "with quenchless optimism essay[s] speech" (37–38). Faulkner is equally effective at portraying the misery and disorientation of Lowe's hung-over awakening the next day, which he assuages by a breakfast of whiskey, as the author also was wont to do on occasion. Faulkner ends this punishing and revealing self-caricature by sending Lowe on his separate way at the end of chapter one. Lowe reappears in the novel only through a series of letters he sends to Margaret from the West, striking in their juvenility, awkwardness, semiliteracy, and even ill-timing, for his most ardent declarations of his intent to marry her arrive as she is marrying Mahon.

The comparison between the childishly romantic and impotent Lowe and the quietly suffering and heroic Mahon seems clearly intended, for Faulkner even places them in symbolically parallel beds during one scene. All of our initial views of Mahon and his "dreadful scar" come through Lowe's eyes, and while the cadet himself is portrayed as ridiculous, we are made to share something of his response to Mahon's tragic glamor by the evocation of similar responses in Joe Gilligan, the train porter, and Margaret Powers. Faulkner's brother Jack had incurred a severe head wound during the war and had been hospitalized in France, causing grave concern to his family and driving his father to talk of killing a local man who reportedly had "bought" his son out of the army (Wells, p. 30). For many years, as we have seen, Faulkner described himself to new acquaintances as having a comparable wound in order to arouse interest and sympathy. Even in the last months of his life, when asked what he secretly wished to be, Faulkner responded, "Why sure, I'd like to be a brave, courageous soldier.''[16] He was speaking at West Point and may have been attempting to please his military audience, but the comment also has a touching ring of nostalgia for what might have been, had his "luck" run differently.

Mahon has symbolic importance beyond that of a vehicle for Faulkner's romantic fantasies of himself as a wounded hero. His very name sounds like "man" and he is obviously a personification of all the terrible physical and spiritual wounds inflicted by the war. Nonetheless, Faulkner revealingly gave Mahon many of his own real or imagined characteristics. Mahon carries Housman's *A Shropshire Lad,* a volume to which Faulkner was also devoted, to war; he reads but has little formal education; he wears the uniform of a British officer; he has small hands; and he even looks like Faulkner, with a "thin face," a "delicate pointed chin and wild, soft eyes" (67). Mahon's taciturnity is but a magnification of the sort of silent face which Faulkner presented to much of the world during the postwar period.

Unlike Faulkner, however, Mahon is the center of everyone's attention, the pivotal figure even in his quiet suffering. Mahon evokes fascination, pity, envy, and self-sacrificing concern, and every other character is tacitly judged as worthy or unworthy by his response to Mahon. Almost immediately after Joe Gilligan and Margaret Powers first encounter Mahon, they become a self-appointed nursing staff of two and give up all personal plans to escort him home to Georgia. There, as on the train, they hover at his side. Gilligan, who begins as a drunken prankster and deflator of any verbal sentiment, is soon moved to say parental things and to evince his aroused concern by sleeping at the foot of Mahon's bed like a nurse. Margaret moves from friendly interest to a nurture-based affection and, finally, to the self-sacrificial decision to marry Mahon in order to lessen the shock of his fiancée's abrupt decampment. Mahon's former childhood sweetheart, Emmy, waits devotedly in the background, and many of the townspeople make a pilgrimage to his bedside.

The tender nursing of Mahon by Gilligan and Margaret is central to their relationship with him; its quasi-parental quality turns them at last into "two Niobes" (203), completely focused on their charge. Their concern is paralleled by a good deal of other nurturing that goes on in the novel. This is important thematically, because it reveals the morally admirable capacity for selflessness. But it also, by its pervasiveness, discloses the desire for loving attention which existed in Faulkner in tandem with his sense that the world was a threatening place. The novel's characters are divided, in one respect, into those who are solicitous of each other and those who are selfish and destructive. In addition to Gilligan and Margaret (whose nursing impulses extend even to Lowe, as they help him to bed or gently tolerate his effusive folly), the railroad porter, Emmy, Mahon's father, and Caroline, his former nurse (who is named after Faulkner's), all are affectionately helpful to the wounded airman. In addition to bedside attention, the act of holding someone on one's lap recurs frequently as a demonstration of caring, and adults as often as children are, surprisingly, treated to this.

Such quasi-maternal gentleness as a unifying force is offset by the self-centered, disruptive, and usually sexual behavior of characters like Cecily Saunders and Januarius Jones. Jones is a ludicrous figure, a fat, feline, and apparently androgynous Latin teacher who spends much of his time in futile pursuit of various females and whose presence in the novel is perplexing, seeming to serve no purpose except as an embodiment of selfishness and pointless sexual aggressiveness. Cecily, however, is intriguing. One moment she is as attractive and lithe as a wood nymph, the next her restlessness and shallow destructiveness appear to anticipate qualities evinced by Temple Drake in *Sanctuary*. In his portrait of Cecily, Faulkner demonstrates the ambivalence he felt toward nubile females, an ambivalence engendered by his "betrayal" by Estelle and before that by his problematic relationship with his mother. He obviously drew on the Oldhams for his portrayal of Cecily's parents, who are prosperous and socially secure, yet faintly anomalous; they are Catholic, which is "almost as sinful as being a republican" (97), which Mr. Oldham was. They warn their daughter, as did Estelle's parents, against marrying a man who is a "pauper" (260) and "probably won't work" (99). Cecily heeds their warnings as well as her own distaste for her now blind and dying fiancé and marries instead the handsome "gentleman" George Farr, who may be patterned on Cornell Franklin, Estelle's first husband. When, many years later, Estelle told an interviewer that her husband used her as a model for one of the characters in his first novel and that it "hurt my feelings terribly,"[17] she was almost certainly referring to Cecily Saunders.

Cecily is not an adequately realized character, and the descriptions of her reveal confused authorial attitudes toward her that may account for the aesthetic failure. Though some critics, including most recently Albert Guerard, have commented on what they view as Faulkner's "misogyny,"[18] a more accurate term for the outlook evident in many of Faulkner's portrayals of young women would seem to be attraction-repulsion. This is a yearning for and even idealization of the female that is directly counterbalanced by fear and a certain distaste. Nowhere is this conflicting attitude, of which Faulkner had yet to make effective use artistically, more obvious than in his depiction of Cecily Saunders. She is, with virtual simultaneity, lovely and repellent. She is a "flower stalk," a "young tree," and frequently a "poplar," like the graceful feminine figures in *The Marble Faun,* a creature of "pliant fragility" (84), whose "clear delicate being was nourished by sunlight and honey until even digestion was a beautiful function" (80). Yet she is also "shallow characterless" and depraved enough to like being called a "bitch" (79, 77). Indeed, her vain coquetry and ultimate abandonment of Mahon confirm that her nature is a destructive one. She is beautiful, but "not for maternity, not even for love," as Jones reflects bitterly (224). To be involved with her is to court the dangers of frustration and suffering.

The book contains derogatory statements about women that are not balanced by equivalent statements about men. "That subtle effluvia of antagonism" that surrounds " 'pretty' women" colors an encounter between the two major female characters, who speak with "malice" and examine each other "with narrow care" (81–82). Even the noble Margaret Powers, one of Faulkner's rare female characters of marriageable age with a capacity for disinterested moral action, does not escape being touched ever so faintly with a bitter brush. First described as a Beardsley woman, "white and slim and depraved" (31), she seems "impersonal" and "self-contained" (32). The length of her thighs, like that of Cecily's, is insisted upon so often, as is her "long body," that her attractiveness becomes slightly ambiguous and she acquires, like Hemingway's contemporaneous Brett Ashley, a certain aura of masculinity.

Margaret has been made cynical by her first experience of marriage. The sexual side of her three-day relationship now seems sordid as she remembers her husband's "ugly body breaking into mine like a burglar" (184), and because her letter asking to end it arrived after he was killed, she is haunted by the "wrongness" of the fact that he died believing in her. Having acquired a sense of futility that is now almost a "curse," she is led to make a second marriage that is doomed to end in death and to refuse, at the last, any easy escape into a third marriage, with Joe Gilligan. Her honesty and her ability for selfless action are the result of the sort of painful experiences Faulkner usually reserves for his male heroes. She is the most complex character in *Soldiers' Pay,* not only because of her singularity among Faulkner's females and of the ambiguities in her portrayal, but also because Faulkner gives her the capacity for both detachment and compassion, for judgment and engagement; she is, in a way, the V. K. Ratliff of this novel. Seeing the ardent Lowe in all his foolishness, she nonetheless treats him tenderly; knowing that Mahon will go blind and die, she still commits herself to him. In an early passage in which she muses about her dead husband, she evinces both objectivity and subjectivity, moving from calm appraisal to moral outrage, and she shows both sides of her character in the course of the novel. Never as fully realized as she might be, Margaret does, sharply and intriguingly, bring together both sides of Faulkner's dualistic vision.

The Reverend Mahon is a similarly "dualistic" character, both inside and outside the action, simultaneously concerned and detached. Piercingly honest in some ways, touchingly vulnerable in others, the minister has a capacity for detachment that allows him moments of wise insight into other characters, but his desperate involvement with his son leads him to be almost willfully blind to the fact that the young man is dying. The Reverend Mahon is obviously in no sense a surrogate for Faulkner himself, but he does serve as a vehicle for some of the author's artistic concerns. His symbolic rosebush, like a work of art, represents a displacement of desire and procreative impulses onto the nonhuman; ultimately it becomes both lover and child, "my son and my daughter, the wife of my bosom and the bread of my belly" (61), a concept Faulkner explored again in his very next novel. Moreover, in speaking of the rosebush, the minister invokes "the old pagan who kept his Byzantine goblet at his bedside and slowly wore the rim away kissing it" (61), an image Faulkner later used to refer to his own attitude toward his work. The Reverend Mahon also expresses the author's vision of man's temporal plight that underlies much of his fiction. Religious faith has become a near-impossibility, and man must assume the terrifying responsibility for his own destiny: he must confront "the facts of division and death" and make his "own heaven or hell in this world" (317–18). Such statements represent only the most explicit of the many ways in which *Soldiers' Pay* can be said to constitute the first substantial work in a lifetime of fictional art that embodied and came to terms with the complexities of Faulkner's own psychology while making important statements about the modern world.

After Faulkner finished the manuscript in mid-1925, he left New Orleans and went to Pascagoula, a Mississippi seacoast town, for the month of June. He then returned to Oxford, where Estelle and her two children were visiting from Shanghai, to prepare for a trip abroad. Like so many artists of the time, Faulkner decided to go to Europe, although he was to be untypical in the rapidity of his return. Accompanied by his friend William Spratling, he sailed in July on a steamer, the *West Ivis,* which was headed for Genoa. After a period spent touring Italy, he went through Switzerland to Paris, where he settled briefly in a room near the Luxembourg Gardens. He liked spending the fall days in the gardens, sitting and writing or watching the children. He was impressed by what he saw as the tender manner in which the French treated their children, and letters to his mother once again subtly reveal his special vulnerability in this regard: "Everything in the gardens is for children," he told her. "Its beautiful the way the French love their babies." He repeated this sentiment in his next letter. "French people are crazy about their children. Its awful nice to see them together on the street and in the gardens" *(L* pp. 13, 14).

Faulkner spent little time attempting to join the fringes of the active literary colony in Paris, which included James Joyce, whose work was to influence his own so greatly, and American expatriates like Hemingway, Fitzgerald, and Gertrude Stein. Instead he began work on a new novel, *Mosquitoes,* which he soon put aside to start "Elmer." He felt the latter work was "a grand one," and "so clear in my mind that I can hardly write fast enough," but he abandoned it when it was little more than a gathering of unintegrated fragments. Though incomplete, the manuscript is remarkable, as we have seen, for its intensely personal quality. Faulkner's attitude toward Elmer is uneven; he satirizes the adult but treats his deprived childhood with such compassion that one senses how closely its psychological aspects parallel Faulkner's own early years. One element in "Elmer" also suggests that Faulkner was aware of the essential relation of his "wound," or frustrations, to his "bow," or creative powers, for when the would-be artist-protagonist gets everything he wants as an adult—good looks, money, a European title, and a desirable marriage—he "never gets to paint" *(L,* pp. 13, 14, 25).

Faulkner returned home at the end of 1925, unwashed and unshaven, but with a new knowledge of European cities and battlefields of the recent war that he would use in short stories such as "Mistral" and "Divorce in Naples" and, much later, in his novel *A Fable, Soldiers' Pay,* accepted by Liveright while he was in Europe, was published in February of 1926, and the caring familial responses he had depicted took on a deeply ironic cast in light of his own parents' hostility to their son's first novel: his mother strongly disliked the sexual byplay in the work, and his father refused even to open it (B, p. 494). This was a restless and generally unhappy period for Faulkner. In Oxford his bachelorhood isolated him, for two of his younger brothers were now married. So did his "vocation," which was not considered honest work for a man approaching thirty. There were rumors of an impending divorce for Estelle, but she would not return from Shanghai until midyear. By February Faulkner had impatiently gone off again to New Orleans, but Sherwood Anderson would not even speak to him. In April Anderson praised Faulkner's work to his publisher but added that he did "not like the man personally very much. . . . He was so nasty to me personally."[19] Faulkner later said, disingenuously, "I never did know why" (L, p. 293), even though the two had quarreled and Faulkner's unkind, if largely accurate, critical survey of Anderson's career had already appeared and he would soon publish the damaging caricatures of Anderson in Creoles and Mosquitoes.

The summer of 1926 Faulkner spent in Pascagoula, where he divided his time between futile pursuit of a young woman and hard work on the manuscript of Mosquitoes. Helen Baird was Faulkner's first serious romantic interest since Estelle's marriage eight years before, but the new romance proved as abortive as its predecessor, for Helen barely tolerated him. She regarded Faulkner as strange, smelly, and disreputable, and frequently lectured him about his drinking, but he was strongly drawn to her, particularly by her childlikeness (B, pp. 511–12). She had many traits in common with Faulkner's mother, which may account for his interest; she was tiny, hardly five feet tall, and known for her candid outspokenness. She was also an artist, and that aspect of her, along with a terrible scar from a childhood burn, Faulkner would use in his portrait of Charlotte Rittenmeyer in The Wild Palms.

In Mosquitoes, Helen is transmuted, in not altogether complimentary fashion, into Pat Robyn, the elusive young woman who is pursued in vain by several of the male characters. Her most ardent suitor tells Pat that "your name is like a little golden bell hung in my heart" (267–68),[20] words which Faulkner wrote in a letter to Helen later that summer but never mailed. Pat, like Helen, has a brother named Josh, and, perhaps vengefully, in Mosquitoes Faulkner gives the relationship incestuous overtones. Faulkner even dedicated the novel to Helen, but with as poor timing as Julian Lowe's marriage proposal to Margaret Powers in Soldiers' Pay, for the work was published just four days before she married another man. Faulkner justified his futile gesture with some bitter words about the opposite sex: "I made the promise some time ago, and you can lie to women, you know, but you cant break promises you make 'em. That infringes on their own province" (L, p. 34). The woman who had jilted him did not invite Faulkner to her wedding and repudiated his book along with his person, telling a friend, "Don't read it, it's no good" (B, p. 549).

Mosquitoes is, as Conrad Aiken pointed out in an early review,[21] a Huxleyan satire directed at the members of a yachting party during their four-day cruise aboard the aptly named Nausikaa on Louisiana's Lake

Pontchartrain. It is also a *roman à clef*. Faulkner based it on an identifiable group of people, the literary and artistic "set" of New Orleans with whom he associated during his brief time in that city, and on an actual occurrence, a boat trip he took with several members of that group. *Mosquitoes* contains Faulkner's harshest satire, and the boatful of urban intellectuals becomes in his hands a ship of fools emptily talking their way from nowhere to nowhere; it is also (if *A Fable* is excepted) his one "novel of ideas," especially of ideas about art and creativity. In neither regard is it fully successful, and most critics consider the novel his weakest. Faulkner undercuts his own satire with an epilogic "explanation" of his characters' deficiencies, a sympathetic afterthought much like the one concerning Popeye that he later appended to *Sanctuary*. This "explanation" leaves us with a confused conception of the characters and of the author's intent, while the book's "ideas," though sometimes psychologically revealing, are something less than fully clarified philosophical statements. In one sense, indeed, they are pursued so emphatically as to threaten to topple the entire artistic structure; the emptiness of words is insisted upon to such a degree that the very raison d'être of this or any novel is called into question and one wonders why Faulkner chose a verbal medium in which to work. The dichotomy between words and action will be implicit and important in every one of his novels, but in *Mosquitoes* he carries it so far that he seriously undermines the foundation of the art at which he worked so assiduously. To some extent this attitude is understandable, for Faulkner often wrote because he was driven to, because his "demons" demanded it, and he never fully accepted his writing as truly "honest" work. Yet it remains perplexing, coming from a serious artist who elected writing over painting or sculpture and art over law or the hardware business, and seems to represent a form of paradoxical self-repudiation.

Faulkner uses verbosity as a criterion for appraising his characters in *Mosquitoes,* placing them on a spectrum of worthiness that ranges from the nearly silent and clearly admirable sculptor, Gordon, downwards to the wordy and bemused Dawson Fairchild, who is based on Sherwood Anderson, and thence to the futile, almost impotent, Ernest Talliaferro, whose endless sexual pursuits and exercises in wordiness yield few results. It seems likely that Faulkner intended Gordon to be a—perhaps the—central male character, because he dominates the early pages and offers a standard by which the other characters are judged and found wanting. Gordon does not talk, he works, and when he does speak it is often to deflate the vain verbiage of someone else. In the opening scene, the foolish Talliaferro tells him, "The sex instinct is quite strong in me," and Gordon responds simply, "Yes. Would you mind moving a little?" (9). While Talliaferro pointlessly talks, Gordon chisels away earnestly at a marble statue of a young woman which splendidly gives a "sense of swiftness, of space encompassed" (11).

Silence is obviously related to masculinity, and here, too, the men are sharply contrasted. Gordon is strong, "muscularity in an undershirt" (9), and his "masculine" jaw, his "hard body," and the "curling vigor of his hair" (10) are sexual and striking. Gordon may represent Faulkner's idealized self-portrait, for he has the author's hawklike nose as well as his taciturnity. Talliaferro, on the other hand, is effete as well as talkative, painfully aware of his own "unmuscled" body as symbolized by his "symmetrical sleeve" (12, 9), and fatuous in thought and action alike. In a scene with sexually symbolic overtones, Gordon gives Talliaferro his empty milk bottle to have refilled. The phallic connotations were clearly intended by Faulkner, and the section is full of clumsy double entendres. The phallic bottle is an object of extreme repugnance to Talliaferro, who regards it as "clammy" and "unbearably dirty" and tries to hide it beneath his coat (13): "It bulged distressingly under his exploring hand" (14). At the grocery he insists on having it wrapped to keep it hidden from public view. Meeting Mrs. Maurier and her niece, Talliaferro desperately attempts to keep the bottle out of sight, but is foiled when the aggressive Pat, another of Faulkner's threateningly long-legged females, snatches the bottle from his hand and exposes it to her aunt. The scene betrays Talliaferro's distaste for the earthier aspects of that sexuality which he verbally professes to desire. Although Faulkner's use of Freudian symbolism here is rather awkward and obviously intentional, it would become more adroit in later works, in which it seems to have been produced more subconsciously, out of the writer's own emotional anguish and his struggle with the residue of old, half-understood personal problems.

Whether dealt with consciously or subconsciously, sexual issues are central to the novel. Most of the narrative movement focuses on sexual relationships, generally thwarted ones, from the proto-lesbian or incipiently incestuous to the conventionally heterosexual. Even some of the descriptions of setting seem sexually charged, like the shore and the river that "curved away like the bodies of two dark sleepers embracing, curved one to another in slumber" (47) or the ferry boats that "passed and repassed like a pair of golden swans in a barren cycle of courtship" (53). Yet sex also has a metaphorical function in the novel, standing for the potency of vital and unself-conscious engagement in art as well as in human relationships. Gordon's sexual attractiveness seems to go hand in hand with his status as the most committed artist in the novel, one who finds the creation of "shapes out of chaos more satisfactory than bread to the belly" (47), while Talliaferro's sexual ineptness appears directly related to his parasitism and need to live vicariously through the creativity of others.

Although Gordon is obviously more potent than the talkative and effeminate Talliaferro, in a world populated by the sort of empty women Faulkner envisages, neither of them is ultimately successful. At points Gordon's sense of futility seems as great as Talliaferro's, and his cynicism is certainly more pervasive. Gordon calls his feminine ideal "a virgin with no legs to leave me, no arms to hold me, no head to talk to me" (26), and later sees himself a crucified Christ-figure, "by his own hand an auto-gethsemane" (48), as he dwells on his hopeless and debilitating ardor. Sexual desire is tantamount to self-crucifixion in the sculptor's bleak heart, in part because he has made realization imposible by identifying Pat, the object of his passion, with his marble statue. Neither is fully formed or humanly real to him, and his pursuit of the ideal almost inevitably ends in incompletion, both sexual and artistic. When Gordon finally turns from marble to clay and molds the head of Mrs. Maurier with "savage verisimilitude" (322), he is at last able to capture the rich individuality of an actual human being. Greater realism of attitude brings Gordon to artistic achievement, but insofar as it also drives him to seek sexual satisfaction in a brothel, the triumph seems a qualified one.

Gordon and his story are paradigmatic; in *Mosquitoes,* the men are generally more sympathetic than the women and more physically attractive; Gordon and David, the yacht steward, evoke unqualified admiration for their muscled manliness or their "young lean splendor" (159), and the thoughts of several of the male characters, even the futile Talliaferro, are explored in a manner that makes them almost fully human. On the other hand, Pat Robyn, who has a clean odor that smells like "young trees" (21) and purportedly represents in the novel the sort of feminine "ideal" that arouses the passions of the otherwise self-contained Gordon, is described as having "shanks" that are "straight and brittle" (19) and a flat-breasted, "sexless" boy's body (24). She is a compromised ideal at best, and later in the book becomes a literal burden to a man who cares for her. Her "elopement" to land with David is an exaggeration of the real event on which it is based, Faulkner's departure from the boat for an amusement park at Mandeville, in the company of a young woman painter, Virginia Nagle. In the novel, when the two become lost in a swamp, Pat's near-hysterical petulance forces the yacht steward to take her on his back and carry her through the broiling heat and assaulting mosquitoes. Involvement with her thus results in physical as well as emotional pain.

Another of the young female characters, Jenny, suggests in her simple earthiness such later Faulknerian women as Lena Grove and Eula Varner. She may, as Olga Vickery proposes, partake of "the secret richness of 'just being,' "[22] but she is also, in her bovine sexuality, a "soiled" creature (55, 104, 127). Once again, as in *The Marble Faun,* the association of sexuality and uncleanliness arises, and Jenny presents a confused image, seeming to be alternately a goddess, in her "angelic nakedness" (140), and an animal, in her inert stupidity. In *Mosquitoes,* the nubile women are ambiguous and the one quasi-maternal figure is little short of oppressive. Mrs. Maurier, the owner of the yacht and organizer of the excursion, plays the role of "mother" insofar as she is the overseer and protectress of her gathered guests, and she is the actual aunt of Pat and her brother. But her "mothering" is ludicrous and her maternal authority ineffective. She feeds her passengers endless vitamin-filled grapefruit and organizes games, but the men ridicule her and constantly escape her smothering attention to stay below decks drinking themselves insensible, fearful of being "captured" by her. Her niece is heedless and disrespectful, constantly deflating her commands with "Oh, haul in your sheet, you're jibbing" (30). Eventually Mrs. Maurier becomes a figure of some pathos, as her early lost romance and entrapment in an unhappy marriage are explained, yet for much of the novel she is a comic Terrible Mother attempting to dominate her imprisoned protégés.

Mrs. Maurier may also represent Faulkner's vision of the suffocating quality of the would-be patron; she offers artists financial support—food, drink, and entertainment—but is emotionally parasitic, faintly vampirish, surrounding herself with vital, productive people to mask the emptiness at her core. Faulkner's punishing satiric treatment of the relationship between Mrs. Maurier and her guest-victims is perhaps related at some level to his earnest need for an artistic declaration of independence from the Maecenas-figure in his own life, Phil Stone. Gratitude to Stone was doubtlessly tinged with rebellious resentment in Faulkner's mind, for the latter quality finds vehement expression in his portrait of Mrs. Maurier.

Faulkner also directs the satire in the novel against various manifestations of affectation, revealing an attitude similar to the one expressed by Fielding: "The only source of the true Ridiculous is affectation . . . [as it] proceeds from one of these two causes, vanity or hypocrisy.[23] In so doing, Faulkner was assailing in his characters what was clearly one of his own prevailing tendencies, proceeding from his sense of the need for a protective mask. When he was writing *Mosquitoes,* the war in which he had failed to participate had been over for nearly eight years, yet he was still talking to New Orleans acquaintances in an assumed British accent about his apocryphal war wounds; in Oxford, he often posed as an English dandy and affectedly told a friend, "The British wear their handkerchiefs in their jacket sleeves. I prefer the sartorial usage also" (B, pp. 421, 255).

The disdainfully presented Talliaferro is like his creator at that time in being something of a false "gentleman" whose attention to externals masks a pitiable insecurity. Talliaferro, like Faulkner's Elmer, has a sister who has vanished, and he has been straitened by his environment, forced "while quite young and pliable to do all the things to which his natural impulses objected" (32); like Faulkner himself, he has wandered to Europe and back to New Orleans and is oppressed by his celibate state. The entire presentation of Talliaferro seems, in fact, to constitute a defensive response to early wounds of which the author makes us aware even while treating the character with mordant wit.

If Faulkner's strong sense of self-directed irony lies behind his portrait of Talliaferro, it is also, though less obviously, responsible for another group of satiric depictions that balance the element of idealized self-portraiture in the presentation of Gordon, the passionate, absorbed artist. The boy Josh, for example, is a comic version of the obsessed craftsman. He is whittling a mere pipe from a small cylinder of wood but will stop at nothing to complete his project. Needing a piece of wire, Josh steals a portion of the yacht's costly steering mechanism and thus causes the ship to run aground, marooning the entire party. Josh's mock objet d'art has both male and female portions, and thus anticipates in a ludicrous way the seriously intellectual depiction of art as basically hermaphroditic. Two additional characters complete Faulkner's self-criticism. Mark Frost is a ghostly poet with prehensile lips who lounges around self-consciously and writes poetry "reminding one somehow of the function of evacuation excruciatingly and incompletely performed" (54), while a character actually named Faulkner is briefly mentioned, a "little kind of black man" who is a "liar by profession" but "not dangerous: just crazy." "Faulkner?" queries another character and then dismisses him flatly: "Never heard of him" (144–45).

Faulkner draws more seriously and continuously upon directly autobiographical material in his treatment of Dawson Fairchild, the Sherwood Anderson figure. Fairchild is a dominant character in the work and, appropriately for a portrait of the voluable Anderson, he is at the center of nearly every significant conversation. But he himself appears ridiculous and pathetic, and the flaws in his vision are underscored. Only in his efforts to define some of the important tenets of artistic endeavor does Faulkner grant him acuity and an occasionally valuable insight. Fairchild/Anderson is physically described as a "benevolent walrus" (33) with a "kind, baffled face" (221), and he even derides himself as "an old racehorse" (49). He is almost foolishly talkative, tells humiliatingly revealing stories about himself—along with some splendid tall tales about Al Jackson, the fish rancher—and betrays an awareness of his waning artistic powers: "Words. . . . I had it once" (248). Faulkner locates a percipient critical voice in Julius, the Semitic man, who repeatedly and accurately points out Fairchild's flaws to him, just as Faulkner elucidated Anderson's in his articles and published statements. Julius calls him "a bewildered stenographer with a gift for people" (51), and astutely says, "His writing seems fumbling, not because life is unclear to him, but because of his innate humorless belief that, though it bewilder him at times, life at bottom is sound and admirable and fine" (242). He thus defines the quality of naiveté that impelled but also marred much of Anderson's fiction, as Faulkner explicitly commented in answering a question about Anderson at the University of Virginia: "A lot of the stuff that went into his stories a man with a harder mind, more sure of himself, would have stricken out and would have gotten rid of some of the sense of fumbling and clumsiness, the heavy-footedness" (*FIU*, p. 229).

Julius represents the critical acuity which Fairchild lacks, Gordon the single-minded dedication which he is beginning to lose, and there is an important symbolic parting of the ways at the end of the novel. Gordon, Julius, and Fairchild have been drinking together in an apparent recapitulation of the *Walspurgisnacht* scene from *Ulysses,* and Fairchild has become very drunk. Gordon, the intense artist, leaves them abruptly, much as Faulkner left his older writer friend. Faulkner's impetus to write novels instead of poetry and his basic ideas about art owed much to Anderson initially, but his work would increasingly depart from that of his mentor and far surpass it in power and complexity. Julius, the critical conscience, stays with Fairchild and supports him, and indeed, in that respect, Faulkner always remained with Anderson. Even after Anderson was long dead and his reputation in almost total eclipse, Faulkner paid sincere obeisance to the older writer. He repeatedly acknowledged his debt to Anderson, singled out the few strong works in Anderson's corpus for special praise, and even said that he had some reservations about accepting the Nobel Prize because he felt its worth was compromised by the fact that it had never been awarded to Anderson. The working artist left his "literary father" far behind, but the conscientious critic remained to pay his respects.

Despite his satirizing of Fairchild/Anderson as one who bumbled in both his life and his art, Faulkner has him offer several generalized statements of artistic philosophy that clearly approximate his own. Fairchild expresses his sense of the limitations of the word when he advises Talliaferro that women "don't care anything about words. . . . They ain't interested in what you're going to say: they are interested in what you're going to do" (112), thus anticipating the authorial impatience with "Talk, talk, talk: the utter and heartbreaking stupidity of words" (186). Further on, however, Fairchild qualifies his antiverbal position with his admission that "words brought into a happy conjunction produce something that lives, just as soil and climate and an acorn in proper conjunction will produce a tree" (210) and his belief that words occasionally have a "kind of fire" that can "invest the veriest platitude with magic" (249). He thus effects a certain healing of the disjunction between words and action that otherwise pervades this novel, a dynamic conciliation of the "abstract and the actual" such as Panthea Broughton has deemed central to Faulkner's art.[24]

Fairchild makes other important observations on the nature of the artist's endeavor. He declares, as Faulkner would later, that "human nature don't change. Its actions achieve different results under different conditions, but human nature don't change" (227), and he talks about the need for consistency in fictional plot and character that stands in paradoxical contrast to the anarchy of "real life"—a need all too strikingly apparent to an apprentice novelist trying to create characters that "cast a shadow." As Fairchild says, "It's only in books that people must function according to arbitrary rules of conduct and probability; it's only in books that events must never flout credulity" (181).

Also given to Fairchild are some provocative statements about the hermaphroditic nature of art. Faulkner had used a hermaphroditic character in his first novel—Januarius Jones, a male in whom "the feminine predominated . . . a woman with a man's body" (222)—and in *Mosquitoes* he expands the idea to stand metaphorically for the fictional artifact. Fairchild first calls poetry "Hermaphroditus," a "dark perversion. Like a fire that don't need any fuel, that lives on its own heat" (252). But he later returns to the subject and invests the "bisexual" process of art with a more positive meaning. He states that because the dominating impulse in the world is feminine and biological, the value of his art to the male is that he "can create without any assistance at all: what he does is his." It is "creation, reproduction from within" (320). One critic has chosen to see this passage as revealing a vision of writing as autoerotic self-destruction, as the devouring of the masculine self by the feminine work of art,[25] and to be sure the metaphor which follows of the female spider who consumes her mate does suggest such an interpretation. But the overriding impression is that Faulkner regarded art as a positive form of generation, as a uniting in the artist of the masculine and feminine principles to produce a "child," the artifact. He often referred parentally to his books as his children, and however ambivalently he may have felt about the hermaphrodite in the guise of a "real" character whose sexual identity is in question, as an emblem of the process that produces art the idea provided him with a major symbol of unilateral self-procreation.

Mosquitoes thus makes some rare explicit statements about art, and its characters, like those in *Soldiers' Pay,* reveal Faulkner's severely mixed feelings toward women during this period as well as his ability to balance irony and earnestness in his self-depictions. Neither of the apprentice works is a mature and integrated piece of fictional art, and yet both have value in themselves and in their anticipation of the later great novels. The earlier novel is the more often cited for such forecasting, with its small-town setting that suggests an embryonic Jefferson and its themes of war and the doomed hero, but *Mosquitoes,* too, is a germinal work in ways that are less frequently pointed out. Minor elements in this novel become major motifs in future ones. The palms in Jackson Square, "fixed in black and soundless explosions" (14), suggest the violence of the controlling image in *The Wild Palms,* while Gordon's assertion that "only an idiot has no grief; only a fool would forget it" (329), prefigures Wilbourne's major speech in that same novel. The swamp road that runs "on like a hypnotism: a dull and endless proression from which there was no escape" (187), would become the road that rules Joe Christmas in *Light in August,* just as the "rabid manifestations" of Protestantism referred to by Julius (42) would dominate that same work. Fairchild's observation on the folly of living by a "code" ("When you've made a form of behavior out of an ideal, it's not an ideal any longer, and you become a public nuisance" [39]), receives full-scale treatment in *Sartoris, The Sound and the Fury,* and *The Town,* while the intense, almost incestuous relationship between Pat and her brother, a theme which Faulkner first touched upon in "Elmer," would recur in a number of his later works, and especially, his two greatest, *The Sound and the Fury* and *Absalom, Absalom!.* The yacht's engine, "terrifying" (like Henry Adams's dynamo) in its "implacable soulless power" (76), introduces the theme of antimechanism found so frequently in Faulkner's later novels, and the stream-of-consciousness technique that Faulkner somewhat tentatively essays at the end of the novel anticipates his reuse of the method with consummate power in *The Sound and the Fury*.

Mosquitoes, for all its singularity in the Faulkner canon, is a sourcebook from which the writer later drew more copiously than is usually recognized. Moreover, its status as a sort of *Künstlerroman* in which Faulkner explicitly confronted his literary milieu and acknowledged some of the ideas to which it had introduced him, even while he satirized and denounced the milieu itself, makes the novel a significant statement of his early artistic credo. Finally, Faulkner defined therein the art of true creative genius in a way that showed how much he viewed it as emanating from emotion, not from reason: it was, he said, "that Passion Week of the heart, that instant of timeless beatitude . . . that passive state of the heart with which the mind, the brain, has nothing to do at all, in which the hackneyed accidents which make up this world—love and life and death and sex and sorrow—brought together by chance in perfect proportions, take on a kind of splendid and timeless beauty" (339). He thus defined both the origins and the glory of his own life's work.

3

Heritage and Imagined Suicide:
Sartoris and *The Sound and the Fury*

WHEN WILLIAM FAULKNER WAS ASKED if his works should be read in any particular sequence, he answered, "Probably . . . begin with a book called *Sartoris* that has the germ of my apocrypha in it" (*FIU,* p. 285). *Sartoris* (or *Flags in the Dust,* as Faulkner first titled it) is the initial novel in the great Yoknapatawpha series, and its inclusive quality bothered one early reviewer, who pointed out its variety, its "widest possible range of characters, situations, moods, effects, and styles." [1] This same quality now makes the work important to critics, who view it as Faulkner's Yoknapatawpha sourcebook, the germinal work in which he introduced characters like the members of the Sartoris and the Snopes families, Narcissa and Horace Benbow, and Doc Peabody; treated both of the wars that haunted his imagination throughout his career as a novelist; presented types that would become recurrent, such as the indomitable elderly woman and the patient black family retainer; and developed such themes as the heritage that is both ideal and curse, the fraternal struggle, and the regenerative power of the land.

These elements alone would make the novel significant in Faulkner's corpus, but *Sartoris* is also notable because it is his first intensely serious fiction and because it contains numerous portents of the great work that immediately followed it, *The Sound and the Fury.* In *Sartoris* he began to probe with earnestness the implications of his own individual inheritance from the past that at once inspired him as a novelist and frustrated him as a man, and to reveal, unconsciously as well as consciously, some of the dark

61

aspects of his response to his family situation. In later writing about the genesis of this novel, Faulkner made a rare admission about its autobiographical nature, confessing that the characters were "composed partly from what they were in actual life and partly from what they should have been and were not," and that when he started it, "I began to write, without much purpose, until I realised that to make it truly evocative it must be personal, in order to not only preserve my own interest in the writing, but to preserve my belief in the savor of the bread-and-salt" (B, p. 532). *Sartoris* seemed especially "personal" to Faulkner because he came home to write it, both literally and figuratively, returning from two years of wandering early in 1927 to begin the manuscript, and finding his material in and around Oxford and in his contemplation of his own and his family's history. The fact that he was approaching his thirtieth birthday no doubt increased his desire to discover some sort of self-definition in the present through an exploration of his past; his developing powers as an artist provided him with the means to embark upon such an exploration.

The emotional energy which Faulkner poured into *Sartoris* distinguishes it from his previous two novels, which, though personal in certain essential ways, were predominantly written in a mood of sardonic detachment. *Sartoris* is much more highly pitched, and this quality gives its particular psychological revelations a special significance. Faulkner was profoundly committed to the work—one of his friends during this period remarked that "William Faulkner cared deeply about *Sartoris*"[2]—and his response to the manuscript's initial rejection betrayed a passionately protective concern. Having written about the hermaphroditic nature of the artist and the procreative aspect of the artifact in *Mosquitoes,* he displayed a corresponding parental attitude toward this fictional offspring that proved so vulnerable.

In the fall of 1927, when Faulkner had finished his manuscript, a longer version of *Sartoris* which he then called *Flags in the Dust,* he sent it to Boni and Liveright, which had published his previous two novels. Horace Liveright sent back a letter of rejection with the cutting comment that "we don't believe that you should offer it for publication." Faulkner wrote of his reaction: "I was shocked: my first emotion was blind protest, then I became objective for an instant, like a parent who is told that its child is a thief or an idiot or a leper; for a dreadful moment I contemplated it with consternation and despair, then like the parent I hid my own eyes in the fury of denial" (B, pp. 559–60). The work is said to have been turned down by twelve publishers[3] before Harcourt, Brace finally accepted it, on the condition that the manuscript be condensed. As if this were tantamount

to a request to dismember his fictional child, Faulkner refused outright to
have anything to do with it, and the job devolved on a friend from
Mississippi, Ben Wasson, who had become his literary agent.

When the much-reduced text was published, as *Sartoris*, in January,
1929, Faulkner dedicated it to Sherwood Anderson, "through whose
kindness I was first published, with the belief that this book will give him
no reason to regret that fact." The dedication reveals Faulkner's self-con-
fident belief in the merits of this crucial novel; it also makes a gesture of
tribute toward the immediate past that seems appropriate as an introduction
to a work whose central theme is the influence of the past, both recent and
distant, on the lives of a series of characters. The pivotal figure is young
Bayard Sartoris, whose problems of living with the legend of "glamorous
fatality" that he has inherited from the first dashing, heroic Sartorises and
with the recent death of his twin brother at the hands of German fighter
pilots have rendered him guilt-ridden and confused. Bayard's story is
paralleled or illuminated by a number of subplots and character-groups.
The black Strothers family, for example, has its own problems in dealing
with the war and with the contrast between past and present, particularly
Caspey—who, like Bayard, has been overseas and returned altered,
godless and insolent, unwilling to accept his second-class citizenship as a
black after serving in the military—and old Simon, who longs for the
irrecoverable glories of the past.

In another quarter of Jefferson, the intellectual Horace Benbow, with his
volubility and his interest in the delicate art of glass blowing, presents a
striking contrast to the taciturn and violent Bayard. Yet Horace, too, has
been overseas and returned to his own postwar "doom," an adulterous
alliance with the married Belle Mitchell, whom he sees as shallow but from
whom he feels powerless to disentangle himself. Narcissa, his sister, links
the stories of Horace and the Sartorises as she edges somewhat reluctantly
toward marriage with Bayard, and the anonymous letters she receives from
Byron Snopes represent the first incursion of the contaminating Snopeses
into the previously closed Sartoris world, though Narcissa's secret titilla-
tion by the letters reveals the capacity of that world to be corrupted and
eventually overtaken. Bayard's acerbic great-aunt Jenny provides a running ironic commentary on the vainglory of her kinsmen, and a group of
doctors and a folkhealer present a variety of medical outlooks ranging from
"outdated" to "modern" whose varied efficaciousness makes another sort
of satiric comment on old versus new.

At the time he wrote *Sartoris,* Faulkner had immersed himself in his
Oxford milieu and was trying to come to terms, at many levels, with the

figurative inheritance passed down by the Old Colonel and his progeny. The burden of the past is the predominant theme of the work, and it is manifested in a number of ways, from the concrete to the symbolic to the psychological. In the very first sentence, "the spirit of the dead man" John Sartoris becomes a palpable presence that joins Old Bayard and old man Falls as they sit musing together, and that lost but vivid past which he represents is embodied, on the first level, in things. The carved pipe which was John's has just been given by Falls to the old man who is John's son, and later Old Bayard goes to the cedar chest with its "scent drily and muskily nostalgic, as of old ashes" (90) to draw out family memorabilia, notably the Bible wherein is recorded "the stark dissolving apotheosis of his name" (92).[4] While Old Bayard has reverence for the family's souvenirs, young Bayard, in a significant scene, tries rebelliously to immolate the past by burning all of his dead brother's mementos. The Sartoris house is full of actual objects that evoke the past, and the parlor also contains imagined ghosts perceptible to all who know the family legend, "figures in crinoline and hooped muslin and silk" (61). In ironic parody of this, the Snopes world is "desolate with ghosts," too, "ghosts of discouraged weeds, of food in the shape of empty tins, broken boxes and barrels" (107), and its detritus counterpoints the glamorous emblems of the Sartorises. Even as the Sartoris past is apotheosized early in the novel, however, there are symbolic suggestions that it can be stultifying. The beautiful house sits "serenely benignant" with its almost memorial "bed of salvia where a Yankee patrol had halted on a day long ago," but its other flora include a rose which is "slowly but steadily choking" a wisteria, whose shattered petals now lie all around (6-7). The glorious past has a strangulating effect on its inheritors, who must find their own growing room in the present, and it is the difficulty of finding just such growing room that finally dooms Bayard Sartoris—and haunts his creator.

Faulkner portrays a whole range of responses to the past which illuminate Bayard's plight. His grandfather refuses to enter the modern world and lives instead behind a wall of deafness with the memories of his father, whose presence is so strong that "it seemed to him that he could hear his father's breathing" (2). Old Simon, watching the decline of his once proud carriage horses, similarly retreats into the past and goes around talking to "Marse John," "mumbling away to that arrogant shade which dominated the house and the life that went on there" (113). Even Aunt Jenny's usual harsh realism fails her when she tells the old stories about the first Bayard, transmuting fact into legend "until what had been a hare-brained prank of two heedless and reckless boys wild with their own youth had become a gallant and finely tragical focal point to which the history of the race had been raised from out the old miasmic swamps of spiritual sloth by two angels valiantly fallen and strayed'' (9). The absurdity of attempting to live by romantic notions is demonstrated by the tale of that Bayard's suicidal reentry into an enemy camp in pursuit of anchovies, but even Jenny cannot resist glamorizing the deed and the dead.

Both this distant past and the more recent and personal memory of watching the foolhardy but glorious flight into enemy skies that led to his brother's death make living in the present an impossibility for Bayard. He can find no outlet for purposeful action, no means of articulating and coming to terms with his anguish, and nothing even in love other than "the temporary abeyance of his despair" (289). He is finally driven to destroy himself. "Perhaps," says the authorial voice, raising Bayard's plight to a higher level, "Sartoris is the game itself—a game outmoded and played with pawns shaped too late and to an old dead pattern, and of which the Player Himself is a little wearied" (380).

The theme of *Sartoris,* a common enough one in southern literature for obvious reasons, is treated by Faulkner with entire seriousness. He uses suggestive detail, careful parallelism and contrast, and tries to balance elegy with irony and the central plot with a secondary one in order to give the novel richness. But the novel has apparent flaws, and no one considers it to be, in either its original *(Flags in the Dust)* or published form, among Faulkner's greatest works. The Horace Benbow plot is inadequately developed as a balance to Bayard's narrative, though much of the responsibility for this lopsidedness is attributable to Ben Wasson, who excised a great deal of the Benbow material from the *Flags in the Dust* manuscript. The novel also has a certain patchwork quality, like Aunt Sally Wyatt's bag of scraps, "odds and ends of colored fabric in all possible shapes" (151) that have been fitted together but not particularly well integrated. Moreover, the tone of the book is uncertain, wavering between earnest romanticism and satiric irony, and Faulkner is not always careful to locate one or the other viewpoint in a particular character, as he would in later works. Hence the authorial voice seems to romanticize the very events it is attempting to satirize.

Perhaps the most severe weakness of *Sartoris* is the inadequacy of Bayard as a tragic hero. Many critics have commented on his tendency to seem glamorous one moment and foolish the next and on the problems created by thrusting the weight of meaning on a central character who is inarticulate and unreflective and whose very motives seem confused. The sense of "doom' which pervades Bayard's psyche as well as the entire novel is referred to constantly but is neither satisfactorily explained nor adequately dramatized. This flaw results from Faulkner's still insufficiently developed literary craftsmanship, but the atmosphere of fatality is itself attributable to the author's own state of mind as he wrote the novel—a condition similar in many ways to that of his doom-ridden protagonist. Faulkner said soon afterwards that he had been "speculating . . . on time and death" and soon "nothing served but that I try by main strength to recreate between the covers of a book the world I was already preparing to lose and regret." Though the "world" of which Faulkner speaks is that of the Sartorises with its fading glamor, the statement has Thanatotic overtones that go beyond the usual "morbidity of the young" that Faulkner described (B, p. 531) and may well be related to some of the darker impulses of his subconscious that are revealed in the book, especially in the portrait of Bayard.

It may illuminate the excessive and unexplained drive of Bayard toward self-destruction and death to refer for a moment to the well-known discussion of similar problems in the portrayal of Shakespeare's most famous protagonist. In writing of *Hamlet* in his 1919 essay, T. S. Eliot criticized the play by saying that there was no "objective correlative" for Hamlet's extreme feelings of guilt over his failure to revenge his father's murder. He suggested that Hamlet was dominated by an emotion "in *excess* of the facts as they appear" and that this artistic flaw was probably related to psychological factors in the mind of Hamlet's creator, "things which Shakespeare did not understand himself."[5] Long before Eliot's essay appeared, two psychoanalysts had already addressed themselves to the problems raised by Hamlet's procrastination. By 1900, aided by his reading of *Hamlet,* Freud had formulated his theory of the Oedipus complex, and he observed that "Hamlet is able to do anything—except take vengeance on the man who did away with his father and took that father's place with his mother, the man who shows him the repressed wishes of his own childhood realized."[6] He goes on to point out that the play was written after the death of Shakespeare's father, which probably had reactivated the playwright's own Oedipal wishes. Freud's follower, Ernest Jones, expanding on this theory of subconscious Oedipal identification in a 1910 essay which was later published in book form as *Hamlet and Oedipus,*[7] went on to postulate that the very reason the play enjoyed such a wide appeal was to be found in its expression of a psychological problem common to males.

Bayard Sartoris, not unlike Hamlet, has an obsessive preoccupation which seems far in excess of the given facts. He reiterates constantly and without provocation that he should not be blamed for his twin brother's death; his very first words to his grandfather upon his return from war are, "I tried to keep him from going up there on that goddam little popgun" (43). Nearly all of his subsequent actions seem based on a deep-seated need to punish himself for some imagined guilt and, in effect, to recapitulate in his own death the brother's death for which he feels responsible, and he moves self-destructively and almost inexorably toward involvement in a violent plane crash which is almost an exact duplicate of that in which his brother died two years before. Bayard obviously regards himself as a murderer, and when he inadvertently causes his grandfather's death from a heart attack during a wild automobile ride, he again accuses himself of the first death even as he is forced to take responsibility for the second. After futilely trying to exculpate himself for Old Bayard's heart attack, he acknowledges bitterly that *"You, who deliberately do things your judgment tells you may not be successful, even possible, are afraid to face the consequences of your own acts."* He then irrationally bursts out "in vindication and justification and accusation; what he knew not, blazing out at what, Whom, he did not know: *You did it! You caused it all; you killed Johnny!"* (311).

Bayard's guilt about his brother is extreme and illogical, and his extraordinary sense of responsibility for a death in which he actually had no hand is undoubtedly related to his subconscious wish that his brother be destroyed: the fulfillment of such secret and forbidden desires almost invariably gives rise to excessive guilt and self-accusation. Faulkner presents many subtle clues concerning the ways in which the brothers were unspoken competitors "in the young masculine violence of their twinship" (47), and indicates that Bayard frequently came off a poor second in the eyes of his small Jefferson world. "His dead brother was the braver," said Bayard's creator later (*FIU*, p. 250), and in the novel John is remembered as more attractive in other ways by those who knew him. Narcissa, who regards Bayard at first with shrinking dread, remembers John as full of laughter, with a face that was "merry and bold and wild"; and she recalls that his youthful ascent in a balloon seemed to show that "the end of wisdom is to dream high enough not to lose the dream in the seeking of it" (73–74). Later, looking at a portrait of John, she sees in his face "not that bleak arrogance she had come to know in Bayard's, but a sort of frank spontaneity, warm and ready and generous" (356).

Several other times Bayard is compared with his dead twin in a way that reveals John's greater generosity, exuberance, and skill, and his remembered warmth makes a sharp contrast with Bayard's chill haughtiness. The MacCallums, with whom Bayard spends several days hunting, recall the time during a fox hunt when John was found drifting down the river on a log with the fox at one end, "singing that fool song as loud as he could yell" (125). They later reminisce at length, in front of his twin, about John's merits—his hunting ability, his warmheartedness, his unfailing cheerfulness, and his consideration of others. Bayard himself painfully realizes his comparative inadequacy when he arrives at the MacCallums' without a present for Mandy, "some trinket of no value which John never forgot to bring her when he came" (314). Whether or not Bayard was ever aware of his wish to supersede his attractive twin, it undoubtedly existed, and it now causes that terrible sense of responsibility which escalates into an irresistible compulsion to destroy himself.

Sartoris took on a terrifying sense of prophecy when Faulkner's own brother Dean died in a plane crash six years after the novel was published, to be buried under a tombstone with the same inscription as John Sartoris's: "I bare him on eagles' wings and brought him unto me." To fully understand the psychological import of *Sartoris,* it is necessary to see just how autobiographical a character Bayard Sartoris was for Faulkner. That he subconsciously transmuted Dean, the brother, born when he was ten, who claimed so much of the parental affection that had been denied to William, into John Sartoris and then annihilated him seems hardly questionable. When Dean Faulkner's own daughter later sought to describe her father in a biographical study, her sense of him made her turn to his brother's portrait of John Sartoris with its "warm radiance" of "something sweet and merry and wild" (Wells, p. 20). And Dean, like his fictional counterpart, was known for his reckless exuberance, his insouciance, and his skill at all outdoor pastimes. William Faulkner, as we have seen, was indulgent and gentle with his youngest brother, playing games with Dean and his friends, sending him affectionate letters whenever he was away, and serving as the scoutmaster of Dean's troop, and Dean adored him in return. Still, *Sartoris* makes it clear that there were some dark undercurrents in William's attitude, and his overwhelming guilt after Dean's 1935 crash in the plane which William had given him was as extreme and illogical in its way as Bayard Sartoris's.[8]

Besides a complex fraternal attitude, the portrait of Bayard reveals several other elements of the psychology of his creator. The mood of despair in which Faulkner said he wrote *Sartoris* is close to that he embodies in Bayard, as Bayard lies in bed in the jail that is both real and self-created and reflects on the "bleak and barren world" through which he must drag his body and in which there is "nothing to be seen" (160). He is the Marble Faun grown older and destructive, driving himself, as did

Faulkner, to ride powerful horses and pilot airplanes on or in which he did not belong. Both show a regressive element in their violent behavior; Narcissa tells the bedridden Bayard that "you do things to hurt yourself just to worry people" (254), and the endless vigils at Bayard's bedside by various kindly figures do much to reveal their creator's need for nurturing tenderness. Bayard, like Faulkner, is an insomniac, and both use alcohol as an anodyne to physical pain. After Bayard hurts his head in a fall from the wild stallion, he turns for relief to corn whiskey and says, "I keep thinking another drink will ease it off some" (146). Faulkner, too, tended to treat his physical traumas with liberal doses of whiskey. During spring planting at the Sartoris place, the brief respite from guilt and anguish Bayard finds through involvement in the rhythms of the farm seems an augury of the relief from writing and restlessness Faulkner would later enjoy on the farm he bought outside Oxford.

It is also significant that Bayard should gain a necessary, if temporary, spiritual sustenance not only from the land but also from nonfamilial human sources, from the MacCallums, who treat him with warmth and acceptance as he lingers with them for several days before fleeing the area, and from the black family with whom he spends Christmas. Such turning to figures outside the family for emotional buttressing would be a recurrent theme in Faulkner's work, an expression of his low estimation of the family as a place for life-sustaining interchange and the consequence of his years in his own strife-ridden household. Bayard cannot find what he needs at the Sartoris place, even with an attentive wife and expected child, and, after a period with the solid country folk, departs for the aimless odyssey that ends in his death. In his rejection of his family, his pessimism, his self-destructive and regressive impulses, and in the powerful guilt that arises from a subconscious need to obliterate his brother, he is an exaggerated psychological self-portrait of the author himself. The picture may be askew and inadequately realized artistically, but it embodies many of the concerns which seem to have loomed large for Faulkner as he wrote the novel.

Sartoris has a number of other important biographical qualities, both psychological and factual. The work probably represents Faulkner's most extensive use of family material. He drew on the family lore about his great-grandfather, the Old Colonel, and divided it between the first Sartoris brothers. He gave to that early Bayard the reckless Civil War exploit against a large enemy force which is adjudged foolish but somehow admirable, transforming it into a suicidal quest for Yankee anchovies, and to John Sartoris the Old Colonel's expulsion from command by his underlings, his killing of two men, his subsequent building of a railroad, and his death at the hands of a former partner on the day of his election to the state legislature. The Old Colonel is, despite comments on his folly or his arrogance, a vivid and romantic personage in the novel, as he undoubtedly then was in William Faulkner's imagination, his legend somehow exerting a more powerful hold on the family than the man himself had during his lifetime: "Freed as he was of time and flesh, he was a far more palpable presence" (1) than many of those who were still alive. Through his depiction of the first Sartorises, Faulkner attempts to enumerate some few of his great-grandfather's flaws and to indict his "useless vainglory," but he is also quite clearly entranced by the legend. The sight of John's "pompous effigy" brooding above the landscape, like the Old Colonel's in Ripley, looking out over his railroad and the valley in which it ran to the very "ramparts of infinity" (375), is an awesome and troubling one to his survivors. Faulkner used this same view of the Old Colonel in some of the short stories which he eventually integrated into *The Unvanquished;* only in "Odor of Verbena" and *Absalom, Absalom!* did he take a severely negative look at the questionable values represented by his great-grandfather.

Old Bayard is closely modeled on Faulkner's grandfather, John Wesley Thompson Falkner, who lived near his grandson in Oxford until his death in 1922. There are almost no points here where fact and fiction diverge. Old Bayard, like the Young Colonel, is a banker whose daily nap is as well-known a ritual as his daily toddy, and the "walled tower of his deafness" behind which he retreats conveniently is known to be a ruse by family members. In his rigid erectness and widower's solitude he is a proud and isolated figure to whom Doc Peabody says, "I don't know anybody that gets less fun out of living than you do" (100), an appraisal much like that the Falkners made of the Young Colonel in his final years. Aunt Jenny, based on Faulkner's outspoken great-aunt Alabama, is angered by his failure to die heroically, feeling he "had committed lese majesty toward his ancestors and the lusty glamour of the family doom by dying, as she put it, practically from the 'inside out' " (354).

Old Bayard's son and his wife are barely mentioned, save for a few words on their death in an epidemic when their twin sons were eight. Faulkner was once asked why this particular Sartoris is omitted from his multigenerational chronicle, and he answered, "The twins' father didn't have a story. He came at a period in history which, in this country, people thought of and think of now as a peaceful one. . . . This John Sartoris, the father, lived in that time when there was nothing that brought the issue to him to be brave and strong or dramatic" (*FIU,* p. 251). This reply is at best equivocal, since Old Bayard (so far as this novel is concerned) is also a Sartoris without a war in which to perform gloriously: indeed, there is an explicit statement to this effect in the novel, about Old Bayard's "having been born too late for one war and too soon for the next" (374). Although Faulkner gives no satisfactory reason for completely glossing over the fictional generation to which his own father belonged, it is conceivable that he did so either because he was as yet unprepared to deal artistically with Murry or because he envisaged omission as some sort of punishment; it is equally possible that the Dean character was a surrogate for Murry Falkner. Buried fratricidal desires often have their origins in an Oedipal wish for the death of the father that is displaced onto the brother, who is more vulnerable. Dean was closely identified with his father—he was the acclaimed favorite among the boys, and son and father shared many interests—and Faulkner's fictional annihilation of his brother thus served indirectly to dispose of his father. The psychic process described is a familiar one to depth psychologists, and the omission of a parental genera- tion in *Sartoris,* like the aesthetic problems in the presentation of Bayard, reveals that Faulkner was at some level coming to terms with deep-rooted difficulties.

Another important element in Faulkner's situation in the late 1920s is represented by his rather harsh portrait of Horace Benbow. Faulkner frequently portrays an introspective artist-figure as well as a doomed man of action, and each objectifies an aspect of his psyche. Horace is referred to as a "poet," although he is a lawyer. His earnest glass blowing, his futile efforts to create one perfect vase, make him almost a parodic artist-figure, like the boy Josh in *Mosquitoes*. Horace's description of "lying" as a creative act definable as a "struggle for survival," "little puny man's way of dragging circumstance about to fit his preconception of himself as a figure in the world" (198), at once recalls and expands upon Faulkner's statement in *Mosquitoes* that he was a "liar by profession." Horace's best work he calls by his sister's name and keeps by his bedside, having shown it to her with a face "a little mad, passionate and fine and austere" (203).

The association of Horace's ardor for his art with his ardor for his sister has a sexual and more than slightly incestuous overtone. Horace evokes the caves where he first discovered glassblowing in images of female sexuality and exults in describing to Narcissa his entry therein: "When you put your hand out to steady yourself against the wall, it's wet when you take it away. It feels just like blood" (171). Though Horace has been carrying on a sexual liaison with the married Belle Mitchell, he does so with a certain distaste, referring to Belle as "cannily stupid" (178) and "enveloping"

(257). His reunion with his sister after a quarrel is tinged with far more loverlike passion than any of his scenes with Belle. "He swept her into his wet arms. 'Don't,' she cried. 'You're wet!' But he swung her from the floor, against his sopping chest, repeating, 'Narcy, Narcy'; then his cold nose was against her face and she tasted rain" (302–303). Horace ultimately goes to live with Belle, but unenthusiastically. The distastefulness of the relationship is suggested by the odorous and dripping box of shrimp he must regularly fetch for Belle (described in a passage which was excised from the original manuscript), and he writes long, loving letters to his sister, whom he calls "thou still unravished bride of quietness" (352). His Keatsian vision of Narcissa's essential chastity contrasts sharply with his sense of Belle's sulliedness, and she occupies, like his fragile vases, some inviolate pedestal in his heart. Horace's emotional ties to his sister reveal the arrested nature of his masculine development and are linked with his incapacity to perform any useful action. Faulkner was occasionally plagued by a sense of the effeteness of art and this attitude is manifested in his portrait of Horace Benbow.

Both of the male protagonists fall prey to their particular "doom" by the end of the novel, Horace to an imperfect relationship with his tainted mistress, and Bayard to a violent end in an experimental airplane which he has been warned against flying. Bayard Sartoris is the modern heir to a family myth so strong that his sense of inadequacy before it, augmented by his guilt over the death of his brother that he may have secretly desired, drives him inexorably to self-destruction. He obviously had a great deal of personal and symbolic significance to Faulkner. It would be a number of years before Faulkner could fully repudiate the glamorous fatality of the legend; he would return again and again to the theme of real or imagined fratricide, and the young male protagonist of his very next novel would, like Bayard, follow a downward course toward suicide.

Unaware of the publishing difficulties *Sartoris* would encounter, Faulkner finished writing it with a sense of exhilaration: "I have written THE book," he told his publisher, "of which these other things were but foals." He knew with certainty that "it is much better than that other stuff. I believe that at last I have learned to control the stuff and fix it on something like rational truth" (*L,* pp. 38, 37). His use of family material and his immersion in the milieu of northern Mississippi in which he was raised had proved imaginatively fruitful and he was ready to begin probing even more deeply into his personal heritage. Sometime around the end of 1927, Faulkner began working on a story he called "Twilight": derived from his childhood memories, it was gradually to evolve into *The Sound and the Fury*.

He soon learned that his previous novel had been decisively rejected, and as it continued to make its frustrating rounds of New York publishers, Faulkner decided to write this next one solely for himself. He plunged wholeheartedly into the work that became, both emotionally and technically, one of his most powerful books. Just a few years later he said of the experience: "With one novel completed and consistently refused for two years, I had just written my guts into *The Sound and the Fury,* though I was not aware until the book was published that I had done so, because I had done it for pleasure. I believed then that I would never be published again."[9] The statement includes the usual Faulknerian hyperbole, for *Sartoris* was on the market for less than two years, and it is unlikely that he wrote *The Sound and the Fury* solely for "pleasure." But his emphasis on the highly visceral nature of the experience is telling, for the work has a depth and intensity equaled by few others in his oeuvre, and the manner in which this full-blown, megalithic artifact virtually erupted out of a fictional landscape of more pallid works is little less than awesome.

The Sound and the Fury is considered by a number of critics to be Faulkner's greatest work and by others to be rivaled only by *Absalom, Absalom!*. All have praised it as an impressive technical achievement in which Faulkner equals or surpasses James Joyce's *Ulysses* in his use of stream-of-consciousness for character portrayal and in which he develops a remarkably effective narrative mode involving both parallelism and incremental expansion. Some critics have further seen the story as sociologically symbolic, signifying, not nothing, but the very decline of southern society itself, with Quentin's suicide revealing the failure of the old code and Jason representing the rapacious standards of the "New South."[10] The splendor of *The Sound and the Fury* is fully apparent and sufficiently definable from an aesthetic and a sociological vantage point. The question may be raised whether psychobiographical criticism can also contribute to an understanding of how and why the seemingly abrupt transition from *Sartoris* to *The Sound and the Fury* occurred, how Faulkner progressed suddenly from writing a promising but flawed novel to creating a superb work of mature fictional art. Yet it is clear that many elements of the greatness of *The Sound and the Fury* emanated from Faulkner's own psychology, from his conscious and unconscious emotional attitudes toward the novel, as well as from his growing craftsmanship.

Much that Faulkner said retrospectively about the novel reveals the extent to which it was an other than rational exercise in artistry, springing instead from the deeper strata of the authorial subconscious. The entire book evinces the war between sense and non-sense, or unreason, and just as the latter dominates the book thematically, so also did it control the work's creation. Faulkner talked about the title, which came "out of my unconscious,"[11] and about the "ecstasy" in which he wrote the book, "that eager and joyous faith and anticipation of surprise which the yet unmarred sheet beneath my hand held inviolate and unfailing, waiting for release."[12] He apparently created the novel without any conscious method: "I had no idea of writing the book it finally became. It simply grew from day to day" (*LIG,* p. 31). Michael Millgate, who has explored the manner in which Faulkner worked, points out that he seems to have written it without notes, just letting the narrative expand and develop under his pen in the direction which the themes and material seemed to demand.[13] Given that Faulkner wrote the novel in a heightened state of emotion, it is not surprising that many significant aspects of its technique and effect should have had their source in the author's personal psychology. The structure, the inwardness, the psychological portraits, and the interrelationships of the characters—all are a product of Faulkner's effort at a crucial moment in his life to understand and depict his personal struggles in a newly explorative and definitive way. Having begun this effort in *Sartoris,* he took it to a much deeper level in *The Sound and the Fury.*

Two elements in the structure of the novel, its quadripartite nature and the constant recurrence of the past in the present, are obsessional and revealing. Faulkner called *The Sound and the Fury* "the book that failed four times"[14]—alternatively, referring to the "Appendix" he added in 1946, the novel "I wrote . . . five separate times trying to tell the story, to rid myself of the dream which would continue to anguish me until I did" (*LIG,* p. 244). "The story" that demanded to be told and retold is obviously that of Faulkner's personal past and the severe problems it had created. Faulkner said that any writer in the early stages of his career "is writing his own biography because . . . at that time all he knows is what has happened to him" and "his only insight in it is into himself, and it's a biography because that's the only gauge he has to measure—is what he had experienced himself" (*FIU,* p. 103). All of Faulkner's previous works had been to some degree "biography" but never in such a compulsive and inward fashion as *The Sound and the Fury.* In it Faulkner began to explore those inner regions of the psyche which had previously been hidden from his readers' eyes (and possibly from his own) and to attempt to describe the turmoil he discovered there. As Faulkner tried to understand some of his own desperate anxieties and to embody them in the structure and characters of the novel, he simultaneously illuminated them for others. Bayard Sartoris had been a somewhat opaque and troubling character because Faulkner apparently neither compehended nor adequately depicted his psychic difficulties, but in creating Benjy and Quentin Compson Faulkner employed a greater psychological thoroughness of presentation and thus made them more vivid and sympathetically human, more fully realized.

With the growth of his willingness to explore the roots of anxiety and motivation, Faulkner also began to trace his protagonists' difficulties to their origins in a troubled childhood. Quentin Compson is, like Bayard Sartoris and like Faulkner himself, subconsciously preoccupied with self-destruction. In *Sartoris* the problem is related to a competitive fraternal relationship magnified by the fact that the parents are dead, but in *The Sound and the Fury* it is pursued to its real source, the parental failure that has left the major character Oedipally arrested and incapable of attaining masculine adulthood. In Bayard we perceive only the symptoms; through the probing characterization of Quentin we discover the causes, the emotional deprivations created by a problematic family situation. We see how the deficiencies of the crucial parent-child interaction, never touched upon in *Sartoris,* affect an entire group of children, all of whose plights are related to the author's own. In *The Sound and the Fury,* Faulkner describes the problems and affixes the blame, as it were, with a completeness and psychological perspicacity which he had never previously demonstrated.

Along with the psychic portraits of the novel, the symbolic relationships of the characters are also attributable to the more introspective nature of Faulkner's concerns. *The Sound and the Fury* marks the beginning of Faulkner's ability to create "linked characters," characters who represent closely interrelated ego fragments rather than fully discrete individuals.[15] The technique, which had its source in Faulkner's new psychological self-awareness, would again be employed in such works as *As I Lay Dying, Light in August,* and *Absalom, Absalom!.* Benjy and Quentin are psychically akin in a way earlier Faulkner characters had not been—they serve as emotional mirror images of each other in their arrested development—and Jason is related to them by more than blood, for he suffers from similar problems whose causes are different. In this approach to character relationships, as in other technical aspects of *The Sound and the Fury,* Faulkner's artistic sophistication is a direct result of his exploration of new psychic territory in himself and, concomitantly, in his fiction.

No single event in Faulkner's life during this period visibly accounts for his sudden delving into the darker substrata of the mind, but rather a series of small occurrences whose cumulative effect drove him increasingly inward. Faulkner told Maurice Coindreau that he wrote *The Sound and the Fury* when he was struggling with difficulties of an intimate nature,[16] thus implying that the problems, whether real or imagined, were primarily sexual. From any standpoint, 1928 was certainly an odd and probably a trying time in the writer's life. That year he became thirty-one, yet he still lived as a bachelor in the house of a father he despised and was confronted daily with younger brothers who were not only married but producing children. He continued to wait for Estelle to end her ten-year-old marriage and worked occasionally at odd jobs, in addition to writing, but his lifestyle hardly pleased his male relatives, and it was in 1928 that his uncle, a local judge, is said to have responded with disgust to an inquiry about him: "What, that nut! I'm sorry to say he's my nephew."[17] Moreover, Faulkner's encounters with alcohol were becoming more prolonged and destructive. It was probably during this period that—in the first of many such incidents—some friends discovered him in an alcoholic stupor, comatose and debilitated from having gone without food for upwards of two days (B, p. 591). Whatever the exact nature of the problems which haunted him at this time, they were obviously disturbing and pervasive, and only through his writing could he even begin to try and confront them.

The Sound and the Fury seems to have been written by Faulkner in a mood of anger and despair. Underlying the book is a sense that all children are betrayed in fundamental ways by their parents and left to flounder helplessly in a world where they can find no succor. Every member of the Compson family is in some degree either a victimized child or a betraying parent. The principal villains are the senior Compsons, who have by their lack of interest or their skewed loyalties damaged all of the children, and the cycle is tragically repeated in the next generation, as Jason proves a cruel surrogate father to his niece, and even Caddy, who nurtured her brothers with such tenderness, allows herself to abandon her own child. Benjy at thirty-three is still a victimized child, and Quentin, despite his superb intelligence, is trapped in the terrible problems created by his sense of parental deprivation. His feeling of masculine inadequacy undoubtedly echoes Faulkner's own. Quentin's father, like Murry Falkner, gives little to his sensitive son but a destructive example, and Quentin's mother—like Faulkner's, during a crucial period—bestows the bulk of her attention on another child. Quentin's consequent lack of self-esteem and his tendency to regard all women as mothers or whores are qualities Faulkner had already shown in his fiction, where he denounced most artists and thus himself as effete and divided the females into troubling either-or categories. There are other autobiographical resonances in *The Sound and the Fury,* for Faulkner patterns nearly every character in the book on some figure in his own life.

Faulkner chose to open the novel with the section belonging to Benjy, the thirty-three-year-old imbecile whom he called "truly innocent, that is, an idiot," and declared his authorial concern about "just where he could get the tenderness, the help, to shield him in his innocence."[18] Faulkner has occasionally been criticized for his decision to begin with a foray into the chaotic mind of a mental defective, but the choice was a brilliant one, both artistically and psychologically. It is not simply that Benjy's section is an aesthetically appropriate means of introducing the story of the doomed Compsons, but that Faulkner's use of a principal character who is "objective" (i.e., who is as different from the author in exterior ways as he is psychologically like him—and thus not merely an exercise in direct self-portraiture) saves the work from the emotional confusion which had flawed *Sartoris* and which occasionally renders impenetrable even Quentin's section of *The Sound and the Fury* itself. Faulkner apparently drew on an actual person for his creation of Benjy— the severely retarded son of an Oxford doctor[19]—but if the idiot thus has his origins in the local milieu, he also has a great deal of psychologically symbolic importance as a mirror of Quentin, and hence, in exaggerated fashion, of Faulkner himself.

The first two interior portraitures seem almost diametric opposites— Benjy focuses on the pure physical sensations of sight and smell and is unaware of cause and effect or "normal" diachronic time, while Quentin explores the abstract and is all too aware of consequences and the movement of time—but they are psychically similar in basic ways. Both brothers are obsessed with their sister, whom they have lost to time and circumstance, but who once offered the sort of emotional nurturing unavailable from their mother. They long to sleep with Caddy. Benjy yearns to share a warm bed with her as he did before the family attempted to separate them when he was thirteen, and Quentin wants to possess her sexually, to commit incest not only as affirmation of their exclusiveness but also as proof that there is some code meaningful enough that violation of it will lead to eternal damnation. Each has, as a consequence, been in some sense castrated:[20] Benjy physically, as a result of his chasing little girls and "trying to say" (63) in an attempt to regain his lost sister;[21] Quentin psychically, because of the extreme attachment to her that prevents him from consummating any other relationship and causes him to see her wedding announcement as a fiat decreeing his death. The olfactory sense is strong in both brothers and triggers their memories of Caddy: to Benjy she smells like "trees" (5); to Quentin, the knowledge of her sexual involvement with someone else is associated with the heavy smell of honeysuckle. Thus Benjy is a psychological double of Quentin, and his experience anticipates, at a more primal level, what happens to Quentin. Their sections are more closely related than any other pair in the novel, and it is obvious that the significant core of that story about himself which Faulkner felt he had to tell over and over appears in the first half of the book. Faulkner may have intended to reveal this dualistic self-portraiture, for Benjy was born the same year as his creator and Quentin, like Faulkner, is the oldest son.

Benjy is psychologically a child, barely more than an infant, and his simple responses give us one view of things before we move into the tortured complexity of his brother's section, while his emotional reactions forecast the outcome of that section. Both are victims: Benjy of his mental deficiency and of the heedless selfishness of most of the members of his household; Quentin, despite his intellectual powers, of his psychic inability to break out of early adolescent sexual attitudes created by those same familial inadequacies. A feeling of endless movement is created by Benjy's memories of being shunted in and out of the house and torn from his accustomed places for sleeping and eating during the period after his grandmother's death—undoubtedly based on Faulkner's remembrance of the upheaval after the death of Damuddy in 1907—and of the physical and emotional uproar surrounding his sister's wedding, no less clearly based on the author's reaction to the marriage of Estelle. The motion and chaos culminate finally in a picture of severe dislocation within the microcosm of the household. This is amplified, in the following section, into dislocation in the macrocosm, which is expressed by Quentin's uprooting from Mississippi and removal to Harvard at his family's behest and his subsequent aimless wanderings around Boston as he moves ever closer to self-destruction.

This physical movement on both the small and the large scale is paralleled by the mental travels between past and present in the minds of the brothers. Benjy's transitions are based on the senses: he hears a golfer yell "caddie" and bellows for the sister who has been gone from him for years; he sees the girl Quentin with a man and recalls a long-ago scene between Caddy and a suitor which disturbed him; he smells death at his father's funeral precisely as he had at his grandmother's years before. Quentin's urgent mental leaps are also triggered by sense experiences, such as the smell of honeysuckle, the overhearing of a key phrase, or the sight of a little girl, but he quickly moves from association to agonized recapitulation of his painful experiences and thence to the conclusion that all possibilities for the future have been destroyed by the past. His journeys backward in time lead him forward to annihilation.

Benjy's section includes just about every crucial piece of family "data" that the later portions amplify. Through his wounded sensibility and uncomprehending eyes we see the physical decline of the Compson place, its decay imaging the emotional disarray of the family itself. The mother querulously treats Benjy as a troublesome object put on earth to punish her, and retreats to her room and her hypochondria. She denies all the children affection; Benjy she denies even the name he was given at birth, Maury, seeing it as a family heirloom inappropriate to bestow on an idiot. Benjy's father is an alcoholic and a nihilist who, though occasionally demonstrative toward his retarded son, is too often overwhelmed by his own problems; his main legacy to his children is his hideous vision of man as "created by disease, within putrefaction, into decay" (53). Benjy's parents generally ignore him, his brother Jason destroys his playthings, and almost the sole tenderness he receives is from his sister Caddy and the black servant Dilsey, who act as mother-protectors.

The only member of the family with whom Benjy does not interact in either a positive or a negative way is Quentin. This underscores the fact that their stories are meant to illuminate rather than to intersect each other. In neither Benjy's nor Quentin's section does one brother have evaluative or emotionally responsive thoughts or images of the other. Virtually the only scene in which Faulkner dramatizes any interaction between the two is after Caddie's wedding, when Quentin tries to sober up his drunken and helpless younger brother. But Quentin's actions are perfunctory, the scene is a brief one, and the importance of Benjy's story in relation to Quentin's remains primarily illustrative and anticipatory; the two narratives run on parallel tracks.

Caddy is the central focus of Benjy's ruminations, as she is of Quentin's, for she has been loving and solicitous to him during the years she lived at home. Benjy's attachment to his sister is understandable, but he makes the same sort of unspoken demands for exclusiveness in their relationship and for sexual purity on Caddy's part that Quentin will make quite explicitly in his section.[22] When Benjy comes upon Caddy and a young man embracing in the porch swing, he cries out and pulls at her dress, continuing to bellow until she abandons her suitor to join him. After Caddy marries, Benjy's association of her wedding with the death of his grandmother signifies that he perceives her liaison as a sort of "death" in the same way that Quentin will later, when the link between sex and death becomes overt. Benjy also moves from an image of Caddy in the pear tree and the "muddy bottom of her drawers," with its suggestion of sexual contamination, to a recollection of her wedding day when, despite her beauty, he "couldn't smell trees anymore" (48). The smell that connotes purity vanishes and his final memory is one in which a remembrance of Caddy holding him is linked with the smell of death. The association of dirt and sex and Caddy and death in Benjy's mind is a powerful one. It comes in part from a sense of loss, but also suggests the fatal aversion that will be a major element in Quentin's narrative.

Quentin's desperate situation is undoubtedly related to the despair that was threatening to overwhelm Faulkner at the time he wrote *The Sound and the Fury*. His section is by far the most high-pitched, and its emotional inchoateness reveals the extreme turbulence experienced by a sensitive intelligence beleaguered by insoluble difficulties; some passages are, as Cleanth Brooks points out, "so private as to be almost incomprehensible."[23] Such privateness may well be a result of the author's having drawn directly from anguished and confused thoughts of his own for much of the material in Quentin's section. Faulkner later admitted his identification with this character: "Ishmael is the witness in *Moby Dick* as I am Quentin in *The Sound and the Fury*" (B, p. 1522). Moreover, Quentin's similarity to Bayard Sartoris, an arrested and suicidal character who has a strong biographical component, and his embodiment of certain attitudes that appear everywhere in Faulkner's fiction suggest a close relationship between author and protagonist which may account both for Quentin's problems and for the special complexities of his section.

By the Freudian definition, Quentin is a classic Oedipal figure who has displaced his yearning for his mother onto his sister, and whose inability to identify with his cynical and ineffectual father has prevented him from attaining masculine adulthood.[24] His prizing of female virginity, his distaste for the sexual act, and his rather feminine behavior are all symptoms of what is now a well-known emotional disorder. Faulkner was certainly aware of Freud at this period of his life. Despite his avowals to the contrary, his knowledge is revealed in his early novels, which contain references to Freud and occasional use and misuse of Freudian terminology. His knowledge was limited, however, and it is most unlikely that he intended to present any sort of "case history" in his portrayal of Quentin; he seems rather to have drawn upon and magnified impulses with which he was directly familiar. Fortunately, Faulkner, unlike his protagonist, conquered his "masculine" problems to a large degree before many years had passed, and if his self-destructive impulses left him with backaches and headaches, they also left him his life. Even so, there are minor manifestations of many of Quentin's symptoms in Faulkner's own life; he too had lost a "sister-lover" to marriage, and certainly his parents' failings had some striking likenesses to those of the Compsons.

Mrs. Compson, weak, hypochondriacal, and primly aware of social proprieties, is in no obvious way a portrait of Faulkner's mother, but she is incapable of giving her children adequate affection, and the one psychoanalyst to whom Faulkner ever consented to talk concluded that the author felt his mother had given him all too little emotional sustenance (B, p. 1454). In his portrayal of Mrs. Compson, therefore, Faulkner may have been drawing upon both his sense of his mother's affectional failings and his memories of a specific period in 1915 when he was Quentin's age and his mother was ill for several months and he and his brothers had to fend for themselves (B, p. 178). Mrs. Compson's detachment is symbolized physically by the time she spends locked away in her room, and her moral inadequacy is revealed by the strong favoritism she shows to Jason, the child who is "my joy and my salvation" (127). Quentin has been deeply affected by her failure. He is very aware of Gerald Bland's devoted mother and says with an anguished sense of loss, "If I could say Mother. Mother" (117) in the midst of his thoughts about Caddy, then repeats, "If I'd just had a mother so I could say Mother Mother" (213) just before his suicide. His yearning is primarily for affection, but it has a sexual component, too.

Quentin's unresolved feelings for his mother have left him with the feeling that all sex is unclean, a feeling Faulkner had also shown in his earlier work. Quentin regards sex as something "nigger women do in the pasture the ditches the dark woods hot hidden furious in the dark woods" (113–14). His sister Caddy has become Quentin's mother substitute by giving him the tenderness he needs, and she has also, as is often the case, replaced the mother sexually in the Oedipal triangle.[25] Faulkner shared Quentin's passion for Caddy; even though he never directly portrays her, described her as "my heart's darling" (*FIU,* p. 6) and said, "I did not realise then that I was trying to manufacture the sister which I did not have."[26] His fervor for this sisterly figure who appears only in the minds of others is revealing, especially since Faulkner had spent much time with a Caddy-like tomboy cousin whom he and his brothers thought of as a sister and was soon to marry a woman who had been in other significant ways a "sister" to him, as well as a romantic object of desire. Caddy is thus a complex, symbolic, and important sister-mother-lover image to both Quentin and his creator.

Mr. Compson is like Faulkner's father only in his alcoholism and detachment, for he is cerebral and articulate, a lawyer who knows Latin—like the author's friend Phil Stone. With a nice touch of irony, Faulkner tended to give more of his father's qualities to the "villain" Jason and to Quentin's drunken Uncle Maury. But though Mr. Compson shows moments of compassionate understanding, he is as destructive a male parent as was Murry Falkner, chiefly because his only legacy to his son is a constant stream of nihilistic statements that fatally undermine Quentin's serious need to believe in something. Mr. Compson's fundamental decency somehow makes him all the more potent a negative force in the realm where Quentin is vulnerable. Mr. Compson calls the watch he gives to Quentin a "mausoleum of all hope and desire" (93) and asserts that Christ "was worn away by a minute clicking of little wheels" (94). Soon obsessed by time and by the watch which is clicking his own life away, Quentin feels that only some sort of heroic encounter can give him the significance he desires. But his father's words ruin any possibility of meaning in that arena, for Mr. Compson has said, "No battle is ever won. . . . They are not even fought. The field only reveals to man his own folly and despair, and victory is an illusion of philosophers and fools" (93). Even Quentin's wish to defend his sister's honor has been deflated by his father, who says, "it was men invented virginity not women" (96).

Mr. Compson is more of a negative voice resounding in his son's head than a palpable presence with whom he feels the need to struggle physically, and Quentin's direct confrontations of an Oedipal nature are with his sister's suitors. Each "rival," poised and confident, may have been based in part on Cornell Franklin, the successful lawyer and businessman to whom Faulkner had lost Estelle ten years before. Quentin relives two of these encounters, with their sexual overtones, and each augments his sense of defeat and emasculation. The first one to surge into memory is his encounter with Herbert Head, whom Caddy married. The suave and assured Head is friendly and somewhat paternal toward Quentin, but like Quentin's father he insists on imparting bitter truth to the younger man, declaring that he "wasn't the first or the last" (134) of Caddy's lovers. Quentin helplessly fantasizes shooting Head, but is prevented from even striking him by the appearance of Caddy. Head's final riposte is to deflate the youth by calling him a "half-baked Galahad" (136).

In a similar encounter, Quentin confronts Dalton Ames, the man he believes responsible for impregnating his sister. Making an appointment as if for a duel, Quentin melodramatically demands that Ames leave town by sundown or else "I'll kill you" (198). Ames, however, disconcertingly reacts with quasi-paternal understanding and the sort of harshly realistic comment that is so destructive to Quentin; "no good taking it so hard its not your fault kid it would have been some other fellow" (199). Ames has a pistol—a symbol of masculinity—which he daringly offers to Quentin, but Quentin, shaking like a frightened girl, tries to slap Ames with his open hand and then faints.[27] Quentin is ineffectual at attempting to best these two substitute father-figures who are replacing him sexually in a relationship with his sister-mother, just as Faulkner, in a more oblique way, proved incapable of "defeating" Cornell Franklin through his failure to take an active role in preventing Estelle's marriage. Faulkner once said of Quentin's unmanliness that "he was such a weakling that even if they [he and Caddy] had been no kin, she would never have chosen him for her sweetheart. She would have chosen one like the ex-soldier she did" (*FIU,* p. 263).

Quentin is vanquished in these confrontations that confirm his sense of emasculation. He almost longs for a state in which he would not have sexual organs to trouble him, remembering a man who castrated himself, but realizes that even that drastic measure would not be sufficient to alleviate his pain: "It's not not having them. It's never to have had them" (143). His sexual incompetence is again revealed in the imagined scene in which he futilely attempts to carry out Caddy's murder and his own suicide. He has a knife and holds its point at her throat as she tries in sexual te:ms to guide him, saying "no like this you'll have to push harder. . . . pu;h it are you going to . . . yes push it" (189). But he cannot perform. He begins to cry, drops the knife, and slinks away.

Quentin has early linked his sister and death in his evocation of "Saint Francis that said Little Sister Death" (94), and the two become irrevocably associated when he is followed by a little Italian girl he calls "sister" while he carries out the preparations for his suicide. Having transformed his sister's wedding announcement into the announcement of his own death, haunted by the memory of the odor of honeysuckle that he associates with sex, and obsessed by the water, "peaceful and swift" (210), that offers the prospect of reabsorption into the ultimate "mother," the ocean, he moves toward death. As he carries on an inner dialogue with his father and his father's destructive ideas, Quentin once again remembers the shadows of his past, "inherent themselves with the denial of the significance they should have affirmed" (211), and in his final memories of his inability to act purposefully, even to the point of committing the incest that was his one great desire, he reveals a consequent loss of a sense of self: "i was afraid to i was afraid," he recalls, with the sense of "i temporary" (220) that is his last important thought before dying. Faulkner uses the lower case *i* to show how pervasive is Quentin's fatal lack of identity.

The anxieties produced in Quentin by the failure of his parents hold him so in thrall as a young man that he is as effectively victimized by them as Benjy is victimized by his severe mental deficiency, and Quentin's psy-

chological emasculation eventually proves to have more serious consequences than Benjy's actual castration. He cannot move outward to act
significantly in the world, even to achieve damnation by committing incest
or slaying one of the threatening father-figures, but turns his anger inward
to carry out the most negative act possible, self-destruction. Sister and
death finally merge as his obsession with the first leads him inexorably to
the second.

With the great poignancy of Benjy's section and the confused intensity
of Quentin's, the most deeply felt half of *The Sound and the Fury* comes to
an end. One sense a certain release, on Faulkner's part, from the weight of
pressing personal concerns, as though his writing about suicide somehow
liberated him from the danger of acting it out in his life, and as though the
depiction of emotional specters from his childhood and young manhood
somehow helped to overcome the threat they offered to his psychic balance. He moves on to tell the story twice more, with no attendant loss of
artistic power, but certainly with greater detachment.

Jason is a Compson sibling, but he is also "logical rational contained,"
as Faulkner said in his 1946 Appendix, and embodies some of Faulkner's
larger concerns, his anti-rationalism and his dislike of the economic rapacity that was emerging in the "New South" of his day. Dilsey is the long-
suffering Compson family servant, but her section is told from an omniscient point of view and she represents to some degree the redemptive
power of self-sacrifice. The movement of the book is thus outward toward
the symbolic and universal, as critics have often noted, and there is also a
corollary movement upward toward maturity, with Benjy and Quentin em-
bodying the painful periods of early childhood and adolescence, Jason the
responsibility of young adulthood, and Dilsey the wisdom and emotional
generosity of true parenthood. While Faulkner shows understanding of human beings in the latter two categories, his greatest sympathy—and hence
artistic energy—tends to be reserved for the innocent and the vulnerable,
and there is a sense in which the expansionary quality of *The Sound and the
Fury* is a paradigm for Faulkner's career as a novelist; as he moved increasingly outward from private to public issues, the work lessened in its
psychological intensity.

Jason is generally regarded as the "villain" of the piece. Indeed, with
his greed, his defrauding of his niece, his harshness to Benjy, and his
pointlessly cruel treatment of all subordinates, he is the most evil figure in
The Sound and the Fury. Faulkner revealingly gave Jason some of his
father's characteristics, his verbal idiom, his temper, his lifelong sense of
having been deprived of a job that he wanted badly, and a gruffness that is

as lacerating as Faulkner undoubtedly once perceived his father's to be. Faulkner's mother readily admitted Jason's many similarities to Murry Falkner. "He talks just like my husband did. My husband had a hardware store uptown at one time. His way of talking was just like Jason's, same words and same style. All those 'you know's.' He also had an old 'nigrah' named Jobus, just like the character Job in the story. He was always after Jobus for not working hard enough, just like in the story."[28] Moreover, Jason is as inadequate a "father" to the girl Quentin as Murry was to his son William.

However, although Jason's bigotry, xenophobia, and absorbed attention to dollars and cents at the cost of human consideration make him a highly unattractive figure, it is insufficient to characterize him as a pure symbol of Snopesism without any virtues. For Jason is a complex and even at points sympathetic character, his humor leavens the novel, and his shouldering of all the responsibilities of running the household mark him as the one real "adult" in the Compson family by 1928. His headaches are both literal and figurative and equally painful in both respects. He has become head of his disorderly clan and must attempt to keep a highly chaotic houseold under control. Moreover, many of his complaints are legitimate. His brother Quentin received the only money available for a college education and promptly killed himself, and now the undereducated and (in his own view) underemployed Jason is in charge of a sickly mother, an idiot brother, and a wayward niece to whom he must necessarily be a "father." He must deal, as he says in his bitterly humorous way, with "Beale Street" and "bedlam" (329), and it is difficult not to be a little sympathetic with him. No opportunity exists in his world for heroic action, and the only dying fall of horns he hears is the "Yahhhh, Yahhhh, Yaaahhhhhhhhh" (302) of the car in which his niece escapes, leaving him spluttering.

Jason is forced to assume "the entire burden of the rotting family in the rotting house," a duty he feels compelled to take on "so that his mother's life might continue as nearly as possible to what it had been."[29] His tie to his mother, who has always shown him special favoritism but who is now querulous, paranoid, and vainly preoccupied with outmoded social distinctions, is as crippling in its way as was Quentin's rejection by that same mother. Jason must listen to his mother's endless talk about the specialness of "we Bascombs," obviously incompatible though it is with the realities of her present situation. She says plaintively, "Thank God it was you left me I can depend on you," and Jason is bitterly aware that "I dont reckon I'll ever get far enough from the store to get out of your reach" (256–57).

Hopelessly dominated by the figure of his mother, he believes all other women are bitches one must manage with a "bust in the jaw" (240). He cannot conceive of any fulfilling relationship with a "decent" woman, for, as he says, "I have all the women I can take care of now" (307). He defrauds his mother of money, which is a criminal act, but her special treatment of and demands on Jason have been "criminal" in another way, for they have emotionally and economically bound him hand and foot. Even the money he has stolen from his niece, and which she steals back in a supreme gesture of comeuppance, symbolizes "the job in the bank of which he had been deprived before he ever got it" (382), the promise broken by Caddy's husband.

A certain eerily prophetic element marks this portion of *The Sound and the Fury,* rather as *Sartoris* can be seen as predicting the death of Faulkner's brother in an airplane crash. The resented responsibilities of running a large family and of paying daily obeisance to a mother about whom he had some emotional ambivalence were soon to be Faulkner's own. When his father died, just four years after Faulkner completed the manuscript of *The Sound and the Fury,* he became head of the clan and eventually assumed economic responsibility for, among others, his mother, his brother John and John's wife and children, and his brother Dean's widow and child. His complaints to his publisher when he wrote asking for more money came to sound almost like Jason's protests that he had to cope with "Beale Street" and "bedlam." In addition, Faulkner was expected to pay a daily visit to his mother whenever he was in Oxford, and though he gave no overt evidence of minding this, a close friend said that Faulkner resented the tie and that it tended to make him resentful of women in general (B, p. 631). The novel makes a third prophecy, in that the elopment of the girl Quentin at age seventeen with a circus showman portends the secret flight of Faulkner's stepdaughter Victoria into marriage at the same age. Faulkner's fiction occasionally deals as vividly with what "will be" in his own life as with what "was" and "is."

The last two sections of the novel are linked, like the first two, by both parallels and incremental development; Jason and Dilsey are both "survivors" and household managers, although the latter has moral strengths— the nobility and redemptiveness of true parenthood—which serve to illuminate the former's deficiencies. Dilsey's role is also significant in that here, as in *Sartoris,* a source of affection and acceptance is found outside the family. Given the serious insufficiencies of the senior Compsons as parents, Dilsey, patterned to a large extent on Faulkner's childhood nurse, Caroline Barr,[30] has been the only one—apart from Caddy herself—to give the children loving attention. Seen from the outside, Dilsey is something of a grotesque, but her "indomitable skeleton" (331) symbolizes the staunchness with which she attends the family, supervising the domestic sphere and making special gestures such as buying a birthday cake for Benjy out of her pitifully small wages. She is the one true mother of the household, and her maternal impulses envelop them all, black and white: "Ef I dont worry bout y'll, I dont know who is" (361), she asserts. As both worrier and sustainer, her role is paramount, and she is, as nearly every Faulkner critic has pointed out, the one character who is not defeated by ordinary time and circumstance. She functions efficiently and caringly in the daily world, but hers is the special clock with only one hand that strikes five times for eight o'clock, and hers is the Easter vision, denied to everyone else, of "de first en de last" as she weeps silently in "the annealment and the blood of the remembered Lamb" (371). Dilsey's freedom from time also symbolizes her liberation from a personal familial past that cripples or destroys the others—she moves to a perception of the eternal verities. She is a worthy and redemptive figure, but the fact that she is racially and biologically outside the family which encompasses the rest of the characters makes the affirmative implications of her portraiture highly tentative.

In the richness of its characterization, the complexity of its interior monologues, the incremental and expansive nature of its structure, and the resonance of its themes, *The Sound and the Fury* is a powerful and mature work of fiction that presents the squalor but also the splendor of humanity in defeat. It was an exhilarating, somewhat cathartic experience for its creator, and he regarded the finished product with pride and excitement. It's "the damndest [*sic*] book I ever read," he told his great-aunt. "I dont believe anyone will publish it for 10 years" (*L*, p. 41). It was, however, soon published, and although one shortsighted reviewer denounced it as a treatment of "imbecility, incest, alcoholism, and insanity" that was "almost unreadable,"[31] another, Evelyn Scott, in a prepublication analysis that was the source of many critical axioms still relevant today, defended the "morbidity" as being "reflected from the impression, made on a sensitive and normally egoistic nature, of what is in the air."[32] In so saying, she put her finger very nearly on the real origin of all the wider social implications of the novel—its exploration of one vulnerable sensibility, Faulkner's, trying to come to terms with the terrors and anxieties engendered by a difficult personal past. Benjy/Quentin is Faulkner, but he might also be any frail and fallen being whose sadness at the loss of past innocence and affection, incapacity to mature emotionally, and failure to believe combine to hold him in thralldom in the present and thus to negate the possibility of the future. Although the psychological portraiture of *The Sound and the Fury* emerged from the most troubled regions of Faulkner's mind, he confronted his problems with such honesty and thoroughness and expressed them with such sensitivity and penetration that they took on, finally, a universal significance.

4
Bleak Epithalamion: *Sanctuary*

FAULKNER ALWAYS DENIGRATED *Sanctuary*, the novel which he wrote after completing *The Sound and the Fury* and which is in many ways his most disturbing work, the vehicle of a vision of corruption permeating every level of society. In 1955, when asked why he wrote the novel, Faulkner answered, "I needed money, and I wanted to buy a horse."[1] This sort of glib dismissal of his motivation by an author some decades after the creation of a work is not altogether uncommon, but Faulkner also repudiated *Sanctuary* almost immediately after it was published. In an introduction to the 1932 Modern Library edition, he wrote, "To me it is a cheap idea, because it was deliberately conceived to make money. . . . I took a little time out, and speculated what a person in Mississippi would believe to be current trends, chose what I thought was the right answer and invented the most horrific tale I could imagine and wrote it in about three weeks."[2]

Faulkner's belittling of his bleak novel as a "cheap idea" is as unjustified as the rest of his statement is inaccurate—he wrote the novel in four months, not three weeks, and used a reported incident as the basis for the work, not an "invented" one—and critics have always considered *Sanctuary* to be one of his major fictional achievements, if not among the very greatest. The story of the bizarre rape of Temple Drake by the perverted gangster Popeye was called in one early essay an allegory of the rape of the Old South, in the person of Southern Womanhood, by amoral Modernism[3] and referred to by contemporary critics as Faulkner's "Inferno" and as a "Manichean morality play,"[4] or, along with *Requiem for*

89

a Nun, as Faulkner's version of *Crime and Punishment.*[5] Even a commentator who was skeptical about the worth of Faulkner's fiction paid him an unwitting tribute by calling him a "moralist with a corncob."[6]

Since *Sanctuary* has led its informed readers to invoke Dante, Dostoevsky, and medieval allegory, what might have caused its author, who was always cognizant of the merit of his art and who wrote this work almost as painstakingly as the monumental fictions like *The Sound and the Fury* and *Absalom, Absalom!,* to renounce it so rapidly and so completely? Faulkner himself never provided any answer, because his responses to such probing ranged from the glibness of his introduction to the prurience of his assertion that when *Sanctuary* was dramatized, he planned to play the role of the corncob. (B, pp. 739, 777). One can only surmise that his over-reactions and discomfort emanated from the fact that *Sanctuary* embodied, in the bleakest possible terms, an emotional and perhaps even physical dilemma in which the author found himself, and that Popeye and Horace Benbow are each artistic reifications of serious psychological problems that Faulkner was facing even as he wrote the novel. The philosophical nadir represented in the novel's portrayal of a southern wasteland is related to the psychic nadir Faulkner had reached as he confronted his own situation.

Though *Sanctuary* was not published until 1931, it was written between January and May of 1929 and completed just before Faulkner's marriage to Estelle Oldham Franklin, to whom he had been a devoted friend and suitor for twenty-five years. This novel must be the strangest epithalamion ever created, for Faulkner imagines a nightmare world of impotence, rape, murder, and moral corruption that pervades every stratum of society. *Sanctuary* is, as a psychologist in an early article pointed out, a horror fantasy that is linked to a subterranean struggle with fears of impotence— an impotence that signifies incapacity in all spheres of instinctual potency.[7] How much of this horror originated in Faulkner's actual fears about his impending marriage and his adequacy as a husband and father cannot be known, but the links between the events of his personal life and the nightmares of *Sanctuary* suggest that the novel may constitute a projective exaggeration of some of his deepest anxieties. In *The Sound and the Fury* he located the responsibility for the problems of Quentin and Benjy in the failure of their parents, but in *Sanctuary* the horror is much greater and much less readily assignable to a given source. It is as though Faulkner's worries had become so intense that he had lost the ability to diagnose and to attribute and could only portray and magnify them.

Faulkner acknowledged that he had experienced difficulties of an intimate nature during the period when he wrote *The Sound and the Fury,*[8] and those difficulties were probably objectified in Quentin's Oedipal struggles and suicide. *Sanctuary* gives the distinct impression that the difficulties had increased, for its world contains terror and despair that are both more extreme and less explicable than in *The Sound and the Fury,* and it seems reasonable to assume that this emotional escalation would have been related to the events of the spring of 1929. On the surface, Faulkner's life appeared ordinary. He wrote, helped his Uncle John to campaign for the post of district attorney, played with Estelle's two children, and waited for her divorce decree to become final in April, after which the couple could at last consider the marriage that had eluded them for more than a decade.

There were, however, undercurrents which revealed that all was not psychically serene in the writer's inner life. Faulkner had always spent a moderate amount of time on the fringes of the demimonde, and he continued this behavior as his marriage approached and he began work on *Sanctuary.* He touted the book he was writing as ''bad'' and claimed that he had to go frequently to Memphis, the city of brothels, in order ''to do a lot of research on it.''[9] Since Faulkner was more or less engaged at the time, such action may have been prompted by his fears about the sexual aspect of his relationship with his fiancée. A man who spends a good deal of time with prostitutes often has severe doubts about his sexual adequacy with ''respectable'' women, as well as the kind of ambivalence about women in general that Faulkner's work and life had already demonstrated. Moreover, in *Sanctuary* Faulkner tends to locate a good share of the evil in the female characters, particularly in the ''decent'' women like Temple Drake, Narcissa Benbow, and the Baptist ladies, who prove to be more destructive and inhuman than any previous Faulknerian females, and shows sympathy only for the debased ex-whore, Ruby Lamar. It seems likely that he felt a certain kinship with the sexually confused Horace Benbow and perhaps also with the villainous and impotent Popeye.

It was not utterly clear, after all, that Faulkner truly wanted to marry Estelle. He had, to be sure, waited doggedly for her over a period of many years, and his early work is full of anguished and thwarted suitors, but perhaps Faulkner, like Yeats, was somehow paradoxically more fulfilled by frustration than by satisfaction. As the actuality of marriage approached, Faulkner's overt reluctance to carry through with the ceremony suggested that he felt a good deal of trepidation, some of which he revealed in his portrait of Horace Benbow. Estelle was divorced on April 29 and Faulkner did not marry her for nearly two months. Presumably, some of his hesitation arose from family objections—Faulkner's mother was opposed to the marriage because Estelle was already an alcoholic, and Judge Oldham was still concerned about Faulkner's financial suitability as a spouse for his daughter—but the opposition on economic grounds was partly specious, for Estelle had received an adequate divorce settlement from Cornell Franklin. Apparently it was William himself who did the foot-dragging, as is not surprising in light of his 1918 refusal to elope with Estelle. His inaction ended only when Estelle's sister Dorothy telephoned Faulkner and declared that it was time he married her sister (B, pp. 619–20). The three of them, the two sisters and the bridegroom, went off to the church together, and Dorothy Oldham, perhaps determined to continue her role as shepherd to her reluctant brother-in-law, prepared the two for their honeymoon.

Ironically, Faulkner's wedding took place on the twentieth of June, the date of the hideous trial in *Sanctuary* that is perverted by the perjury of Temple Drake and results in the martyrdom of the innocent Lee Goodwin. Faulkner's marriage, too, would prove an arduous trial, and the parallel between these crucial dates is unnerving: the stark opening of chapter twenty-seven, "The trial was set for the twentieth of June," could have served as the author's announcement of his impending marriage.

The honeymoon in the resort town of Pascagoula was catastrophic. Not only was it overpopulated—by a servant, stepchildren, and even Estelle's ex-mother-in-law—but the bridal couple spent much of their time drinking heavily. One night Estelle evidently attempted to commit suicide by wading out into the ocean. Faulkner yelled to a neighbor, "She's going to drown herself!" The neighbor rushed out and rescued her, despite her efforts to fight him off, just before the beach dropped off into the deep waters of the channel (B, p. 630). Whether Estelle's suicide attempt was related to her new husband's adequacy as a sexual partner is unknown, but clearly at least a few of Faulkner's worst fears had been realized, and the grimness of his vision in *Sanctuary* received some justification from the outcome of occurrences in his personal life.

The dark action of the novel centers on two culminating events, each containing a form of perversion and a murder—the rape of Temple Drake and shooting of Tommy at the Old Frenchman Place, and Lee Goodwin's travesty of a trial and subsequent immolation by an angry mob. The gangster Popeye is ultimately responsible for these happenings, but the guilt is shared by nearly every character in the novel, each contributing his evil portion to the universal corruption. What few there are of the good, the innocent, and the well-meaning are overcome or destroyed, and the triumph of baseness by the end of the novel is virtually complete. From the opening scene, with its ominous confrontation between the voyeuristic, almost mechanical figure of Popeye and the frail and vulnerable Horace Benbow, to the final subdued but terrible vision of Temple Drake in the Luxembourg Gardens under "the sky lying prone and vanquished in the embrace of the season of rain and death" (250),[10] Faulkner gives us a bleak vision of life and of man's capacity for evil.

The despair at the core of Faulkner's outlook is revealed in manifold ways in the novel—in images of entrapment, in the general confusion over sexual identity which is related to the central impotent perversions, in Faulkner's self-portraiture as Horace/Popeye, and in his depiction of the female characters. As in previous works like *Sartoris* and *The Sound and the Fury,* the author parallels, contrasts, and expands outward to create an amplified picture of his personal plight that becomes at the last a *Weltanschauung,* a portrait of life in the modern wasteland. His style in this work is unique in the Faulkner canon, highly objective and precise, almost wholly free from his usual poeticizing and entirely appropriate for anchoring in concrete reality a series of horrific excesses. Madame Bovary's death is invoked early in the novel, and Faulkner makes use of a Flaubertian exactitude to project a dark vision of life itself comparable to Flaubert's. The third-person omniscient narrator describes the exteriors of people and settings succinctly, records the dialogue, and creates scenes that are brief but powerful, enabling the horrors of the novel to be at once minimized and maximized.

The effectiveness of this understated yet incremental technique emerges in the way Faulkner makes use of images of enclosure. These images are psychologically related to the author's own sense of entrapment by an impending marriage about which he had serious reservations and to his central characters' entrapment by evil or by circumstance, yet they also appear in a highly concrete form. Early in the novel, Ruby's baby is described, not in human terms, but in terms of the container in which he lies. "Behind the stove, in shadow, was a wooden box" (5). This brief sentence, with its overtones of darkness and interment, portends the death of the frail being who lies within. Later, Temple lies on her cornshuck mattress at the Old Frenchman Place with "her hands crossed on her breast and her legs straight and close and decorous, like an effigy on an ancient tomb" (54). Temple's deathlike appearance anticipates her symbolic entombment in the corncrib where she invites her brutal rape. Subsequently, her face becomes a "dead-colored mask" (83), emblematic of the death-in-life she soon undergoes at the Memphis bordello as she willingly accepts further assaults on her body. It also suggests her complicity in the deaths of others.

Popeye, another death-containing and death-purveying figure, is shown enclosing himself in the hayloft in order to spy on Temple, and he will later keep her prisoner in a locked room. After presenting the figurative encapsulations of the baby, Temple, and Popeye, Faulkner escalates the violence and gives us literal death and entombment. The dead victims both of Popeye's murderous anger and of the larger corruption of society include the idiot Tommy, whose body lies pathetically in death at the undertaker's parlor, the gangster Red, whose mortal remains are arrayed in garish, macabre splendor at his uproarious funeral in a roadhouse, and Lee Goodwin, whose charred corpse is testimony to the perversion of justice. The narrative thus moves inexorably from symbolic to real death, and the scale of horror mounts.

Another suggestive symbolic presence in *Sanctuary* is the clock on the mantel of Temple's room in the Memphis bordello. With its one hand and air of having "nothing whatever to do with time" (118) it ironically recalls Dilsey's kitchen clock in *The Sound and the Fury,* which signifies her freedom from ordinary time. And with its china nymphs arrested in "attitudes of voluptuous lassitude" (119) it ironically evokes Keats's Grecian urn, with which Faulkner was so intrigued. By its location and its lack of the affirmative qualities of the other two objects it evokes, the clock serves to emphasize the bleakness of Faulkner's vision in this novel.

Just as the images of enclosure and the symbolic clock suggest the death-in-life at the core of the world of *Sanctuary,* so the early hints of skewed sexual identity and strange familial associations prepare us for the larger distortions of Horace and Popeye and of the bizarre "family" which Temple joins at the brothel. Ruby Lamar, the one truly womanly female of the novel, wears large and ill-fitting men's brogans, appurtenances which undermine her femaleness; Van, an assertive male member of the enclave at the Old Frenchman Place, has hair that is "long as a girl's" (55); while Temple, the woman who arouses a series of sexual pursuers, has a "boy's name" (117), according to Miss Reba. These minor "data" of sexual dislocation are related to the major sexual confusion experienced by Popeye, the man who cannot function properly; by Horace, the male who is perpetually defeated by the female element in his world; and by Temple, who alternates between ravenous sexuality and the desire to be desexualized.

The weird "family" at the Old Frenchman Place augurs the even stranger group in Memphis. That first "family" includes Ruby, who is "wife" and "mother," but not married to the father of her child and forced into mothering "crimps and spungs and feebs" as well as the nameless frail being in the box; a series of "children" that includes the idiot Tommy and the helpless old blind man as well as the one actual child;

and a group of male "father-protectors" whose brutality and violence make a travesty of their purported role. The still more perverted group at the brothel also includes a "mother," "father," and "child." Miss Reba, the madam of the house, is an obvious mother-figure, with the "lush billows of her breast" (114) and her efforts to reassure Temple about her post-rape bleeding and comfort her with food and drink. But she heartlessly colludes with Popeye in keeping Temple prisoner and allows him to use her house to carry out his perverted sexual assaults on the girl. Temple, under the duress of her rape and confusion, regresses to childhood even as she becomes a lascivious woman. She punishes her "parents" by refusing to eat, later cries "like a child in a dentist's waiting room" (119), hides under her bedclothes like a frightened little girl when Horace comes to visit, and destroys all of her clothes and cosmetics in a moment of petulance. Temple's childish behavior has evil consequences, however, as she taunts Popeye into killing her lover and wantonly refuses to offer the honest testimony that would save Lee Goodwin from an undeserved death. In the absence of the biological parent on whom Temple is so dependent, Popeye becomes her "father," ordering her around like an authoritative parent and provoking her into calling him "daddy" (184). Yet Popeye is undoubtedly the most pernicious "father-figure" in Faulkner's fiction. He murders the childlike Tommy, sexually violates the childish Temple and forces her into a depraved existence, and eventually kills the one man about whom his "daughter" cares in any way.

Even the outwardly respectable Benbow is not without his distortions. Horace Benbow is married to a woman with a teenaged daughter and acts more seductively toward his stepchild than toward his wife, becoming obsessed with the "urgent mammalian whisper of [her] curious small flesh" (132). Possibly frightened of his own impulses toward the girl, he flees the family he has acquired by marriage, but only to return to his biological family, which contains its own potential for perversion. Horace is drawn almost incestuously to his sister Narcissa, despite his awareness of her stupid bovinity, and he allows her to violate his moral principles by turning the beleaguered Ruby out of his house. Ultimately Horace returns to his wife, but when he does his first action is to make an eager telephone call with sexual overtones to his stepdaughter.

The "families" of *Sanctuary* are as distorted as the sexual identity and impulses of most of the characters. These distortions are focused in the three main figures of the novel, all of whom bear disconcerting similarities to figures in Faulkner's own life. They thus betray the darkness of the problems with which he was grappling at the time he wrote the book. Both Horace and Popeye are at least partial exercises in authorial self-portraiture, and Temple, along with her counterparts, the other female nemeses, Belle and Little Belle, has some troubling likenesses to Faulkner's bride-to-be. As always with Faulkner's "biographical" characters, he alters and exaggerates their real-life models, but in this particular nightmarish vision the disguises seem more than usually thin.

Using a technique common to many of his other novels, Faulkner posits a "real man" and a "worthy woman" with whom he contrasts his severely flawed protagonists. However, the distortions evident in even these "ideal" characters show how troubled the author's outlook was in early 1929. The martyred Lee Goodwin is the "real man" of *Sanctuary,* and his very name suggests his worth. Like Donald Mahon and John Sartoris, Goodwin is a military hero who has proven his valor in combat; unlike them, he has killed outside of battle, brutally murdering a fellow soldier in an argument "over one of those nigger women" (45). Like Gordon in *Mosquitoes,* Goodwin is silent and stoic in the face of adversity, refusing to elicit sympathy for his plight or to "squeal" on the actual villain. Yet he is a lawless bootlegger, not a hardworking and productive sculptor, and his leadership qualities are accompanied by a heartless disdain for lesser beings that allows him to deal gratuitous blows to men and women alike. He knocks down the drunken Gowan Stevens in a moment of anger and even strikes his devoted mistress when she betrays jealousy of Temple. " 'That's what I do to them,' he said, slapping her" (76), declaring what sounds like a general policy of harshness toward women that identifies him with the "villain" of Faulkner's previous novel, Jason Compson.

Just as Goodwin's stature is compromised by his bent for needless violence, so Ruby Lamar's role as the "worthy woman" is marred by her background and her personal unattractiveness. Like Margaret Powers and Dilsey, Ruby is motherly and devoted to nurturing the flawed and helpless creatures who depend on her for sustenance. Nonetheless, she is a debased female with little sense of self-worth, an ex-prostitute who can offer only her body in return for favors, as in the scene with Horace Benbow when she tries to "pay" him for his defense of Goodwin. She is sordid in much of her conduct, if not in her essential nature. She jealously taunts Temple for being a "cheap sport" (45), and her brutal idiom corresponds to Goodwin's physical brutality. In the rat-infested wasteland of *Sanctuary,* even the "ideal" figures have more flaws than strengths.

By contrast with the manly Goodwin, Horace and Popeye are both impotent. Horace is an inhabitant of the "respectable" world and his impotence is portrayed as largely spiritual, while Popeye is a denizen of the underworld whose impotence is physical, but they are equally crippled.

The two males have fundamentally a great deal in common and serve almost as mirror images of each other in the same way as did Quentin and Benjy in *The Sound and the Fury,* two other Faulknerian protagonists whose problems were significantly related to those experienced by their creator. Some of Faulkner's emotional anxieties are expressed by Horace and some of his external physical attributes are embodied in Popeye, and the two male characters together form what must be in some sense a composite portrait of the author at this time in his life.

Horace is a husband and a lawyer and thus far from a failure in the eyes of society, but the private truth is that he is inept in nearly every possible way. He is Quentin Compson grown up, in bondage to the past and to a sense of personal inadequacy, yet with an adult sense of responsibility that makes him want to put things right. It also allows him, unlike Quentin, a commitment to the larger issue of injustice, although Horace is as maladroit in carrying through this commitment as he is in every other sphere of his life. Like his immediate fictional predecessor, Horace is focused on his sister and jealous of her entanglement with another man. In a passage which recalls similar ones in *The Sound and the Fury,* Horace associates the smell of honeysuckle with female sexuality and links this sexuality in turn with thoughts of death. He sees a couple caressing each other and muses, "Perhaps it is upon the instant that we realise, admit, that there is a logical pattern to evil, that we die" (175). The rich fragrance of the flower "writhe[s] like cold smoke" as Horace goes on to invoke his stepdaughter, Little Belle, onto whom his incestuous yearnings have recently been displaced. Looking at her picture "beneath the slow, smoke-like tongues of invisible honeysuckle," Horace imagines a rape scene with the victim roaring away into "darkness" and "nothingness" (177).

Sex, evil, and death are all related in the mind of Horace, and honeysuckle is the *fleur du mal* which reveals his entrapment by an inhibiting image of women and carnality. Horace is again like Quentin in dwelling on memories of an earlier time, when he and his sister were joined in innocent comradeship, playing in the rain-soaked streets with their whittled boats and the "muddy bottoms" that presaged their later corruption by time and circumstance (97). In the 1929 manuscript of *Sanctuary,* which Faulkner was to change substantially before its publication, Horace was the central protagonist, and his psychosexual problems were explored with a thoroughness approaching that which the author brought to bear upon Quentin in his previous novel. His strong incentuous attachment to his sister, with its complicated mixture of nurturing and sexuality, is made clear, as are its origins in a childhood trauma, Horace's loss of his mother and subsequent yearning for her.[11] Like Caddy Compson, Horace's sister has become the major female figure in her brother's emotions. In his adult life, Horace's unconscious identification of his sister with his mother intrudes on his relationship with Belle Mitchell, who is associated in his mind with Narcissa, and later is displaced onto his yearning for Little Belle. Sister, mother, wife, and stepdaughter all merge in a manner that is twisted, but psychologically plausible. In the original version of the novel, Horace's gradual discovery of his own sexual problems becomes tantamount to a recognition of his potential for evil that makes him sensitive to the evil he perceives in others.

In his sexual confusion and hopeless idealism, Horace Benbow is much like Quentin Compson, who embodied many of the late adolescent problems faced by his creator. Horace, however, is officially an adult and must confront difficulties much like those facing the thirty-one-year-old Faulkner in early 1929. He is married to a divorced woman, and his bitter statement that ''when you marry somebody else's wife, you start off maybe ten years behind, from somebody else's scratch and scratching'' (10) may reflect Faulkner's own feelings on the subject, for the sentiment is later echoed by Aunt Jenny's comment that ''if a woman dont make a very good wife for one man, she aint likely to for another'' (86). In what is perhaps a wish fulfilling portion of the novel, Faulkner allows Horace a period of escape from his oppressive wife—and from the weekly shrimp-collecting ritual that causes his life to seem objectified as ''a fading series of small stinking spots on a Mississippi sidewalk'' (12). Horace's respite is only temporary, however, and he is eventually forced into capitulation by the strong-willed women in his life, much as Faulkner was virtually marched to the altar by his willful future sister-in-law. Horace's surrender to Narcissa's demand that he cease to house the ex-whore Ruby during his client's murder trial augurs his later abject and defeated return to Belle, who merely looks up and says disparagingly, ''Did you lock the back door?'' (236).

Horace is thus in many ways a personification of Faulkner's present and of his imagined immediate future; in his evocation of Quentin, he also embodies Faulkner's past. But he is in addition a harbinger of the Faulkner of the distant future, in that he tries gamely, if ineffectually, to fight the evil he perceives in the world around him. Believing firmly that Goodwin is innocent, Horace tracks down Temple and attempts to build a valid defense for his client, but he is utterly defeated—by his sister's betrayal, by Temple's perjury, and by the refusal of Goodwin to accuse the real murderer. Faulkner later would make an equally valiant yet hopeless effort to combat the injustice of racial segregation, in which he was beaten not only by the inertia of a rigid southern caste system, but also by his own brother's attempt to sabotage his public statements on the subject. In this respect, Horace is a figure of dark prophecy, and he presages other activist yet ultimately ineffective men of conscience, like Gavin Stevens, who would appear in Faulkner's later works.

Despite his failings, Horace is a figure with some redeeming qualities; Popeye, on the other hand, appears initially to be in almost every respect a monster, and Faulkner on one occasion called him just that. The character is based on an actual Memphis gangster, probably Popeye Pumphrey, said to have been responsible for the perverted rape of a female victim. Faulkner heard stories about the real-life Popeye during visits to Memphis during the 1920s when he was spending time socializing with raffish figures on the fringes of the underworld there. With his evil ways and black suit, the Popeye of *Sanctuary* often seems to be a cardboard villain straight out of nineteenth-century melodrama; he is Faulkner's most repellent evildoer. Portraying him from the start as a vile creature retrieved from the noisome squalor of the modern world, Faulkner "thingifies" Popeye by comparing his eyes to "two knobs of soft black rubber" (2) and his stiffness to that of a "modernistic lampstand" (3), and by asserting that he has "that vicious depthless quality of stamped tin" (1). Popeye is a thing, and one whose psychology is as antihuman as his appearance, for he is voyeur, arsonist, rapist, and murderer, and his final obliteration removes from the earth a creature whom any human moral standard must condemn.

Sexual impotence, however, in itself grounds for sympathy as the most grievous trouble for a male short of terminal disease, is at the root of all of Popeye's psychopathic behavior. It is possible that the author himself was struggling either with actual impotence or fears thereof which he attempted to exorcise by creating and then annihilating his frightening gangster figure. Popeye has a curiously striking physical resemblance to Faulkner. He is short, carries his body stiffly, has dark eyes, "little doll-like hands," a nose that is "aquiline," and almost "no chin at all" (2)—terms that would all be used to describe the author. Temple taunts Popeye for being a "little runt" and Horace refers to him as "that little black man," descriptions which recall, almost word for word, Faulkner's self-portrayal in *Mosquitoes*. In his dutiful devotion to his mother and his free hand with money, Popeye is also similar to his creator.

Perhaps for these reasons, Faulkner gradually came to see Popeye as more than a symbol of evil: as he later said, "He was to me another lost human being" (*FIU,* p. 74). The epilogue which Faulkner added the following year (possibly after he had made some peace with the sexual horror represented by the gangster), through an afterthought insufficiently integrated with the rest of the novel, makes a step toward humanizing Popeye by showing him to be the victim of a disease-ridden mother and of a severely deprived childhood and suggests, finally, that the proper response to Popeye is pity rather than terror. Moreover, after Popeye's wanton rape of Temple and two murders, for which he goes unpunished, he is, ironically, condemned to hang for a murder he did not commit. Thus he, too, becomes a recipient of the injustice which has crippled or destroyed other characters such as Benbow or Lee Goodwin.

In portraying Popeye, at the last, as the son of a man who impregnated his mother, infected her with venereal disease, and then deserted her, and as a child who was abandoned by his grandmother at the age of three, Faulkner makes him a lost child like those earlier characters Elmer and Benjy, though "a sullen and sick child" (87). His birth on Christmas Day also suggests that he is one of "the least of these," like Joe Christmas. He faces his execution stoically and refuses to escape, thus becoming identified with the generally admirable Lee Goodwin. His final request to the sheriff-hangman, "Fix my hair, Jack" (249), injects a note of pathos and makes yet another step toward the rehabilitation of Popeye from a figure of pure evil into one who was sinned against as well as sinning and who shares the minor weaknesses and strengths of ordinary men.

At least one of Popeye's victims, Temple Drake, shares a complicity in the crimes perpetrated by him against her, and she is an equally disturbing figure. One of her most troubling aspects, as Faulkner envisaged it, was her insensitivity, the manner in which "all this evil flowed off her like water off a duck's back"; his additional comment, "Women are completely impervious to evil" (B, p. 613), constitutes one of the bitterest generalizations he ever made about the opposite sex. Certainly Temple is the most depraved of the gallery of nubile women that Faulkner created, beginning with Cecily Saunders. Like Cecily and Pat Robyn, Temple is a "tease," a hypocritical "good girl" who seduces even as she repels, a long-legged child-woman who is both attractive and repulsive. She is slim and pretty, but her eyes are "cool, predatory and discreet" (21) and she is easily drawn into a life in which she becomes unattractive when sexually aroused. In the scene with Red, her mouth is "gaped and ugly like that of a dying fish as she writhed her loins against him" (190).

In *Sanctuary*, Faulkner's previously ambiguous young feminine "ideal" becomes fully debauched, a name on a lavatory wall; and her taunting of Popeye and "grimace of taut, toothed coquetry" (38) can be seen as at least partially responsible for her subsequent rape. Temple's provocative actions just before the assault with the corncob, as well as her later willing submission to life in a Memphis bordello, reveal a subconscious desire to be violated. [12] Moreover, Temple is a death-dealing woman who anticipates Norman Mailer's assertion that all women are killers, for she essentially causes the deaths of two "real men," her lover Red, whom Popeye had threatened to murder if she saw him again, and Lee Goodwin, whom she falsely accuses of killing Tommy and thus condemns to death. Sexuality is figuratively associated with death in the phrase she uses to urge Red to intercourse, "I'm on fire. I'm dying, I tell you" (191), and the two become literally fused as that sexuality causes the murder of two innocent men. Faulkner's vision of women reached its nadir in *Sanctuary* and would never again be as bleak.

Temple is almost as horrific a female as Popeye is a male, and like him she begins to appear as an object, an evil thing, with hair "like clots of resin," rouge like "paper discs," and a "parrotlike" manner of speaking (225–27). Yet she is, like Popeye, to be pitied, for she has evidently been led into her irresponsible and provocative behavior by her unresolved feelings for her father, which have made her incapable of any healthy relationship with a male. In this respect she bears an intriguing relation to Quentin Compson, who was similarly inhibited by yearnings for his sister-mother. Temple's perennial focus on her father has led her, in the absence of any sustaining religious sense, almost to deify him. In moments of crisis she recites her solacing incantation, "My father's a judge," which has supplanted prayers to the heavenly father. Her obsession with her absent father leads her almost inevitably to seek a substitute, and in the Memphis underworld she takes Popeye as her father-lover. In a highly suggestive scene, sex and paternal yearning are linked as she attempts to coax Popeye's pistol away from him. " 'Give it to me,' she whispered. 'Daddy. Daddy.' She leaned her thigh against his shoulder, caressing his arm with her flank. 'Give it to me, daddy,' she whispered" (188). But the sexual relationship with her surrogate father can never be consummated, because of his impotence, and Temple is eventually rescued by her real father, Judge Drake. He retrieves her from the witness box at Goodwin's trial and the scene as they leave the courtroom is a parody of a wedding procession—the two "moved on down the aisle" (229) attended by Temple's four brothers, who, like groomsmen, "moved and surrounded the other two, and in a close body" (230)[13]—after which the "couple" go off to Paris together. Temple has been trapped into a perpetual sexual adolescence by her constant longing to be exclusively with her father, and her plight is a pathetic one.

In creating his portrait of Temple Drake, Faulkner used several of the attributes of his bride-to-be, Estelle Oldham Franklin—her slimness and reddish hair, her popularity and fickleness as a college belle, and her influential judge-father. Whether he also meant to suggest that Estelle had an unnatural dependence on her father which accounted for her failed marriage and early decline into alcoholism cannot be ascertained. Like the other portraits in *Sanctuary* which have biographical elements, that of Temple is so disturbing that one does not know where the line between reality and horror fantasy falls, if indeed such a line can ever be drawn.

Faulkner hoped that the publication of *Sanctuary* would solve some of his pressing financial problems (B, p. 618). He may also, at a more subconscious level, have wished that the writing of it would serve to confront, order, and thus exorcise some of the worst personal terrors he had ever known. After the novel appeared, Faulkner was accused of founding a "cult of cruelty," but the work appears even more deeply disturbing once its place in his personal chronicle is realized. For it is, in effect, Faulkner's epithalamion, and its strange darkness is suggestive of the anxieties which seem to have threatened the prospective bridegroom. Though perhaps personal in its origins, his awful vision of a world in which there is no sanctuary from physical and spiritual impotence emerges as so nightmarishly powerful that it becomes an allegory of a land laid waste by corruption at every level of existence.

5
Work as Redemption:
As I Lay Dying and *Light in August*

THERE ARE STRIKING DIFFERENCES between *Sanctuary* and the two novels
Faulkner wrote between late 1929 and 1931. Both *As I Lay Dying* and
Light in August reveal a new emotional quality, affirmation. Both also contain a new narrative element in the presentation of the committed craftsman
who is able to make a valid moral statement through his own actions and
affect positively the lives of those around him, rendering his achievement
worthwhile in the public sphere as well as the private. Horace Benbow of
Sanctuary attempted this sort of affirmative action but failed dismally in
both spheres; the eventual successes of Cash Bundren and Byron Bunch
thus mark a significant departure from the pervasive negations of Faulkner's earlier works.

   In both novels, too, Faulkner begins to make greater use of some of the
structural elements of comedy such as the bumbling yet triumphant naive
rustic, the mock-heroic odyssey, and the classic comic resolution of marriage. He also reveals an increasingly sophisticated capacity for self-portraiture by tripling, rather than doubling, his partially autobiographical male
characters and thus achieving an even greater measure of artistic balance
and objectivity. The pattern created by the configuration of Mahon-Lowe
in *Soldiers' Pay* or Benbow-Popeye in *Sanctuary* is amplified into that of
Cash-Darl-Jewel and Byron-Joe-Hightower, with the first character in the
constellation acting as a sort of moral fulcrum to which the others are
anchored and by which their difficulties are illuminated. Because these
central author-related characters are neither bitterly satirized nor impos-

sibly idealized, as they often were in Faulkner's earlier work, they themselves have a quality of "roundedness," of being equilibrated between flaws and strengths and thus capable of evolving into figures of true moral stature. If *As I Lay Dying* and *Light in August* do not have the power and brilliance of *The Sound and the Fury,* which was written at some sort of mysterious white heat and which delved into the deepest substrata of consciousness, they are nonetheless major works and notable for the introduction of psychically balanced protagonists. The overdrawn and inadequately realized central characters of previous novels—Bayard, Quentin, and Horace Benbow—whose anguish and sense of defeat cannot be completely accounted for, do not dominate these new works.

Asked on one occasion which of his novels he liked the least, Faulkner answered, "The one that gave me no trouble, that I wrote in six weeks without changing a word, that was *As I Lay Dying.* That's pure *tour de force,* that was no trouble."[1] He is uncharacteristically accurate about the time he spent writing *As I Lay Dying,* which was begun on October 25, 1929, and completed by December 11. The "no trouble" phrase he uses to describe the novel's creation may sound dismissive, but it also reveals his sense of technical mastery over devices like the interior monologue and the ease with his basic material which he brought to the writing of it. With this work, Faulkner reveals for the first time a fully developed sense of vocation, in which his compulsion to write is accompanied by a positive image of himself as a working craftsman whose art is beginning to make a contribution to the world beyond the four walls of his study. The redemptive carpenter Cash Bundren and his successor Byron Bunch constitute a newly affirmative self-portraiture and herald the new direction in which Faulkner's fiction was beginning to move, with consequences that may have been personally positive for the writer but would ultimately prove artistically problematic.

A number of developments in Faulkner's personal life probably account for the appearance of these more positive psychic components of his art. To begin with, he had married Estelle in June and thus faced two of the horrors which he had envisioned in *Sanctuary,* the entry into "violated" terrain entailed in marrying a divorced woman, as expressed by Horace Benbow, and the possible fear of impotence embodied in the portrayal of Popeye. Faulkner and his bride had had a turbulent honeymoon, but he revealed great determination to make the marriage last. He told a friend, "They don't think we're gonna stick, but it is gonna stick" (B, p. 626). Survive it did, through extraordinary vicissitudes, over the next thirty-three years. How many of Faulkner's dark apprehensions were realized during that summer and early fall is unknown, but the important thing from a psychological vantage point is that the marriage had in fact taken place and the specters had been confronted. Once the traumatic honeymoon was over and the couple was back in Oxford, Faulkner obviously found the reality to be less terrifying than the anticipation of it, for a new-found sense of equilibrium underlies his first post-marital fiction.

Shortly before he began work on his new novel, Faulkner started a night job at the powerhouse of the University of Mississippi, which he often described afterward as "shoveling coal" but which actually involved the supervision of two Negro laborers. He also said that he wrote *As I Lay Dying* on the back of a wheelbarrow, "in a coal bunker beside the dynamo between working spells on the night shift. . . . If I ever get rich I am going to buy a dynamo and put it in my house. I think that would make writing easier" (*LIG*, p. 8). Despite the usual leg-pulling, Faulkner conveys the impression that the powerhouse job was an ideal one for him in some ways. It gave him the first regular income he had received in five years and allowed him to feel he was making some sort of economic contribution to the upkeep of his recently acquired family. It also provided him with free time and solitude in which to write, although this was undoubtedly a fringe benefit of which his employers were unaware. During the long nights, with the dynamo humming constantly in the background, Faulkner was occupied simultaneously with "real work" and with his art. This unexpected synthesis of a recurring dichotomy must have been satisfying to him, for the portrayal of regular and fulfilling work is important to *As I Lay Dying*.

At this point, Faulkner's achievements as an artist were beginning to offer their own significant satisfactions. *Sartoris* had been published at the beginning of 1929 to at least a modicum of critical approval, and then, on October 7, little more than two weeks before he began his new novel, *The Sound and the Fury* appeared. A perceptive and laudatory essay written for the occasion by the novelist Evelyn Scott compared *The Sound and the Fury* to Greek tragedy, invoked Dostoevsky, Blake, and the Bible for further comparisons, and extolled the superlative nature of Faulkner's achievement. Scott's praise could only have augmented Faulkner's sense that *The Sound and the Fury* was something extraordinary and that he merited recognition as an artist, and it helped to energize him for his next act of creation.

As I Lay Dying is often linked with *The Sound and the Fury*—and not simply because they were published sequentially or because they later appeared together under one cover. Though the one concerns a poor rural family and its difficult, but concerted, quest to bury one of its dead, and the other an aristocratic family which has fallen into disunity and driven one of its members to suicide, the two novels have many points in common, both technically and thematically. In each Faulkner uses the interior monologue extensively and skillfully, emphasizing the individual's responses to events rather than the events themselves. Each work contains movements in space which are corollary to interior movements into memory or tangential concerns. In both novels, the emotional, often obsessive focus of the various characters is on a woman who herself receives little or no direct portrayal, and both contain triangles formed by a deranged brother, a promiscuous sister, and the sister's seducer[2]—though the triangle in *The Sound and the Fury* is more pivotal and has more devastating consequences. Each contains a truly innocent being, a child or an idiot, whose poignant sense of loss and ignorance of cause and effect offers a singular perspective on the action and the adults. In each work the parents are largely or completely responsible for the trials of their children, whether by showing favoritism or by being remote or ineffectual. And in each, self-interest is a centrifugal force which works destructively against the more desirable centripetal pull toward family unity.

The likenesses between *As I Lay Dying* and its predecessor show Faulkner's continued preoccupation with certain artistic and emotional issues. The presence of Cash Bundren, however, makes for a major difference. He is like Dilsey in being the redemptive figure of his novel, strong in his capacity for suffering and self-sacrifice, but very much unlike her in being a biological member of the nuclear family and a young male with an essential similarity to his creator. Cash, in fact, is the first of a series of carpenter-figures who appear in Faulkner's fiction. The author's choice of vocation for this central character has multiple significances, because it relates him to Faulkner's own experiences with carpentry and to his figurative description of himself as a word-carpenter, and, beyond that, to the incarnate Christ. Faulkner was drawn to the satisfactions offered by working with wood; the many odd jobs he held during the 1920s included a number that were related to carpentry. He was also on the verge of many more woodworking projects, for shortly after finishing *As I Lay Dying,* he bought a gracious old house in urgent need of repairs, many of which he undertook himself, with an impulse toward thoroughness like that revealed by Cash Bundren. Further, the carpentry work on the church roof courageously undertaken by Cash before the novel opens, at the cost of his first broken leg, evokes Faulkner's own somewhat foolhardy project of 1921, when he painted the steeple of the law building at the University of Mississippi, a job which no one else was reckless enough to accept.

There are other similarities between Cash and his creator. Cash is the oldest son and clearly not the favored one, yet he maintains a dignified silence on the subject and carries out his duties as the eldest with devotion and a strong sense of responsibility—as did Faulkner, whose unhappiness and feelings of rebelliousness about the injustice of his family situation surfaced almost exclusively in his fiction. Cash's limp may be seen as a badge of the psychic wounds he has undoubtedly suffered in his role of inadequately rewarded family provider, just as the limp which Faulkner affected as part of his "wounded hero" role betrayed his need for another sort of recognition. Despite Cash's status as the devoted son who sees the bulk of his mother's affection given to a younger child, he deals evenhandedly and fairly with that sibling, never revealing his possible resentment, a pattern exactly like that of Faulkner's own interactions with his parentally favored youngest brother. Again, Faulkner's sense of inequity was rarely revealed except in his novels.

Many aspects of Cash's situation thus have their origins in Faulkner's own work experience and familial position. But he is also both a metaphoric embodiment of Faulkner's concept of himself as an artisan of language and, even more important, a man who develops during the course of the narrative both cognitively and morally. His growth is symbolic of what was taking place within Faulkner the man and the artist. Cash is a diligent worker in wood whose concern for precision and functional aesthetics compels him to labor all night in the driving rain, and he describes all transactions, even human ones, in terms rooted in balance and measurement. So Faulkner frequently used the terminology of carpentry to discuss his own efforts to solve artistic problems. He characterized the writing process as "scratch[ing] around in my lumber room" and suggested that reading great works was a good way to learn the craft of writing, "just like a very good way to be a carpenter is from watching a seasoned carpenter do it." When asked about the sources of material, he answered "imagination, observation, and experience," which he uses "as the carpenter reaches into his lumber room and finds a board that fits the particular corner he's building" (*FIU,* pp. 109, 117, 103).

Faulkner may have used such woodworking language as a simple, even self-consciously humble, means of effectively communicating his vision of the artistic process. Nevertheless, it recurs with such frequency in his public comments that it must be related to a sincerely held concept of the conscious aspect of artistic creation as a procedure much like the careful building of a shed or animal pen. The "demons," or the unconscious promptings, were always there too, making their own demands and often capable of bursting the sides of the carefully wrought structures intended to house them, but the diligent, conscious craftsman worked constantly on the exterior, building solidly and carefully, and attempting to keep things under control.

Faulkner was increasingly aware of this craftsmanlike aspect of his art, and the selection of a carpenter hero to dominate his work is revealing. The manner in which Cash develops is also of importance. Most critics tend to consider Addie Bundren the emotional focal point of *As I Lay Dying,* and indeed the macabre journey to bury her body constitutes the main narrative strand, just as the nature of her family's response to her death reveals the intricate workings of their individual consciousnesses. But these critics often overlook the way in which Cash occupies the moral center of the novel and the extent to which his personal growth offers the major ethical message. Cash is a "developing" character who matures into a figure of real moral stature—the first such character to appear in Faulkner's fiction, which had hitherto been peopled with more static types. Cash's expansion, during the course of the novel, from a creature of somewhat narrow sensibility and limited moral horizons into a fully conscious, sympathetic participant in the sorrows and struggles of his fellow men may signify Faulkner's own growth in perceptive sympathy through his commitment to family and artistic responsibility. In any case, Cash's presence is chiefly responsible for that affirmative note which makes its first entrance in *As I Lay Dying*.

The initial limitations of Cash's sensibility and, correlatively, of his moral potential are carefully delineated by Faulkner through linguistic devices. Rigidity is suggested by the propensity of the carpenter for expressing himself in language and imagery drived from his trade. At the outset of *As I Lay Dying,* Cash is inarticulate, preoccupied with his careful carpentry of the coffin for his dying mother. He is literal and precise, making the coffin exactly to Addie's "measure and weight" and replying with absurd precision to a question about the length of his fall from the church roof that it was "twenty-eight foot, four and a half inches, about" (85).[3] The first section in which Cash speaks directly contains merely his list of thirteen reasons for the careful beveling of each board in the coffin, and the second reveals his obsession with balance.

Despite the restrictiveness of such an outlook, Cash is capable of recognizing the inadequacy of his formulas to deal with human emotions. He shows his sense of where measurements fail when he admits that "a body is not square like a crosstie" and reveals his superstitious belief in the "animal magnetism" of a dead person (77, 78). Moreover, Cash's concept of the tensions between vertical and horizontal stress lines and their ultimate irreconcilability forms, in one respect, the linguistic and philosophical foundation of the entire novel. It is closely related to Anse's idea that when God "aims for something to be always a-moving, He makes it longways, like a road or a horse or a wagon, but when He aims for something to stay put, He makes it up-and-down ways, like a tree or a man," and to Addie's sense of "how words go straight up in a thin line, quick and harmless, and how terribly doing goes along the earth, clinging to it" (35, 165). Cash is the one character in *As I Lay Dying* who not only perceives these stressful oppositions but is actively concerned with achieving equipoise between them. The ultimately balanced nature of his vision constitutes a form of moral triumph.

In each of the Bundrens, self-interest clashes with the sense of wider obligations and usually prevails. Even Cash's initial preoccupation with the coffin can be seen as a form of selfishness, for it encloses him in a hermetic world and blinds him to everything else. His silent stolidity early angers the volatile Jewel, who shouts, "Goddamn your thick-nosed soul" (90), but though Cash never loses his stoicism, his self-containment is gradually supplanted by a wider view of the imperatives of family and society. From the outset, Cash is determined to bury his mother according to her wishes, motivated by a fidelity that persists in the face of the fact that she has obviously cared only for Jewel among her children. The broken leg Cash suffers in his heroic effort to get the wagon bearing Addie's coffin across the flooded ford engenders the sort of continuous suffering that provides a psychic baptism into a new state of consciousness. His determination increases and he refuses to delay the trip, despite the unspeakable pain caused by the inept setting of his leg by a veterinarian and his family's absurd attempt to mitigate his suffering by pouring concrete on the broken limb. Sacrificing his own need for surcease to what he perceives as the needs of the family, the martyred Cash suffers in silence, blaming no one.

Early in the book, then, Cash's limitations are both linguistic and, to a lesser degree, moral, but by the end of the arduous journey, he has become a figure both articulate and ethically impressive. He comprehends that the pure verticals and horizontals of carpentry are inadequate and offers a view of Darl's insanity both more generalized and more sensitive than any of his previous utterances. "Sometimes I aint so sho who's got ere a right to say when a man is crazy and when he aint. Sometimes I think it aint none of us pure crazy and aint none of us pure sane" (223). He acknowledges the destructiveness of Darl's barn burning and his unfitness to live any longer in the ordinary world, yet perceives the difficulty of simplistic judgments where human beings are concerned.

By the end of *As I Lay Dying,* Cash's enlarged capacity for selfless actions has been further augmented by his ability to generalize the nature of the experience undergone by his family. Faulkner's novel is as much about the nature of consciousness as about the need for affirmative moral action, and the character of Cash develops significantly at both levels. Cash literally and figuratively finds his voice and discovers his commitment to issues that extend far beyond his private obsession. His growth serves as a paradigm of the discoveries as an artist that Faulkner was making at this time. The writer would always continue to treat his most personal concerns, for they were the perennial source of his "inspiration." Still, the expanded ethical outlook developed by the somewhat autobiographical Cash and the increasing objectification revealed by the author's successful treatment of members of a social class utterly unlike his own together signify Faulkner's sudden progress toward wider moral horizons and a greater engagement in the life beyond the anguish-filled prison of the self in which he had heretofore been trapped.

Cash Bundren thus has psychological importance as a self-portrait of his creator; he represents both actually and metaphorically Faulkner's growing awareness of his own artistic and human possibilities. In addition, Faulkner's carpenter has a relationship to religious myth that increases the resonance of his portrayal, just as similar religious allusions had amplified that of Benjy Compson in *The Sound and the Fury.* Faulkner is careful to qualify the portrait by giving his carpenter a Christian name that is unattractive and has negative connotations, so that Cash Bundren seems complexly human rather than a figure of religious allegory. The mythic overtones are nevertheless suggestive. The baptism by suffering undergone by Cash constitutes a form of palingenesis that relates his story to those in Genesis and the New Testament. The carpenter is an earnest artisan, but he is also in some sense an Adamic or Christ figure whose regeneration has wider implications. Cash subtly reenacts in a humanistic way portions of the terrestrial experience of mankind's first father and of the Nazarene carpenter.

Cash has a literal, if only faintly Adamic, fall before the novel begins when he plunges from a church roof and acquires the knowledge of severe pain, together with an injured leg whose subsequent rebreaking makes him a cripple. Though Faulkner deleted a passage from the book that explicitly associated Cash with the New Testament Savior—in which Darl says, "Not all men are born carpenters, good carpenters, like Christ" (B, p.

640)—there remain suggestions of a Jesus-like aura surrounding Cash. Vardaman, whose concern for the fish is suggestive of Christian faith in the Risen Lord, sees Cash as "going up and down above the saw, at the bleeding plank" (62). Moreover, Cash, making a selfless sacrifice for the good of the family, which represents in its way fallen mankind, twice reenacts versions of the Crucifixion. When he is pulled from the flood water into which he had fallen trying to save his mother's coffin, he appears dead. His face is "sunken a little" and his eyes are closed. The tableau as Faulkner presents it is like the Descent from the Cross, with Dewey Dell as Magdalen wiping Cash's face tenderly with the hem of her dress. Cash's subsequent journey atop his mother's coffin with a painfully broken leg becomes a second crucifixion. He is immobilized there as if nailed to a cross and suffers silently for the sake of his fellow man, but is finally "resurrected" by the ministrations of Doc Peabody, who repairs the dangerously damaged leg.

These Adamic and Christ-like associations with which Faulkner invests the character of Cash Bundren have a personal significance as well as an evocative connection with the most powerful Christian myths. They suggest that the self-enclosed "autogethsemane" of Faulkner's earlier autobiographical figures, which can end only in frustration and death, has become, with the all-important figure of Cash, closer to a true "gethsemane," in which the suffering is accompanied by real engagement and an awareness of the needs of other equally vulnerable human beings.

Cash is the crucial figure in *As I Lay Dying,* and he has much autobiographical importance, as well as a relationship to mythic antecedents, but he is part of a tightly woven novelistic fabric, the threads of which interconnect in a pattern both technically and psychologically complex. There are, for instance, links between Cash and his two brothers which go beyond the usual emotional interactions of siblings into the realm of intuitive and psychically symbolic interrelationships. With his portrayal of the Bundren brothers, Faulkner refined his technique of creating what I will refer to as "linked characters," those closely intertwined sets of individuals whose connections are both dramatically and symbolically intimate. Each Bundren brother represents a differing response to problematic situations and thus embodies an aspect of Faulkner's own emotional world view, but the ties between them are so close that even within the context of the novel they seem at points to be facets of a single being rather than fully autonomous and self-contained individuals. Faulkner's use of these linked characters gives his work a singularly effective form of psychological unity.

Darl has the closest emotional and symbolic connections to the pivotal
Cash. Darl is a creature of pure, disengaged consciousness, and his poetic
ruminations mark him as the thinker in this version of Faulkner's recurrent
thinker-doer dichotomy. Still, the schism between Darl and Cash is far less
complete than it would have been in an earlier work, and the strong
connection Faulkner maintains between the two marks a significant stage
in his psychic development.

The first section is given to Darl. His observations of the physical setting
and human actions on the Bundren place are sometimes poetic, but they are
also, for the most part, thorough and accurate, as is appropriate for the
character who serves as a detached recorder of the life around him (the
artist as mirror) until his descent into madness and destructive behavior
ends his function in that respect. When Darl carefully, and articulately,
notes the silent diligence of Cash's sawing of the planks for his mother's
coffin, the scene initially appears to be the characteristically Faulknerian
one of the man of words commenting admiringly on the man of action, as
in the opening scene of *Mosquitoes,* with each man almost totally enclosed
in his own psychic sphere. But such is not truly the case here. Much of the
language used by Darl in this very first section is related to the linguistic
and, eventually, emotional norm established by Cash and thus portends the
ultimate symbolic assimilation of Darl by Cash. Darl describes the path
from the field as "straight as a plumb-line" and as passing the cottonhouse
at "four soft right angles" (3). The cottonhouse itself is "square," with a
roof "set at a single pitch" and "a single broad window in two opposite
walls," and he and Jewel walk "in single file and five feet apart" (4). This
sort of precise concern for measurement comes from Cash, who speaks at
the outset only in such mathematical language. Thus the two men are
closely linked at the first, as they will be at the end, when Cash himself
takes over Darl's function as observer and generalizer.

The two brothers, interconnected linguistically, are also closely linked
emotionally, with an intuitive understanding that is so powerful that their
dialogue and interactions often seem to be those of a single person. When
the two men wait in the wagon before the flooded stream, they "look at
one another with long probing looks, looks that plunge unimpeded
through one another's eyes and into the ultimate secret place where for an
instant Cash and Darl crouch flagrant and unabashed in all the old terror
and the old foreboding, alert and secret and without shame" (135). Later in
the same scene, the two sit looking at Jewel, and Cash's spoken words
ensue from Darl's unspoken thoughts. " 'He can swim,' " muses Darl
aloud, before continuing silently, "When he was born, he had a bad time of

it. Ma would sit in the lamp-light, holding him on a pillow on her lap. We would wake and find her so. There would be no sound from them. 'That pillow was longer than him,' Cash says'' (137), astonishingly certain of what Darl has been thinking.

Darl is thus in many ways an intimate "part" of Cash, but he cannot function effectively on his own. His problems are like those of Quentin Compson in that his feeling of motherlessness gives him a crippling sense of loss: "I have no mother" (89), he says, in a phrase evocative of Quentin's poignant outbursts. He, too, has become intensely aware of his sister as a sexual being; he sees her breasts as "mammalian ludicrosities" (156) and her leg as the "lever which moves the world" (97). Darl's intuitions are strongest about sex and death, and thus the two seem to be linked in his consciousness as they so destructively were in Quentin's. Darl knows about Dewey Dell's impregnation by a field hand "without the words" (26). His awareness of sex and death is shown again in his reflection that "it takes two people to make you, and one people to die" (38). Darl has also, like Quentin, become too cerebral, unable to convert knowledge into action in any useful way.

Here, as in *The Sound and the Fury,* the psychological portrait of the intellectual is illuminated by the use of a childish character, an innocent who is equally helpless. Like Darl, Vardaman is lost and bewildered, and the actions of both are desperate and destructive. Vardaman drills holes through his mother's coffin so she can "breathe," thus mutilating both coffin and body, and Darl burns the barn that contains his mother's odorous corpse in an anguished effort to be rid of what is both a physical and emotional burden. Darl's act signals the breakdown of his capacity to live in the "normal" world and precipitates his incarceration in the state mental asylum. Yet Cash above everyone sympathizes with him, making his crucial "balanced" statement that "aint none of us pure crazy and aint none of us pure sane" (223). He thus admits how indeterminate and mysterious is the line that separates himself-sanity from Darl-insanity, how close is their contiguity and affinity. The two brothers continue to exhibit real kinship and mutual concern, as Darl generously offers to drive Cash, who is suffering with his concrete-enclosed broken leg, to the doctor's, and Cash selflessly refuses to deflect the family from its goal of burying Addie.

Cash's willingness to shut away the brother to whom he is so intimately tied seems in the deepest sense "wrong," despite his effort to justify it on moral grounds: "I dont reckon nothing excuses setting fire to a man's barn and endangering his stock and destroying his property" (223). His act can only be seen as a symbolic one, the banishment of the disconnected intellect. With the breaking of the all-important link to the brother who is firmly rooted in reality, Darl becomes completely mad, utterly dissociated from a sense of self. He goes off on the train to Jackson, referring to himself in the third person and invoking dichotomous symbols, like the guards riding back to back, the nickel with two faces, and the pig "with two backs and no face" (244), that betray his own psychic splitting.[4] With Darl gone, Cash assimilates his brother's function as recorder-commentator and thus expands his role as man of action into that of actor-thinker, the artist who is fully engaged and fully aware.

Jewel, the other important brother-symbol of *As I Lay Dying,* undergoes a similar process during the course of the narrative in relationship to Cash, though Jewel's fate might be described as "taming," whereas Darl's was banishment-assimilation. The angry and kinetic Jewel is a somewhat problematic character who is less adequately realized than the two brothers to whom he bears a close kinship. In his later public statements, Faulkner used approbatory terms to describe this character, calling Jewel "the toughest" and admiring his relinquishment of his horse in exchange for mules to pull the wagon containing his mother's coffin because "he sacrificed the only thing he loved for someone else's good" (*FIU,* pp. 109–10). These qualities are not as effectively dramatized as they might be, however, and one suspects that some of the problems in Jewel's portrayal are related to his creator's tendency to romanticize the type of character he represents. With his tallness, angry silences, and reckless heroism, Jewel is an embodiment of virility, and aspects of his presentation seem related to earlier, somewhat idealized self-portraits, such as those of Gordon the sculptor and the Sartoris twins: for instance, Jewel's attraction to the violent driving energy of beautiful horses was certainly Faulkner's own.

Jewel plays an important role in illuminating the figure of Cash. Just as Darl is Cash's "other half," Jewel is in a way Cash's "twin," one whose hostile taciturnity and defiant bravery offer a more extreme version of the modest carpenter's quiet heroism. He is also alienated, albeit invisibly, from the family by his status as the product of his mother's adulterous relationship with the Reverend Whitfield, just as Cash is unfairly set apart by his status as most-exploited and least-loved child. At the same time, Jewel's initial harsh judgment of Cash gives us another viewpoint on the dogged devotion with which Cash prepares his mother's coffin.

Initially described by Darl in terms of the linguistic standards tacitly established by Cash—his eyes "like wood" are "staring straight ahead" and his manner suggests "the rigid gravity of a cigar store Indian" (4)—Jewel seems a creature of pure verticals and horizontals. Once fused with his steed, however, he becomes a figure of motion and grandeur, who "flows upward in a stooping swirl like the lash of a whip, his body in midair shaped to the horse" (12). Thus Jewel partakes of both stasis and motion. His position, which has a certain quality of equipoise, lends credibility to his anger at Cash for "hammering and sawing on that goddamn box" under his dying mother's window, "where she can see him saying See. See what a good one I am making for you" (14). Jewel's outburst is a result of his own wish for exclusivity with his mother, with whom he wants to be alone, "just . . . me and her on a high hill" (15). Nevertheless, his judgment complicates our response to Cash, who *is* in a way flaunting his fidelity, and thus intensifies our sense of the effectiveness of Cash's gradual emergence as a decent and selfless person.

During the efforts to get the wagon across the flooded ford, Jewel's actions parallel, with strategic differences, those of Cash and serve to amplify our understanding of the nature of Cash's achievement. Jewel urges the group to act, without concern for the specifics of implementation, "Just so we do something" (139), while Cash methodically undertakes the necessary preparation, tying ropes and stowing gear as if for a sea voyage. The two men bravely enter the water almost simultaneously, but it is Cash who is responsible for the wagon and team—which he manages "carefully and skillfully" (140)—for his passenger Darl, and for the coffin, which he holds with one hand. When nemesis strikes in the shape of a log, Cash stays in the water, even though he cannot swim, trying to retrieve the coffin and rescue Jewel's horse. When Cash finally emerges he seems almost dead. As if his self-sacrifice has inspired his family, they all participate in the efforts to salvage his beloved tools, led by Jewel's repeated heroic dives to the bottom for the saw and chalkline.

Beginning with this incident, Jewel's actions seem increasingly selfless, as he starts in essential ways to emulate Cash, sacrificing his horse when further progress necessitates it. Yet his solitary, almost fierce heroism continues to be contrasted with Cash's more durable and solid bravery during the journey to Jefferson. Cash suffers quietly but continuously from his broken leg while urging the group onward, assuring them that he feels "fine" (205), whereas during the barn fire, Jewel heroically but frenetically rescues a horse, a cow, and the coffin from the inferno in what seems a matter of seconds, heedless of his scorched back.

At this point the brothers visibly become "twins," both with blackened wounds that represent their heroic sacrifices. Vardaman makes the parallel explicit when he says, "Your back looks like a nigger's, Jewel," and immediately reflects that "Cash's foot and leg looked like a nigger's" (214). By the final scene, Jewel appears almost docile and communicative, evincing concern for the proper care of Cash's healing leg and willingly taking charge of the team and wagon as the family waits for Pa to appear with his new wife and new store teeth. Cash's exemplary behavior thus gradually subdues and ethicizes Jewel's lonely violence, just as he assimilates Darl's capacity for cerebration and subordinates it to right action. Cash morally dominates the triad of brothers at the end of the novel as he did linguistically at the outset.

The psychic integration revealed by the evolving interconnection of the three brothers also underlies the portraits of the parents. Anse and Addie Bundren have, like the Compsons, essentially failed their children in every possible way, but Faulkner treats their flaws with a compassion that in *The Sound and the Fury* is reserved for the children, the parents' victims. Anse's humpback symbolizes his defective moral sense and ineffectuality as a parent and husband, yet those around him respond to him with patience and a readiness to help. He himself shows moments of muddled concern, as in the wonderfully touching and funny scene in which he tries awkwardly to smooth the quilt that covers his dead wife before finally giving up to say, "God's will be done. Now I can get them teeth" (51). Addie is an equally inadequate parent, proud and isolated, affectionate only to Jewel, but Faulkner renders Addie sympathetic by showing her as the victim of a nihilistic father who told her "that the reason for living was to get ready to stay dead a long time" (161). She married in a desperate attempt to escape the teaching she despised, only to discover painfully that love was a "word . . . like the others: just a shape to fill a lack" (164). And, as Faulkner later said, she found that there was "nothing ahead of her but a dull and dreary life" (*FIU*, p. 114). Where Faulkner's portrait of the senior Compsons offered a scathing indictment of parental inadequacy, that of the Bundrens is far more moderate and humane. They appear, like their children, to be rounded and sympathetic human beings.

The characterization of Anse and Addie Bundren, like the moral triumph of their son Cash, signifies a form of psychic victory for the author. It shows him taking a first crucial step toward displaying an integrated sense of himself as an artist and as a man, as his developing sense of craftsmanship and awareness of responsibilities beyond himself emerged to balance those deep anxieties which were the wellspring of his art but so often hampered him as an individual. *As I Lay Dying* may not exhibit the dark power of *The Sound and the Fury*, but it treats similar material, shows much of the same technical brilliance, and creates in Cash Bundren a figure with subtle tones of the Incarnate Redeemer capable of standing at the center of the family and modifying or assimilating some of that family's darkness. In so doing it suggests that Faulkner had begun his own form of psychic "redemption" by making a full commitment to his family and his art.

The next novel Faulkner wrote, *Light in August,* is a "companion work" to *As I Lay Dying* in certain essential ways, despite the fact that the attention of readers and critics usually focuses either on the figure of Joe Christmas and the horror of his descent into a personal hell of sexual pathology and murder or on the theme of the perversions of southern Protestantism. Both of these major elements of *Light in August* are introduced in a minor way in *As I Lay Dying.* Jewel Bundren, with his angry aloofness and fierce outbursts, is to some degree a precursor of Joe Christmas, and the theme of Christian hypocrisy and distortion appears in those wrongheaded judgments made by the pious Cora Tull and in the self-delusions of the Reverend Whitfield. Faulkner develops these elements much more fully in *Light in August.*

Light in August, indeed, has many similarities to its predecessor. Both treat the major theme of death and birth in a manner which invokes the eternal natural cycle of decay and regeneration, and both present a series of personal responses to central crises in the present. Each contains the same constellation of characters—the male triad composed of a detached "intellectual," a conscientious doer of the word, and a man of solitary violence; misguided parent-figures; a pregnant unmarried woman; and a "chorus" of local people who offer running commentary on the action and judgments of the central characters. In both, the doer, who is also a worker in wood, serves as a mediator between the other characters and as a moral standard by which they may be appraised. (*Light in August* differs from the earlier work, of course, by being at once more affirmative, in that the "intellectual" moves from a position of detachment to one of moral commitment, and much darker, in that the man of lonely violence commits a gruesome murder and is himself killed and castrated.) Finally, both novels seem to be based more directly than his previous works on acts of conscious craftsmanship. Faulkner described his writing of *Light in August* in phrases reminiscent of his "no trouble" description of *As I Lay Dying:* he was writing consciously, he said, "without that anticipation and that joy which ever made writing pleasure to me. . . . Now I was deliberately choosing among possibilities and probabilities of behavior and weighing and measuring each choice by the scale of the Jameses and Conrads and Balzacs."[5]

This movement away from purely personal obsession toward emotional and artistic balance can be seen in Faulkner's revision of *Sanctuary,* which he undertook not long before he began writing *Light in August.* When the galleys of the novel arrived in Oxford in late 1930, the author began altering them more extensively than was usual with him. He changed the nature of the relationship between Horace and his sister so that the incestuous element was reduced, he made Temple Drake the central character in place of the semiautobiographical Horace, and he added the epilogue which "explains" and thus serves to humanize Popeye. All of these revisions reveal Faulkner's sense of the need for modifying the personal and obsessive component of *Sanctuary* and for greater "roundedness" in character presentation, an awareness which underlay the creation of *Light in August,* as of *As I Lay Dying. Light in August* itself shows increasing efforts at objectification, for personal sexual pathology is emobdied in, and thus partially masked by, the religious issues so central to the novel, and the voice of the town as spokesman for the generalized response is more evident than it had been earlier.

The origin of the qualities common to *Light in August* and its predecessor, most of them new developments in Faulkner's fiction, has already been discussed in the section on *As I Lay Dying.* The figure of the committed craftsman, the sense of regeneration, the growing efforts at balance, objectivity, and generalization—all emanated from Faulkner's own increasing sense of personal engagement and satisfaction. The events in his life between the end of 1929, when he completed *As I Lay Dying,* and late 1931, when he was hard at work on *Light in August,* served to augment in many ways his feeling of worth and responsibility as an artist and as a man, but also contained a tragic disappointment which probably accounts for the singular darkness of portions of *Light in August.*

Having finally made the commitment to marriage and determined to make it last, Faulkner looked for ways to make his new family, which included two active young stepchildren, more comfortable. In April, 1930, he purchased for $6,000 from a family named Bryant a gracious antebellum house known as the Old Shegog Place. Large, becolumned, and situated on wide lawns, the house was impressive but badly in need of rehabilitation. Faulkner moved his family into the house in June and, with help from friends and relatives and fortified by a large supply of whiskey, began the extensive repairs that were necessary. These included replacing the roof and the foundation beams, installing plumbing, wiring, and new screens, and painting the place inside and out. Faulkner almost immediately acquired a staff of black servants to help run his "plantation"—a general factotum, a cook, and Mammy Callie Barr, who had been Faulkner's own childhood nurse and who now undertook the same function for the wards of her former charge. Within barely a year, Faulkner had become husband, stepfather, homeowner, renovator, and chief-of-staff to a tiny army of servants, and the final affirmation of his newly masculine role came when he made his wife pregnant during the summer. The man who was so sympathetic to children looked forward to having one of his own.

Along with visible "progress' in nearly every aspect of his private life, Faulkner's satisfactions in the public sphere were also increasing. He had been writing and mailing out short stories at a great rate, but to no avail, until he finally sold his first one in early 1930, when *Scribner's* accepted "A Rose for Emily." Magazine sales were at this point Faulkner's main hope for substantial economic gain, since his books had been selling poorly, and this first acceptance seemed a promising step toward prosperity. *Sanctuary* appeared in February of 1931 to a roar of mingled approval and outrage—a notoriety which caused large sales and started talk of Hollywood contracts for its author. Faulkner was soon invited to a conference of southern writers to be held in Virginia, which somehow made his vocation "official," and New York publishers began to squabble over the rights to his future novels. Faulkner was becoming a personage. His art was receiving the sort of general public recognition it deserved, and his financial prospects seemed excellent. He wrote with wonderment to his wife from New York about his new status: "I have created quite a sensation. I have had luncheons in my honor by magazine editors every day for a week now, besides evening parties, or people who want to see what I look like. In fact, I have learned with astonishment that I am now the most important figure in American letters. That is, I have the best future" (*L,* p. 53).

But personal tragedy also struck Faulkner that year and undermined any tendency he might have had toward complacency. Estelle's pregnancy was difficult, for she suffered from anemia and continued to drink heavily, and the baby, a girl, was born suddenly in January, 1931, two months prematurely. Faulkner named her Alabama, after the favorite great-aunt who served as a model for the indomitable older women of his fiction, and watched intensely the tiny girl's struggle to survive. He put a bold face on things in a letter written when Alabama was a few days old, in which he reported telling a farmer she weighed three pounds and receiving the reply, "Well, dont feel bad about that. What with this Hoover prosperity and the drouth last summer, a fellow does well to get his seed back."[6] But the local hospital did not have an incubator, and Alabama lived just a few days longer. Her father wept openly for the first time in his life and carried her small casket on his knees all the way to the cemetery.[7] Faulkner's grief was terrible, but he refused to assuage it with his usual anodyne, alcohol. Though he suffered, it was a new kind of pain, grief as much for Alabama's loss of life as for his own deprivation. Faulkner's tragedy increased his awareness of others, seeming to lessen his concentration on the purely self-centered anguish which had previously preoccupied him and to involve him instead in the universal cycle of procreation and death.

When Faulkner sat down to begin his new novel in August of 1931, he was still haunted by his recent loss and entitled the work *Dark House*. Byron Bunch is the positive self-portrait of the work, but Faulkner also identified himself in part with Hightower, a watcher at the window of his dark house, whose burial of his dead wife bears similarities to Faulkner's of his tiny daughter: he oversees it alone, forgoes a church funeral, and takes the body "straight to the cemetery" (59).[8] Faulkner also probably felt certain affinities with his third male protagonist, Joe Christmas, who lashes out angrily at an environment he perceives as hostile: Joe is "crucified" at the age of thirty-three, and the author, also thirty-three at the time, undoubtedly felt himself undergoing an emotional gethesemane as he contemplated the tragic death of the child for whom he had longed.

Both the darkness and the affirmation which were produced by the events of this period in Faulkner's personal life come to the surface in *Light in August*, where they are intensified and placed in what seems an eerie juxtaposition. The balance between despair and hope often appears to be an uneasy one, and only Faulkner's skillful interrelation of the separate narrative portions with their disparate emotional "messages" and his close connection of the three male protagonists through psychological likenesses and contrasts hold the work tightly together.

Faulkner is often most effective when he creates a doomed male who has been crippled and distorted by his early upbringing, for he obviously identified with the psychic wounds incurred by such men. In the figure of Joe Christmas, Faulkner portrayed this sort of character at his darkest and most powerful, aided, as he had been in his creation of Benjy Compson, by knowledge of a similar "real" character which helped him to avoid the inchoateness of his more direct self-portrayals. The story of the arrogant and alienated murderer who spends fifteen years wandering "a thousand savage and lonely streets" (192) haunted by his suspected black blood reaches a violent climax based on an actual incident that occurred in Oxford when Faulkner was a child. Nelse Patton, a black, slashed the throat of a white woman with a razor and was brutally lynched by an angry mob.[9] Joe Christmas meets a similarly brutal fate at the hands of Percy Grimm, but Faulkner gives him a carefully drawn psychic history and complicates it with suggestions of parallels to Christ, with the result that Joe becomes finally a figure of ambiguity to whom our response is mingled distaste and sympathy. He is one of Faulkner's most memorable victim-victimizers.

The portrait of Joe Christmas is the richest of the book. Faulkner achieves this fullness by describing nearly every stage in Joe's early life and presenting a number of varied personal responses to Joe by other characters. Faulkner has been criticized for omitting from Joe's history the years between ages eighteen and thirty-three, but his method seems essentially correct for portraying a figure whose early childhood traumas culminate in his present violent outburst. Those "missing years" are in a way superfluous to the psychoanalyst, and Faulkner uses means that are basically psychoanalytical to delineate Joe Christmas. His history is a more extreme version of Quentin Compson's and has also resulted in sexually arrested development. But Joe learns to turn his anger outward upon his environment and moves toward murder rather than suicide.

When Joe first enters the novel, he gives the appearance of being contemptuous, with an aura of "something definitely rootless" which he carries like a banner with a "quality ruthless, lonely, and almost proud" (27). Like Popeye, he is ominous and rather objectlike: "He carried with him his own inescapable warning, like a . . . rattlesnake its rattle," and his flesh is a "level dead parchment color" (29, 30). Unlike Popeye, however, Joe is soon presented from an interior as well as exterior vantage point, so that he becomes more quickly someone who arouses our sympathy. Even as we learn of that terror and dislike of the "lightless hot wet primogenitive Female" (100) which portends Joe's murder of Joanna Burden, we hear him thinking quietly, "Something is going to happen to me," the cue phrase for the fear of sexual imminence that Faulkner had already given to his rape victim, Temple Drake. And we listen to Joe's pathetic assertion, identifying him with other helpless, yearning human beings, that "God loves me too" (91). Faulkner presents quite early in the book the horrifying events that comprised Joe's childhood, not waiting until an epilogue to do so, as he had with Popeye. By the time the topic of Joe's vicious murder has been reintroduced it is almost impossible not to understand and even empathize with him.

The child Joe is the ultimate isolate, orphaned and bearing the taint of suspected black blood. He is, as was the young Faulkner, small for his age, "sober and quiet as a shadow" (104), and some of Joe's early experiences recall those of Faulkner's first autobiographical fictional child, Elmer. Joe also loses a sister-mother at an early age, a girl of twelve named Alice whom he had allowed to "mother him a little" (119) and who vanished one night, leaving him bemused and bereft. In "Elmer" there were hints of a Freudian "primal scene," the accidental viewing of sexual intercourse by a small child, which often causes emotional trauma. The five-year-old Joe unwillingly becomes a captive witness to such a scene, and the experience of overhearing the sexual encounter causes him to regurgitate the tooth-paste he has been eating and leaves him with a permanent negative association of food, sex, and women. Afterward Joe is misunderstood and cruelly mistreated by the terrified dietician, and this engenders a distrust and hatred of the female principle which is dramatized in the boy's later relations with women. The maternal gestures of his gentle foster-mother meet brutal rejection; he brushes her aside and dashes her proffered platters of food to the ground. Even though Mrs. McEachern is in no way like the dietician, Joe sees her as "casting a faint taint of evil about the most trivial and innocent actions" (147). He does not differentiate nurturing impulses from sexual urges in women and hates both. Just as his foster-mother's unwanted kindness leaves him with an "aftertaste," during his first sexual encounter he senses "something in him trying to get out, like when he had used to think of toothpaste" (137). The revulsion created by the scene's association with his early disturbing memory causes him to kick the girl brutally and escape. By late adolescence, women have become for him "suavely shaped urns" which are fissured, with cracks that effuse "something liquid, deathcolored, and foul" (165). Fittingly, Joe's first sexual liaison is with a debased waitress-prostitute, whom he calls "his whore" (174) and who almost inevitably mistreats him.

While the women in Joe's early life after his initial trauma appear as creatures of defilement in his distorted psyche, the men become figures of terrifying righteousness, a quality which is also evinced by the dietician during Joe's traumatic encounter with her. When she discovers him behind the curtain, she angrily calls him a "little rat" for "spying" and makes him believe that he is the one who has sinned. Thus he feels "tortured with punishment deferred" and yearns to "get his whipping and strike the balance and write it off'' (107). To Joe, the dietician embodies rigorous masculine justice as well as female sexuality, and when these masculine-feminine qualities again coalesce in a woman, Joanna Burden, the merger has catastrophic consequences both for her and for Joe.

Mr. McEachern, the foster-father who removes Joe from the orphanage, appears to embody the merciless righteousness for which Joe longs as punishment for his "sin." McEachern has the aura of a mythical judge-figure, with his thick hair and beard, his black suit and his cold eyes. He makes Rhadamanthine pronouncements and enters a scene angrily as "representative of the wrathful and retributive Throne" (178). Mc-Eachern's belief in harsh punishment fulfills Joe's needs, which have become masochistic and homoerotic. Joe identifies the whipping strap with McEachern; both have "an odor of clean hard virile living leather" (130) and Joe receives his chastisement with a "rapt, calm expression" (131). He and his punisher become almost as one, "the two backs in their rigid abnegation of all compromise more alike than actual blood could have made them" (130), and Joe receives subsequent whippings with an almost sexual satisfaction, "remote with ecstasy and selfcrucifixion" (140).

Although the psychically fulfilling links between the two males, judge and victim, are so strong and so bizarre that sexual pathology and zealous religiosity become identified with each other, Joe also has a need to destroy his oppressor. During their violent confrontation at the dance to which Joe has secretly gone, the son beats the father into unconsciousness and virtually "becomes" the man whom he has destroyed. He intuitively finds McEachern's horse with "something of his adopted father's complete faith in an infallibility in events" (180), wears the older man's "implacable urgency" like a "cloak" on his own shoulders (181), and willingly leaps into another fight "with something of the exaltation of his adopted father" (190).

In some sense Joe has thus overthrown and assimilated the masculine principle with these actions, just as he had earlier rejected the female yet become almost feminine in his submission to McEachern. Joe's sexual identity suffers from the profoundest ambiguity, and when he meets Joanna Burden fifteen years later, his vacillation is so extreme that it can be resolved only by a murderous outburst against the woman who provokes it.

Though the connection between Joanna and the dietician who so disastrously influenced Joe as a child is never made explicit, Joanna, like her predecessor, seems to be both righteous male and sexual female. When Joanna and Joe first enter their liaison, he is drawn to those masculine qualities in her that recall his foster-father, her "manlike yielding," her "strength and fortitude," her "mantrained muscles and the mantrained habit of thinking," the absence of "feminine vacillation" and "coyness" (205). The next day he thinks, "My God, it was like I was the woman and she was the man" (206). He is determined to reverse the roles, but that has still graver consequences. Soon Joanna becomes ultra-sexual, a greedy nymphomaniac. She begins to exude a "rotten richness" (229) and Joe feels himself "sucked down into a bottomless morass" (227) in which his sexual life becomes a "sewer" (224). Joanna again reverts to a masculine role, almost like that of Joe's foster-father, her face "cold, dead white, fanatical" (242) as she attempts first to force him to go to a Negro law school and then to coerce him to pray. Their confrontation—as emphasized by the symbolism of the duelling pistols—is like one between two determined male antagonists, akin to that between Joe and McEachern at the dance, and Joe again erupts into murderous violence. He slashes her throat and flees.

His murder of Joanna, an irrational effort to annihilate the confused response to her produced by his early traumatic experience with the dietician, thus has connotations of both patricide and matricide. He tries to eradicate the troubling masculine and feminine qualities in her which threaten him, but his attempt and subsequent flight are futile, for he returns almost inevitably, and perhaps even deliberately, to the town where his grandfather lives and is there captured. The circle out of which Joe has been unable to break closes irrevocably at a place symbolically linked to his origins and thus to the psychic wounds which have trapped him. When Joe escapes a second time, he again seeks refuge in a past-haunted place, Hightower's house, where his death and castration are only exaggerated emblems of what had already been done to him by a brutal heritage.

Joe's story is a dark and terrible one, and some critics have faulted *Light in August* for failing to reconcile the theme of hopeless injustice which dominates Joe's tale with the blithe renewal of Lena Grove's journey toward motherhood and instinctive satisfaction. Yet Byron Bunch provides a crucial link between the stories which offers a form of implicit resolution. Byron's own story surrounds and makes a hopeful contrast with that of the desperately estranged Joe Christmas, and Byron also acts to free the imprisoned Hightower from his obsessions. Byron is a true mediator, almost Christlike in his capacity to act selflessly and helpfully toward others, but he is also a man who increases in stature as he discovers his own personal involvement in life. Olga Vickery's description of Byron as the one uncommitted character in the novel seems far from accurate,[10] since he is committed from the outset of the novel and the nature of his commitment only increases. He is, moreover, the moral center of the novel from beginning to end, offering by his own actions an implicit commentary on the deficiencies in the actions of the other characters.

Byron Bunch has some smilarities to his creator, as did Cash Bundren, about whose artist-craftsman role much has already been said that also holds true for Byron. Byron is, like Faulkner at that time, a "slight, nondescript man" (42), relatively remote from his fellow workers but intensely loyal to his own private vision of work. He stays alone on Saturday afternoons at the sawmill where he is employed, working conscientiously even when no one oversees him—like a novelist in his study. Faulkner told an interviewer in 1926 that he had spent the summer working in a lumber mill (*LIG*, p. 3), and though there is no record of such employment in Blotner's biography, the statement suggests that he identified with this particular form of manual labor. Byron is also a true doer of the word in a religious sense, regularly riding thirty miles on a mule to spend every Sunday leading the choir in a rural church, and these quiet, solitary labors at both mill and church make him the very model of the committed artist who devotes himself to his work without asking for recognition, while his capacity for "commiseration and pity" (77) shows the sympathetic awareness of man's follies so necessary to a writer. Byron, however, is a character without a personal history, as if at this point Faulkner envisaged that only a man carrying no burden from the past could live in tranquility.

Byron is at first relatively detached, although compassionate, as he reveals in his reflections on Joe Christmas's arrival at the mill. He acts essentially as observer-recorder, but also realizes that Joe "had lived on cigarettes for two or three days now" (30) and readily offers him some lunch. With the arrival of Lena Grove, however, Byron's involvement becomes earnest and personal in the fullest sense. Lena is to the reader almost comical in her implacability as she pursues the father of her child like a relentless force of nature. There are also ironic suggestions that in her patience and singlemindedness she is a Penelope who has taken to the road, while her "husband," Lucas Burch, with his "white scar" (31), seems an unheroic Odysseus, weak and fleeing from his female pursuer. As Lena's odyssey comes to an end, Byron falls in love with her, "contrary to all the tradition of his austere and jealous country raising which demands in the object physical inviolability" (42). He at once takes an active responsibility for Lena and her imminent child—even as Faulkner himself had assumed that of another man's wife and children—finds Lena a place to stay, carefully protects her from the knowledge that the object of her search is in jail, and eventually camps outside the cabin where she has gone to have her baby. Thus committed to Lena, he moves to a more intense level of engagement, one that is personal and emotional as well as religious and idealistic.

This involvement brings an enhancement of Byron's masculinity and personal force. "As though he has learned pride or defiance Byron's head is erect, he walks fast and erect," and Hightower realizes that "he has taken a step" (272). Later, as he sits with Hightower and Joe's grandparents, "Byron alone seems to possess life" (338). His complete entry into the sort of instinctual physical life represented by Lena increases his sense of himself as a male to the point where he is willing to do battle with the man who refuses to accept the responsibility for Lena's child. If Byron's masculine determination is fortified by his love, so is his willingness to extend himself to others in need of help. Byron becomes the one person in Jefferson who works actively to aid the imprisoned Joe Christmas, and he undertakes the nearly hopeless job out of selfless compassion. He brings Joe's grandparents to Hightower and makes the outrageous request that the minister testify that Joe was with him the night of the murder, to allow Joe a moment of freedom and reunion with the grandmother who has not seen him for thirty years. Though the request is denied, it signifies Byron's increasing engagement in the world immediately around him. Byron is in a way an artist-figure, committed to "good work" in every sphere, personally involved and morally idealistic and capable of fusing the crucial action-observation dichotomy, able to act and yet to "stand aloof and watch himself" (344) all at the same moment, to be simultaneously both in and out of life.

Byron's influence, both direct and indirect, on the course of Hightower's life only amplifies the nature of his personal achievement. The two men are closely related, psychically as well as narratively, much as were Cash and Darl in *As I Lay Dying*. They initially appear to represent the action-thought disjunction, with Byron the man who is in life and Hightower the man who is out of it, and their mutual ties are crucial to their existence. Each is the only one whom the other sees on a regular basis. Both are isolated, Byron by his quiet self-sufficiency, Hightower because he is a "fifty-year-old outcast who has been denied by his church" (42). They serve as friends and sustaining forces in each other's lives, and Byron acknowledges their extreme interdependence when he gropes for a word which he knows Hightower would supply and realizes, "It's like I not only cant do anything without getting him mixed up in it, I cant even think without him to help me out" (366). Because of their close relationship, Byron's greater involvement in the life around him augurs Hightower's reentry into the world from which he has been detached for twenty-five years.

At the outset, tragedy and his own volition have set Hightower utterly apart. As an artist-figure, he is like the Lady of Shalott, watching from afar and unable to participate. He sits in his window staring at the sign announcing art lessons that is "his monument" (49), signifying a moribund art and the entombment of any real participatory impulses. He is blind to the beauty of living nature as he sits "waiting for nightfall, the moment of night" (51), which will presage the approach of death.

One of Faulkner's past-obsessed characters, Hightower is a middle-aged version of Bayard Sartoris in that his pathological awareness of an heroic ancestor has stunted his ability to live in the present, just as it had to a lesser degree daunted the author. He is a minister, but even when actively preaching "it was as if he couldn't get religion and that galloping cavalry and his dead grandfather shot from the galloping horse untangled from each other, even in the pulpit" (53). Because Hightower cannot escape his compulsive reliving of his ancestor's heroics, he is unable to carry on his own life. He has become merely a watcher for death, his burden from the distant past made even more weighty but that from the recent past, his wife's scandalous suicide, which forced him out of his ministry. There are suggestions that her misery was a result of Hightower's sexual incompetence—"that he couldn't or wouldn't satisfy her himself" (51), that "he was not a natural husband, a natural man" (61). She was apparently on a quest for sexual satisfaction elsewhere the night she killed herself. Here, as in *Sanctuary,* impotence has disastrous consequences for others besides the man himself; the theme was continuing to be an ominous one for Faulkner, who had perhaps not freed himself from its specter in his own life.

Hightower has bravely remained, like Hawthorne's Hester Prynne, in the town which ostracized him. Though stoical, he declares that he is "not in life anymore" (263) and refuses to be involved in any current crisis because "I have bought immunity. I have paid" (270). Nonetheless, the omens of Hightower's eventual reinvolvement in daily life are evident almost from the beginning. He displays a generalized moral awareness in his sympathetic comments about "Poor man. Poor mankind" (87) and his feeling that "man performs, engenders, so much more than he can or should have to bear" (262). In addition, he has a dim sense of his contribution to his wife's disaster that eventually flares into a full-scale recognition of the interconnection of guilt and responsibility, taking him beyond the enclosure of self. Finally, on a singular occasion just four years before the central narrative action, Hightower delivers a baby by himself. Even though the child dies, as had Faulkner's, Hightower experiences participation in the cycle of birth and death which augurs his culminating action at the end of *Light in August.*

Appropriately, Byron himself initiates Hightower's symbolic reentry into life. When he comes to tell the minister about the capture of Joe Christmas and his guardianship of Lena, Hightower derides him as "the guardian of public weal and morality" (319) but begins suddenly to weep in a moment of cleansing emotion that heralds his willingness to be directly involved. Soon after, when Byron arrives panic-stricken at the minister's house to announce the impending birth of Lena's child, Hightower rushes without thinking to her side. Once again, armed only with "his razor and his book" (347), he singlehandedly officiates at a birth. This time the baby lives, its cries signaling the vigorous beginning of a new life. Hightower becomes a father in the spiritual sense, if not the physical. For him, too, life begins anew as he regards his achievement with "a glow, a wave, a surge of something almost hot, almost triumphant. 'I showed them!' he thinks. 'Life comes to the old man yet' " (355). The experience gives him a sense of purpose. He imagines that the baby might be named after him and envisages many more babies being produced by Lena's healthy young body, "the good stock peopling in tranquil obedience to it the good earth" (356), even as Faulkner, in his hour of disappointment, looked hopefully to the prospect of again fathering a child.

Descending from his figurative aerie above the street, Hightower is filled with a sense of personal and general regeneration. His new feeling of engagement is given real meaning when his actions are followed by a recognition scene. He travels once again back into the past, realizes that he "grew to manhood among phantoms" (415), and admits that his grandfather's glorious deed was in reality a foolhardy prank for which he almost deserved to be shot. He moves from understanding his family past to comprehension of his wife's unhappiness and of his own complicity in her death: "Perhaps in the moment I revealed to her not only the depth of my hunger but the fact that never and never would she have any part in the assuaging of it; perhaps at that moment I became her seducer and her murderer, author and instrument of her shame and death" (427). Hightower knows that for fifty years he has been "a single instant of darkness in which a horse galloped and a gun crashed." With his full self-recognition comes his illumination, his light in August, a "halo" full of all the faces of his life, now at last "peaceful, as though they have escaped into an apotheosis" (430).

Hightower, though he may be at the point of death, has achieved the most that is possible in a generally meaningless modern world for a man who has been emotionally crippled by personal difficulties. In a moment of self-comprehension, he has seen fully and with understanding the past which stultified his own development and eventually contributed to his wife's death. This comprehension constitutes a form of release from the past, as Faulkner himself was vividly aware. Moreover, Hightower finds another sort of meaning in his progress toward engagement in the world from which he has been so long apart. His accomplishment is considerable, and at the end he is both in life and at the same time fully conscious of all its complexities. Hightower is, however, like Henry James's John Marcher, an old man whose awareness of his "beast" comes almost too late. The real affirmation of *Light in August* comes with the gentle comedy of Lena's departure from Jefferson, her baby at her breast and Byron in eager and resolute attendance. They constitute a true family, even though they are a somewhat ludicrous group and Lena still insists she is searching for Lucas. Byron's look, "hangdog and determined and calm," and his assertion that "I be dog if I'm going to quit now" (443) bode his ultimate attainment of his goal to continue as father-provider for the woman and child.

Thus *Light in August,* for all the darkness at its center in the doomed figure of Joe Christmas, begins and ends with the tranquil comedy of Byron and Lena, which provides a hopeful note never before found in a Faulkner novel. The work offers much of the moral commitment found in *As I Lay Dying,* but goes even beyond it: Byron becomes engaged in a deeper way than Cash, and Hightower achieves an involvement and awareness of which the mad Darl was incapable. The hopefulness is qualified because Byron and Hightower are not as fully realized as they might be, remaining in some sense comic caricatures and dramatically secondary to Joe Christmas, but the doer and the intellectual both discover a form of personal salvation. *Light in August,* in short, shows Faulkner emerging from a moment of personal darkness to manifest a greater sense of moral and artistic achievement.

6
Portraits of the Artist at Work:
Pylon and *Absalom, Absalom!*

Absalom, Absalom! IS FAULKNER'S MASTERPIECE, a towering work that overshadows nearly every other American novel written in the first half of the twentieth century. *Pylon* is usually considered to be among his least successful works, marred by uncertainty of purpose and ineffectual lyricism. The disparity between the effectiveness of these novels is mysterious, for they were written during the same period of time in virtual counterpoint. When Faulkner began having difficulty with *Absalom, Absalom!* in mid-1934, he turned to *Pylon;* when that was completed, he returned to the first novel with fresh energy and finished it within a year. As the author himself put it, with somewhat arch simplicity, "I wrote that book *[Pylon]* because I'd got in trouble with *Absalom, Absalom!* and I had to get away from it for a while so I thought a good way to get away from it was to write another book" (*FIU*, p. 36).

Given this chronology and the essential similarities between the two in fundamentals of technique and subject matter, how can one account for the differences in achievement which they represent? One cannot, really, and the novels themselves are about the difficulty of "accounting for" anything in a simple way, but there are a number of possible answers to the question. Some critics would respond that Faulkner, once he had found his true material within his mythical Yoknapatawpha County, was bound to encounter artistic problems whenever he "left" the county, as he did in *Pylon.* This answer seems legitimate until one realizes that another of Faulkner's non-Yoknapatawpha novels, *The Wild Palms,* is more successful artistically than works like *Requiem for a Nun* or *The Town*. The "true" answer, insofar as there is one, may well come from somewhere within the realm of psychological speculation.

Both novels constitute portraits of the artist at work and thus are personal in an essential way. But *Absalom, Absalom!* is the more deeply and painfully autobiographical. *Pylon* is based on Faulkner's observation of the opening of a new airport in New Orleans in early 1934, as well as his lifelong fascination with airplanes and flying. It is thus more a product of perception than of participation, the outcome of an interest that was, so to speak, extracurricular. *Absalom, Absalom!*, on the other hand, had its origins in personal suffering and in Faulkner's efforts to comprehend the distorted dynamics of the family in which he had grown up. The novel contains an immense amount of psychopathology and violence—monomania, fratricide, incest, miscegenation, wife-abandonment, and the slaying of a new father by his enraged "grandfather-in-law"—few of which had direct antecedents in Faulkner's own life. Yet its gothic excesses are only a dramatic amplification of the tensions that had marked his family during his formative years. Moreover, the most painful scene of the work, Bon's desperate quest for paternal recognition, and the most triumphant, Quentin and Shreve's integration of the pieces of the past in a splendid creative burst, as well as the dominant character, Thomas Sutpen, did have direct sources in Faulkner's personal history.

Pylon thus emanated from concerns which were peripheral to the writer, while *Absalom, Absalom!* came directly from the essential man, from a century of family history and nearly forty years of his own experience. This psychological difference between the novels cannot completely explain why the one should have been a partial failure and the other a masterpiece, but it unquestionably accounts for much of the unique emotional power of the second work. What a comparison between the two reveals is that, as always in Faulkner's fiction, as long as the conscious craftsman is in control, the delving into the dark strata of the psyche produces the most powerful art.

Faulkner seemed to be writing his novels in pairs during this period of his life. *Pylon* and *Absalom, Absalom!* are linked in many of the same ways as were *As I Lay Dying* and *Light in August* and have, as a pair, similarities to the previous pair.[1] They were written in the same manner, the first of each couple done quickly, in a matter of weeks, with great technical adroitness but without the dark power and broad emotional range of the second. In addition, they are related by central male protagonists who carry the weight of meaning if not of narrative action: thus the reporter and Quentin-Shreve have functionally a great deal in common, as had Cash Bundren and Byron Bunch of the earlier pair.

As portraits of the artist, *Pylon* and *Absalom, Absalom!* figuratively pick up where *As I Lay Dying* and *Light in August* ended. The woodworkers Cash and Byron were metaphoric embodiments of the artist as careful craftsman and moral paradigm, while the reporter and Quentin-Shreve are actual "novelists" at work, receiving information, weighing alternatives, and attempting to create a finished artifact which contains real meaning. They are both inside and outside the action, trying to be objective but also aware of their own emotional tendencies to distort and to project. They attempt to reconstruct and to understand the events that inundate them and to recreate the past, thus making order out of chaos. Their goal is to pass finally through the symbolic door which serves as a barrier to the truth. Though they fail in one sense, in achieving personal certainty, they succeed in another, in responding fully and inspiredly and thus discovering the essence of the creative process.

The theme of the quest for imaginative understanding is borne out by the experience of the artist-protagonists and is at the core of both *Pylon* and *Absalom, Absalom!,* evinced in technique as well as in subject matter. In each Faulkner uses a poetic style in which the theme of the elusiveness of truth is underscored by submersive language and rich imagery so that everything is suggested, nothing defined.[2] The narrative rhythm of the novels also contributes to the quest theme. The motion is both linear and circular, as action and response alternate and the work progresses to a climactic moment. The method is vastly more successful in *Absalom, Absalom!,* where subject and style fuse at every level, from the single complex sentence to the total intricate fiction. In this work Faulkner achieves a technical brilliance that is approached only by *The Sound and the Fury. Pylon,* on the other hand, can be seen as the author's unsuccessful testing of his new technique, in which the reporter's experiences alternate with his compulsive reiterations of them in his effort to comprehend and to achieve an integrated vision—precisely the method Faulkner refines and amplifies with such skill in *Absalom, Absalom!.*

The renewed energy Faulkner brought to his technical experimentation in *Pylon* and *Absalom, Absalom!,* as well as his failure in the first attempt, may have been the result of a two-year "vacation" he took from novel writing between his completion of *Light in August* and the start of his new book. In 1932, as a consequence of the publicity accorded Faulkner after *Sanctuary* was published, executives at Metro-Goldwyn-Mayer invited him to come to Hollywood and write movie scripts. They added the inducement of a princely salary which the hard-pressed Faulkner had little will to refuse. Thus he began long years of shuttling back and forth between Mississippi and California, doing work that offered some satisfaction at least on the occasions when he collaborated with the talented Howard Hawks. The economic rewards were also high—Faulkner earned more from one week's work in Hollywood than he did from his fiction over several months—but the strains and distractions of his movie work ultimately exacted a toll upon his productivity as a novelist.

Some major family events also kept Faulkner from his fiction during this period. In August of 1932, his father died. Although Murry Falkner's life had become more tranquil in his late years, after he accepted a sinecure as assistant secretary of the University of Mississippi, a job procured for him by his father, and gave up alcohol, he was presumably always haunted by his lost dreams, for he never showed signs of contentment. "He just gave up," said Faulkner, "he got tired of living" (B, p. 782). Nor did Murry ever achieve a state of mutual affection or open communication with his oldest son; he maintained his hostility toward William and his chosen vocation to the end of his life. Murry's death offered Faulkner a sense of liberation, along with a bleak feeling of filial possibilities forever lost, for the constant contact with a father who neither accepted nor understood him had been oppressive and frustrating. Faulkner now acquired patriarchal stature, for as the oldest son he became the head of the Falkner clan, which was rapidly becoming "Faulkner." Ironically, in Murry's obituary, a local newspaper gave William's "u" to the father who had always been so negative toward him,[3] and two of William's younger brothers eventually added the "u" in deference to his fame. Along with titular leadership of the clan came financial responsibility and a series of family demands that would increase as the years went on. The first of these was the pressure to support his mother; the author quickly saw that "Dad left Mother solvent for only about 1 year. Then it is me" (L, p. 65).

In June of the following year, what was probably the most joyous event of Faulkner's adulthood occurred when his daughter Jill was born. Fair and delicate in a way that made her physically as much her father's daughter as her mother's, Jill would also soon show a reticence that strongly identified her with her father. Faulkner adored this child, who was to be his only issue, and heaped upon her, albeit somewhat erratically, the affection he had never received from his own father.

Finally, at the beginning of 1934, Faulkner sat down to write what would become *Absalom, Absalom!* He initially called it *A Dark House,* a title left over from his previous novel, and fashioned it from material in three earlier short stories, "Wash," "The Big Shot," and "Evangeline," which told the tale of Sutpen, Henry, and Bon, of Sutpen's seduction of Jones's granddaughter, and of the subsequent retribution he receives. The writing did not go smoothly, as the complex structure gave Faulkner a good deal of difficulty, and after some time in Hollywood during the summer of 1934, he turned to *Pylon* to "get away from" the other novel.

Faulkner was by now familiar with the flying culture on which *Pylon* was based. It seems ironic that his first flying story that is "legitimate," i.e., based on direct personal experience at the controls of an airplane, is not really about flying per se. In February, 1933, after fifteen years of having claimed a history as a pilot in World War I, Faulkner began taking his first flying lessons. Incapable of real honesty on this sore subject, he told his Memphis instructor that he was a former combat pilot trying to regain the nerve he had lost in two plane crashes. Within two months, Faulkner was soloing, and he soon spent some of his Hollywood earnings on a Waco biplane so that his youngest brother, Dean, could also take lessons. During the next year, despite one near-accident in which he turned the plane over during a landing, doing minor damage to it and none at all to himself, Faulkner had flown to places as distant as New York and been exposed to the barnstorming subculture and the actual incidents which took fictional form in *Pylon* (B, pp. 795, 817).

In February, 1934, Faulkner attended the opening of Shushan airport in New Orleans on land reclaimed from Lake Pontchartrain. The very first day of the festivities was marred by a fatal crash; near the end, another tragedy occurred when a parachutist's silk became entangled with the plane from which he jumped and both he and the pilot were killed in the ensuing crash.[4] The constant danger in which such "barnstormers" lived and the novelty of their vocation made them glamorous and intriguing figures. Faulkner had already used them as subjects for at least two of his short stories, "Honor" and "Death Drag," and felt ready to give them full-scale treatment in a novel. Faulkner's brother Dean, who became a skillful pilot soon after he began flying, was quickly drawn into the life as an instructor and barnstormer. Faulkner himself skirted the edges of it, sponsoring two aerial circuses in Oxford in the spring and fall of 1934 in which he participated slightly. By the time he began to write *Pylon* in the fall of 1934, he had extensive material of both a general and specific nature on which to draw, and he wrote the work rapidly, amplifying his basic plot with imagery derived from the poetry of T. S. Eliot.

Faulkner later spoke thoughtfully about his fascination with the aviators in a passage which reveals how closely his attitude is allied with that of the reporter:

To me they were a fantastic and bizarre phenomenon on the face of a contemporary scene, of our culture at a particular time. . . . There was really no place for them in the culture, in the economy, yet they were there, at that time, and everyone knew that they wouldn't last very long, which they didn't. That time of those frantic little aeroplanes which dashed around the country and people wanted just enough money to live, to get to the next place to race again. Something frenetic and in a way almost immoral about it. That they were outside the range of God, not only of respectability, of love, but of God too. That they had escaped the compulsion of accepting a past and a future, that they were—they had no past. [*FIU,* p. 36]

To Faulkner, men without pasts are truly free, but in a strange way, for their trials occur in a historical vacuum. They have nothing weighty to battle against or to anchor them to the present moment. Thus their freedom is as troubling as it is desirable. Faulkner and his reporter are alike fascinated but disconcerted.

Faulkner's choice of a reporter as a protagonist is an interesting one, for literary as well as personal reasons. The idea of the novel as a form of reportage has been implicit in the works of many writers from the time of our first novelist. Daniel Defoe spent a long life as a journalist before he began to write fiction, and his novels constitute, in a special sense, a "news report" on the life experiences of members of the demimonde and the newly emerging middle class, and on the problems of economic survival in a changing society. Faulkner, by placing a working reporter at the center of his fiction, allies himself with this tradition and illuminates the basic problem common to both journalists and novelists, that of making a story out of chaotic data and subjective impressions. Faulkner himself had worked briefly for a newspaper in the 1920s, the *New Orleans Times-Picayune*. Even though he did "features" rather than news stories, he spent time with the reporters and became familiar with the difficulty of achieving balanced reportage. Moreover, the title of his first sketch, "Mirrors of Chartres Street," also served as the subtitle for most of the other pieces he did for the newspaper and revealed his intention to "mirror" in a particular way the life of the French Quarter, where he was then living.[5]

The role of the reporter in *Pylon* as a mediator between two worlds, the special microcosm of the aviators and the macrocosm for which the editor is spokesman, is a role much like that Faulkner had in his relationship with the flying subculture of northern Mississippi and southern Tennessee. He was involved in a limited way through his ownership of an airplane, his sponsorship of local aerial circuses, and his occasional flying. But his pilot brother, Dean, on whom Roger Shumann seems to have been modeled, and Dean's vivacious wife, Louise, whom he married just before Faulkner began *Pylon,* were at the real center of the subculture, spending nearly all of their time in and around airports. Faulkner was intrigued by this life and by the bravery implicit in the constant piloting of what were still dangerous vehicles, but he never became fully involved. *Pylon* reveals his position as a relative outsider who views aviation in the same ambivalently romantic way as he did the deeds of the Civil War cavalry.

Though the aviators are products of modern technology, they often appear as anachronistic creatures from an earlier age, lonely and glamorous figures who seem displaced in a conformist middle-class society. Their planes seem to be fragile steeds bearing these modern-day knights into solitary battle in the skies. The airplanes are characterized as "a species of esoteric and fatal animals" (7);[6] the one being repaired in the hanger looks like "the halfeaten carcass of a deer" (19). The animal analogy continues, and when Shumann crashes his plane for the first time, it is seen "lying on its back, the undercarriage projecting into the air rigid and delicate and motionless as the legs of a dead bird" (164). The airport has gold-and-purple flapping pennons, the aura of which always surrounds Faulkner's doomed horse-borne heroes, and the pilots are often seen as the sort of brave and masculine knights of action whom Faulkner tended to idolize. The parachutist Jack Holmes has a "bleak handsome face whose features were regular, brutally courageous" (34), and the reporter sees Roger Shumann as a pilot-hero who "can fly anything" (222). The pilots frequently appear as silent, dedicated men of action who "have never learned to talk at any time" (61).

Shumann, however, also gives the impression of being "without any trace of introversion or any ability to objectivate or ratiocinate" (171). After his fatal crash, the folly of dissociating thought from deed receives a piercing comment. One reporter says, "If he had been a man that thought, he would not have been up there in the first place." But a second one replies, "Meaning he would have had a good job on a newspaper, huh?" (289). The deflation of the doomed heroics of the aviator is mixed with the reporter's self-deprecation and thus the balance of romanticism with irony is as uncertain as it was in such earlier Faulkner work as *Sartoris.*

The reporter, like Faulkner, is entranced by the fliers, but he is also answerable to his editor and to a wider public. Here his role becomes symbolic of that of the artist, as he attempts to integrate all of the claims on his attention and emotions and still produce a worthy artifact. The editor Hagood's demands seem to be contradictory, yet they offer what is in essence both a prescription for writing novels (as well as news articles) and a statement about the dilemma of the artist. Hagood first criticizes the reporter because he "never seem[s] to bring back anything but information. . . . it's not the living breath of news" (42). Next he tells him that the paper's owners are uninterested in literature, "since what they want is not fiction . . . but news" (50). Mere information is inadequate, and so is highflown fiction. True "news" (the word, after all, from which "novel" comes) lies somewhere in between. The problem of the writer is related to the problem of discovering that elusive midline between data and fantasy and of infusing the "living breath" into a word-creation. It is a problem with which Faulkner would deal on a much larger scale in *Absalom, Absalom!*.

Hagood also represents the impatient reading public. When the reporter, in an interminable telephone call, breathlessly and obsessively relates every single detail of his day with the fliers, his exasperated listener can stand it no longer, screams, "Fired! Fired! Fired! Fired!" (74) and hangs up. Nothing, however, can inhibit the reporter in his need to verbalize, and the editor eventually, though reluctantly, allows himself to become involved. What is partly a comic parable about the difficulties for a novelist of satisfying the demand for "true news" and of heeding the needs of both self and audience comes to an ending that offers no resolution.

The reporter leaves behind him in the newspaper office two inadequate versions of the story of Shumann's death. One is impossibly romantic, the other version awkward, brutally dessicated, and fact-ridden. The reporter knows that neither approach will do and decides to assuage his sense of artistic deficiency by getting "drunk a while" (315). The problem of integrating romance and fact would be more fully resolved in *Absalom, Absalom!*. But the anguish of attempting to do so would not.

Even as *Pylon* treats some of the technical difficulties faced by the working novelist, it also raises the question of emotional involvement in one's material, of achieving the proper distance and the necessary equilibrium between objectivity and subjectivity. The theme of the onlooker is suggested in the very first paragraph of the novel, when Jiggs the mechanic looks longingly through the store window at a pair of boots. The situation subtly presents the basic problem which the reporter will face. Jiggs stands amid the dirt and detritus of the morning reality, and the boots offer an attractive, even glamorous, contrast in their "umblemished and inviolate implication of horse and spur," like the romantic-seeing lives of the fliers to which the reporter is drawn. But the glass, "the intervening plate," distorts the boots, making them "slantshimmered" (7) and suggesting the symbolic door through which Quentin has to penetrate to meaning in *Absalom, Absalom!*. Jiggs must circumvent the window in order to retrieve the boots, but he never fully owns them, and finally is forced to give them up, now flawed and devalued. Jigg's experience with the boots is a correlative of the reporter's encounter with the fliers. The reporter sees, desires, and attempts to penetrate "the intervening plate" to achieve understanding and full participation in their lives—an effort which proves futile and leaves him empty-handed, overwhelmed by a sense of loss.

The reporter, a bizarre creature six feet tall and ninety-five pounds in weight, enters the aviators' world at Feinman Airport with an expression "leashed, eager, cadaverous" (27) which bodes his ardent and rapid immersion in the fliers' lives. His skeletal appearance suggests his hungry need to be connected to some "real men." The reporter soon compulsively shares his perceptions about them with his editor, his sense that "they aint human like us" (45), that they have "no ties; no place where you were born and have to go back to it now," and that "it aint money they are after anymore than it's glory" (46). He is especially intrigued by the fliers' relations among themselves, by the child who was supposedly born on an unrolled parachute to Laverne and a legal father chosen by a role of the dice, and by the *ménage à trois* of Laverne, Shumann, and Holmes. He tries to imagine their sleeping arrangements, "the three of them in one bed or maybe they take it night about or maybe you just put your hat down on it first like in a barbershop" (54).

The reporter soon moves from bemused fascination to complete involvement. He appoints himself the fliers' patron, buys them cigarettes and absinthe, gives his apartment to them for the night, lets them steal his money, and finally cosigns a $5,000 note in order that Shumann may obtain a new airplane. He even endangers his own life to crouch in the fuselage while the plane is brought to New Valois. The reporter's abject devotion is based partly on self-interest, for he is attracted to Laverne. It also seems to ensue in part from some general concept of himself as "patron (even if not guardian) saint of all waifs, all the homeless, the desperate and the starved" (183).[7] His involvement is so complete that when Shumann dies he, too, finds himself almost dead inside, suffering "the taste not of despair but of Nothing" (241), returned to his previous empty state. As the reporter becomes increasingly immersed in the fliers' world, he loses his ability to judge them with the objectivity which he showed at the outset,[8] ceases to pay attention to his job, and becomes the victim of his purely subjective responses. Only the fliers' death and departure send him back to his desk. He has lost his artistic perspective and the capacity to remove himself voluntarily from their world, and the world must remove itself from him. Thus *Pylon* also becomes a parable about the dangers for an artist of overinvolvement.

The reporter's obviously selfisih motive in attaching himself to the fliers raises an interesting psychological issue that relates this novel to earlier works like *Soldiers' Pay* and *Sartoris*. The pilots are strongly associated with masculinity and sexuality, as they were for Julian Lowe of *Soldiers' Pay*, who felt that their symbolic wings connoted manhood. The incredible scene in which Laverne makes love to Shumann in the moving airplane and then parachutes half-naked to the lascivious yells of the crowd below is a wild sexual fantasy which might have been imagined by Julian Lowe and which suggests the irresistible sexual attraction Faulkner felt to be an attribute of the pilot as quintessential "real man."

The reporter's awe of the masculine fliers and his desire to enjoy the sexual favors of their woman leads finally to a subconscious wish on his part to supplant Roger Shumann, a wish not unlike the secret desire of Bayard Sartoris to obliterate his brother, though in *Pylon* the issue is much more explicit. Both works seem related to Faulkner's subconscious problems with his youngest brother, and Dean's life was by now so much like Shumann's that the augury of his death is almost terrifying. The reporter's efforts to procure a new plane for Shumann after he has demolished his and the fact that the new one seems dangerous begin to alarm the pilot. "Here, for Christ's sake," Shumann tells the reporter, "you'll have me thinking you are ribbing me up in this crate of Ord's so you can marry her maybe" (175). When Shumann does crash, the reporter immediately rushes to Laverne, who is for him "the bright plain shape of love," but she shouts at him furiously, "God damn you to hell! Get away from me!" (235). The reporter's sense of responsibility leads him to borrow some money and give it to the child Shumann left behind, just as Faulkner later financially supported his dead brother's daughter. The reporter's gesture is altruistic but perhaps founded in guilt, as Faulkner's too may have been.

It is difficult to separate generosity from self-interest in the reporter's patronage of the fliers, and it is uncertain whether Faulkner himself had a clear idea of his attitude toward them. *Pylon* is a parable about an artist at work, and it unintentionally, as well as intentionally, reveals some of the major problems faced by that artist. The reporter himself is not clearly conceived and alternates between being an anguished modern man of sensibility and a ludicrous Ichabod-Crane-like caricature.[9] The image of the fliers is even more problematical, as the reporter and Faulkner himself vacillate between attraction and vague distaste. If at some points the fliers appear to be modern knights on a hopeless quest, at others they seem helpless nomads who can find no refuge in the wasteland, evincing "that irrevocable homelessness of three immigrants walking down the steerage gangplank of a ship" (79). At still other points, the fliers' distorted family relationships and skewed sexual identities recall the fantastic relationships of *Sanctuary* and seem symbolic of personal and social dislocation in the culture at large. Laverne is an adequate mother to her child and an object of sexual desire, but she is also very mannish. She wears greasy coveralls and men's underwear, wolfs down her food, and is "like a man about not bumming from just any guy" (250). Holmes is handsome and masculine, yet his mouth is "much more delicate and even feminine" than Laverne's (34). The child has two "fathers" and rarely acts filially toward either of them.

The family as a whole seems almost bizarre, and its individual members are often harsh, even physically brutal, to each other. Yet at other times they show consideration. When Shumann discovers Holmes nursing a wounded leg, he readily offers to give up his own sleeping accommodations. "You better sleep in the bed tonight," he says concernedly. "That blanket will give that skinned place hell" (187). And the group frequently seems tightly knit, unified against an unfriendly world. The "family" is ambiguous, and so are the fliers themselves. One moment they are almost thoughtless machines who function blindly; the next, brave men of action like Shumann, who shows himself capable of self-sacrificial heroism by crashing his plane where it will not injure anyone else. Our uncertainty about how to respond to and interpret the aviators and their unusual family obviously derives from a similar confusion on the part of the author himself.

Pylon makes an admirable if flawed effort to deal with issues that concern any working artist—how much to participate in "life" and how much to remain an onlooker, how to balance objectivity and subjectivity in portrayal, the need to integrate data and poetic truth, and the effort to break through "the intervening plate" to meaning and order. The book's major importance is as a precursor of Faulkner's masterpiece, *Absalom, Absalom!*, in which he would again raise the same issues, but with a sureness and emotional depth almost unparalleled in American fiction.

Faulkner finished *Pylon* in late 1934 and returned, after a brief respite, to the partially completed manuscript of *Absalom, Absalom!*. He had the latter almost finished in November, 1935, when his brother Dean was killed in a plane crash. Dean had taken a student up for some flying instruction, and the plane apparently stalled while the student had command. Dean was unable to wrest the controls away, the plane went into a fatal nose dive, and the men perished.

The incident proved a ghastly fulfillment of the prophecy implicit in the death by flying of Dean-figures in both *Sartoris* and *Pylon*. It also bore a subtle relationship to the fratricidal theme of the novel on which Faulkner was working at the time, for he was, in a way, indirectly responsible for his brother's death, having given him the airplane in which he died. Dean's death was a devastating experience for Faulkner. Immediately afterward, he underwent the horror of attempting to put his brother's shattered body back together. Then he was obsessed by guilt during the ensuing year. His siblings tried to reassure him that he had no share in Dean's death, yet Faulkner kept insisting, "But I bought him the plane, I paid for his lessons," and that *"It is my fault"* (B, p. 916; Wells, p. 184). The loss of the carefree and talented though erratic young man caused grief to all the Faulkners, and especially to his pretty wife, who was pregnant. William immediately shouldered all the financial responsibility for the young widow and her unborn child, a burden which he carried for a considerable time. At the deepest level, however, Dean's death served as some sort of catharsis. Confronting the actual demise of his exuberant young brother, whose physical attributes and special claims on parental affection may have evoked Faulkner's subconscious jealousy, was awful but somehow purgative. The theme of the dead brother-rival, a relatively dominant one in Faulkner's work up to 1935, would never recur in his fiction, except in *Intruder in the Dust,* where it appears in a subordinate way.

Work proved a partial refuge for Faulkner from the guilt he suffered after his brother's death, and he gradually managed to put the finishing touches to the manuscript of *Absalom, Absalom!*. He probably regarded the novel with satisfaction, for it is a superb work as well as a deeply personal one. In it Faulkner deals with the highly charged emotional topics that are found in all of his strongest novels and relate to the essentials of his own psychic biography—family-centered cruelty and violence, the emotional deprivation of a young man, individual obsession, and the themes of the burden of the past and the divided self. *Absalom, Absalom!* is stark, almost completely unleavened by the humor found in Faulkner's other novels, and its unmitigated intensity makes it a unique work in his oeuvre. Despite its darkness, this story of a monomaniac and the outrages visited by him upon his family and his environment, as seen by his posthumous interpreters, offers evidence that its author had reached a crucial point in his maturity as a man, even as he attained a peak of accomplishment as an artist.

Absalom, Absalom! has some obvious links with *The Sound and the Fury,* for it deals with Quentin Compson's exploration, just six months before his suicide, of a haunting story from the past. Two recent books have been devoted to a study of the relationship between the two novels, between Quentin's experience as a narrator and his role as the doomed protagonist of his own story.[10] There is, however, a striking emotional difference between the two novels that reveals the positive strides Faulkner had made psychologically in the seven years since he wrote the first of them. Though *Absalom, Absalom!* narratively antedates *The Sound and the Fury* and the two stories are ostensibly continuous, *Absalom, Absalom!* was clearly written with a much greater sense of mastery and by a man of greater maturity.

Although the artistic and psychological advance which *Absalom, Absalom!* represents over *The Sound and the Fury* is most obvious in the characterology, it is also evident in the narrative movement of the novel. *The Sound and the Fury* is technically dazzling, the "same story told four times" in brilliantly executed and differing modes. But while the four sections have a cumulative effect of wholeness, each segment is virtually autonomous and self-contained. The whole is similar to a group of separate portraits on a wall. *Absalom, Absalom!* is narratively more closely integrated, more like a mural which must be seen in its totality and cannot be separated into component units. There are no sharp divisions in the flow of this novel. Though each chapter tends to focus on a single character's interpretation of events, all are closely intertwined and mutually interdependent, and each portion of narrative merges with and augments its predecessor. A series of dramatic revelations serve as focal points, but a constant circular movement around and through the linear progression creates an effect both incremental and expansive. Everything is part of an almost irresistible forward motion, and the novel progresses like one of Yeats's gyres spinning toward its inevitable climactic point.

Faulkner may well have been consciously using the methods of vorticism, a phenomenon in the visual arts which received a fair amount of publicity in the 1920s and which attempted to draw the viewer into the center of kinetic sworls of action. In Paris in 1925, he had visited an exhibit of vorticist paintings which made enough of an impression on him that he wrote about it to his mother (*L,* p. 13). This technique, as adapted by Faulkner to a verbal medium so that the reader is virtually sucked into the narrative and surrounded by the taletellers, is more sophisticated than the one he used in *The Sound and the Fury* and less closely related to the type of fictional work which influenced it; though *Absalom, Absalom!* is rather Conradian, it is less so than *The Sound and the Fury* is Joycean.

Absalom, Absalom! is also more cerebral than *The Sound and the Fury* in many ways. During the writing of *Absalom, Absalom!*, Faulkner told his publisher that it was about the "violent breakup of a household or family from 1860 to about 1910" (*L*, p. 78), a description which in modified form would also be applicable to *The Sound and the Fury*. However, an extra element marks the later work. While the earlier novel is a rich one, it focuses on a series of desperate emotional problems engendered by a tumultuous personal past. *Absalom, Absalom!* deals with the same sort of basic emotional concerns, but it additionally treats the question of epistemology, of how one acquires knowledge and how one moves from "facts" to "truth." The characters in *Absalom, Absalom!* represent modes of perception as well as distinct individuals, and the differing manner in which they reach their conclusions comments on the relationship of intellect to emotion and of seeing to feeling. The characters in *Absalom, Absalom!* also analyze each other, unlike those in *The Sound and the Fury*, who are self-enclosed, trapped in their separate worlds; hence, all of the later novel's figures become artists at work, creating their own fictional artifacts in accordance with their unique visions. Thus, while *The Sound and the Fury* evokes responses that are emotional and morally judgmental, *Absalom, Absalom!* also produces intellectual responses which add to the complexity of the novel's impact.

The theme of the burden of the past is a powerful one; in both novels it called out some of Faulkner's strongest writing as he struggled to come to terms with his own turbulent family heritage. But here, too, subtle differences between the two books reveal the more mature emotional stage that Faulkner had attained by the mid-1930s. In *The Sound and the Fury*, the past is a crippling psychological force which makes the two principal characters, Quentin and Benjy, completely incapable of living in the present. Reverting continually to memories, Benjy remains locked in eternal childhood, and Quentin, who is trapped in perpetual adolescence, commits suicide. Even Jason is deeply affected by early family dynamics and is partially incapacitated by his ties to his mother.

In *Absalom, Absalom!*, the past is also a potent force, but it eventually coalesces with the present in a more constructive way. The characters—Rosa Coldfield, Mr. Compson, and Quentin—are all obsessed with the past, but they also make an emotional and intellectual effort to come to terms with it and, even more, to "explain" it. Their quest is to peel away the distorting layers of seems-like to get to the essential core of what-is, to discover the important truths about events and human motivation. Most of the characters show comprehension of the others' tendency to project and to distort emotionally, and thus reveal tacit awareness of their own tendencies in that direction. The attainment of understanding of self and other with regard to the onerous past is much richer in *Absalom, Absalom!*. Moreover, in this novel the past is faced directly, as Quentin and Rosa make their symbolic trip back into time to visit the rotting Sutpen mansion and find the past revealed incarnate in Henry Sutpen. Soon afterwards, he and all that he represents are destroyed by fire. The living past is confronted and then immolated in a moment of catharsis that has no counterpart in *The Sound and the Fury*.

Rosa Coldfield is the character who is least capable of being freed from her bondage to the past. At points she seems almost like a character from *The Sound and the Fury,* a vestige of Faulkner's earlier frame of mind. Her oversimplified and obsessive responses to the events of years before are much like those of Quentin Compson in the earlier work. Thomas Sutpen is Rosa's bête noire, and her obsession with him is a darker version of Quentin's preoccupation with Caddy. The intensity of Rosa's continued responses to Sutpen makes her virtually unable to do anything but relive her grief and outrage. Her psychic rigidity is evident from the very outset, when Quentin finds her in a room made stifling hot by her adherence to an old concept that closed blinds make things cooler. The airless dark in which Rosa sits and the stiff black dress she has worn for forty-three years mirror the inner darkness in which she is trapped and stultified as she forever curses the memory of Thomas Sutpen.

Yet Rosa is pitiable in her self-entombment, for her plight has largely been created by forces outside herself. She is early shown to be physically frail and vulnerable, "resembl[ing] a crucified child" (8),[11] and we later learn that she was emotionally stunted by a difficult childhood. Rosa's mother died in childbirth, and she grew up regarding herself as the cause of "the sacrifice of her mother's life" and as "a living and walking reproach to her father" (59). She spent her formative years with a silent, moralistic father who apparently gave her no affection and "whom she hated without knowing it" and with a viciously negative aunt, "in a grim mausoleum air of Puritan righteousness and outraged female vindictiveness" (60).

Rosa's emotional stunting is essentially like that undergone by Quentin. Rejection by the parent of the opposite sex left both of them with mingled fear of and longing for all members of that sex and resulted in a displacement of desire onto a surrogate parent-figure. Quentin is fixated on his sister, and while Rosa overtly rejects her strange, conscientious objector father—who nailed himself in his attic during the Civil War—by composing odes to Southern soldiers, she finally turns her hatred, with its subconscious element of desire, obsessively onto Thomas Sutpen. She sits now recounting her long decades of outrage at Sutpen's request that she prove her ability to bear his son before he marries her, "the lonely thwarted old female flesh embattled for forty-three years in the old insult" (14). However, she unconsciously reveals his attractiveness to her as a surrogate-parent-lover by admitting her readiness to become engaged to her dead sister's husband, a union often viewed as taboo, and her admiration for him as a brave man with "the stature and shape of a hero" (19). Quentin shows his perception of the psychologically ambiguous nature of her presentation of Sutpen when he says that her story has "that logic- and reason-flouting quality of a dream" (22).

Sutpen's outrageous childbearing proposal to his young fiancée provokes the sort of absolutist response which had been inculcated in Rosa by her Puritan father and dour aunt. She repudiates Sutpen utterly, as she had her father, and now pictures him as a Satanic figure ("the light-blinded bat-like image of his own torment cast by the fierce demoniac lantern up from beneath the earth's crust"), furiously denying the sexual element in her attraction to him: "I never owned him; certainly not in that sewer sense which you would mean by that" (171). Rosa becomes, like Sutpen himself, "cold, implacable, and even ruthless" (10), turning the dark light of her anger on everyone in Sutpen's world, using extreme terms to describe them all. She sees everything in startling black and white, and it will require the more considered and rational viewpoint of Mr. Compson to moderate the excesses of her vision.

As is the case with Quentin in *The Sound and the Fury*, Rosa's judgmental absolutism and emotional stultification, the unfortunate result of a deprived childhood, have left her incapable of living purposefully. Unlike Quentin in the earlier novel, however, she is an embryonic novelist. Rosa's emotions lead her to eloquence and generalization, and she has a true sense of mission about getting her story told. She seems to know, as, obviously, did Faulkner, that only in the telling does personal history achieve order and meaning. Rosa is actually, in a minor way, an artist, "the county's poetess laureate," but she cannot write this story herself and so summons Quentin to her side. She subtly charges him to act as guardian of the tale, saying "maybe you will enter the literary profession . . . and maybe some day you will remember this and write about it" (9–10).

Although Rosa is unable to commit her narrative to paper, her verbal powers are so considerable that she creates a character who is rich and autonomous, something far more than a mere emotional appendage to herself. As she speaks about Sutpen, his "invoked ghost" begins to "assume a quality almost of solidity, permanence," and seems to "possess sentience" (13). This verbal creation of an autonomous being is the consummate achievement of a fictional artist, and Rosa proves herself capable of such accomplishment. Her Sutpen has more "reality" than Quentin's Caddy in *The Sound and the Fury*. What is even more important, she makes someone else "see" him in all his vigor. Thus, even at the outset of *Absalom, Absalom!,* its crucial difference from the earlier novel is apparent.

Quentin receives his charge to take possession of the tale with seriousness. He knows part of the story already and identifies emotionally with Rosa because he, too, is in thrall to the past, "an empty hall echoing with sonorous defeated names. . . . a barracks filled with stubborn back-looking ghosts," (12). Moreover, because of his grandfather's allegiance to Sutpen, Quentin realizes that he is perhaps "partly responsible through heredity for what happened to her and her family through him" (13). For these moral and emotional reasons Quentin is receptive, and he proves an excellent choice because of his sensibility. Though Quentin suffers his own psychic problems, he is alert and responsive to the story, readily able to see the characters and to watch the story taking shape, as well as to understand Rosa's difficulties in presenting it fairly and fully.

Having received from her a version that is excessively emotional, Quentin turns to his father for a more rational presentation. Mr. Compson has always accepted his own father's view of Sutpen, which possesses a rational humanism that serves to counterbalance Miss Rosa's demonology. Mr. Compson relates the "actors" to figures in the *Oresteia* and invokes "the mask in Greek tragedy" (62) before recounting his father's version of Sutpen as a hero whose "trouble was innocence" (220) and whose misguided and hubristic efforts to put right the world into which he "fell" brought about his demise. The Compson males see Sutpen as a resourceful man whose childhood mistreatment by a caste-ridden society that literally and figuratively sent him around to the back door led to his vengeful creation of a "design" to acquire the power that would prevent him from ever again being similarly humiliated. Like any tragic hero, Sutpen suffered from *hamartia,* or the fatal flaw, which in his case led him to consider only what was "adjunctive or incremental to the design which I had in mind" (240), until he committed the outrage that resulted in his murder. Influenced by this concept of Sutpen, Mr. Compson rationally and plausibly fills in details of the quarrel between Sutpen and his son Henry. But he is helpless to account for Henry's later killing of Charles Bon.

There are limits to his approach, just as there were to Rosa's, and in both instances many of these limits are attributable to the tendency of the narrator to project his own deficiencies onto the narrative. Mr. Compson understands, for instance, Rosa's "projecting upon Judith all the abortive dreams and delusions of her own doomed and frustrated youth" (71), but does not comprehend that he himself has the same propensity. He sees everything from the southern past as "more heroic" and its people as "distinct, uncomplex" beings (89). With this vision of a simpler, more heroic past, it is almost inevitable that Mr. Compson will see a striking personage from that past (such as Sutpen) as a figure of tragic grandeur, a rebellious man silhouetted against the sky.

Since Quentin's father also tends to emphasize concrete data, it is not surprising that he should see Sutpen as having a vision rooted in calculation, with an "alertness for measuring and weighing event against eventuality, circumstance against human nature . . . choosing and discarding" (53). After Mr. Compson presents his projective version of the story, based on his own romantic vision of the past and his own rationality, he is baffled by the things that still remain unexplained. He sees the characters as "possessing now heroic proportions, performing their acts of simple passion and simple violence, impervious to time and inexplicable. . . . Yet something is missing; they are like a chemical formula . . . you bring them together in the proportions called for, but nothing happens" (101). The inadequacy of Mr. Compson's "formula," heroic or not, is obvious, a result of his too-ready adherence to his own father's ideas about Sutpen and about society and of his own failure to develop fully his emotional participation in the life he observes. He remains always the speculative observer, like Hightower before his final "conversion."

Yet Mr. Compson is, despite his blind spots, also a metaphoric working novelist, his recurrent phrase "I can imagine" attesting to the excitement of creation. He presents as much data as he is capable of, about both the individual and the society with which he was in conflict, much as would a nineteenth-century social realist. Moreover, he understands Rosa's emotional difficulties and Sutpen's limitations, if not his own, and portrays them fully and evenhandedly. Finally, and most importantly, he comprehends that art offers one of the few solutions to the human dilemma of attempting to find meaning in a world of unmeaning. As he says, art is "a scratch, something, something that might make a mark on something that *was* once'' (127), a posthumous mark on human beings who can think and feel, and thus an ''undying mark on the blank face of the oblivion to which we are all doomed'' (129). Mr. Compson's testimony to the long-range worth of art anticipates public statements on the subject by Faulkner himself, who spoke years later about his work as a small but immortal gleam in the dark void, as a ''scratch'' on ''the face of the supreme Obliteration,'' the ''one and only way on earth you can say No to death'' (*L*, p. 125, B, p. 1461). From the statements he has given to Quentin's father in *Absalom, Absalom!*, it is clear that by 1935 this philosophy was already a fully developed justification of his writing as giving meaning not only to his own life but to the lives of others.

For Rosa, art is a symbolic weapon of rebellion against an oppressive figure or a means of preserving the past; for Mr. Compson it is a psychically necessary attempt to create order out of chaos or to utter an everlasting cry that can be heard in the eternal nothingness. Their viewpoints are different but essentially compatible as statements about the great potency of art in both personal and general terms. With their words echoing in his head, Quentin himself becomes, during the course of *Absalom, Absalom!*, a fully committed artist who makes the final creative leap of which neither of the other two were capable and discovers for himself the enormous potential of the artistic process.

Faulkner obviously envisioned Quentin as the pivotal figure in his story. He stressed to his publisher that Quentin ''tells it, or ties it together: he is the protagonist so that it is not complete apocrypha. . . . I use his bitterness which he has projected on the South in the form of hatred of it and its people to get more out of the story itself than a historical novel would be'' (*L*, p. 79). Thus Quentin's centrality and the projective quality of storytelling were apparent to Faulkner from the outset; he was fully conscious of his method in *Absalom, Absalom!* in a way he had not been in *The Sound and the Fury,* which was an outpouring both compulsive and ecstatic. Faulkner also shows an understanding of Quentin's problem which he had not evinced in the earlier novel and thus clarifies his character as well as his role in the storytelling process.

Faulkner's ability to create characters who are closely related psychologically and who illuminate different aspects of a single world-view had been evident from his very first novel. There, though handled clumsily, it revealed, as did all his other works, his own contradictory waverings between romantic and ironic self-characterization. The approach is a central part of his novelistic method, and it gives his finest works a remarkable intricacy and plenitude. Faulkner had used this technique of ''linked characters'' subtly in the antecedent work most closely related to *Absalom, Absalom!* by having Benjy act as a psychic mirror of Quentin, with problems like those of his older brother but in a more primitive and childish version. The technique was developed in *As I Lay Dying* and *Light in August,* where the linked characters are not only psychologically interrelated in a mixture of parallelism and opposition but also narratively interdependent, acting upon each other in important ways and coming together symbolically at the end.[12] In *Absalom, Absalom!* Faulkner employs the method still more extensively and skillfully, so that the psychological revelations are amplified and the work attains an extraordinary resonance.

Linked characters and their relevance to the development of Quentin as man and as artist constitute both theme and method in *Absalom, Absalom!*. The permutations of the interrelationships between Bon-Henry, Henry-Judith, and Quentin-Shreve attain the imaginable limit. Self-division is shown to be Quentin's problem almost the moment he is presented; there are ''two separate Quentins,'' ''the Quentin Compson preparing for Harvard in the South'' and ''the Quentin Compson who was still too young to deserve yet to be a ghost, but nevertheless having to be one for all that'' (9). As the Sutpen story unfolds, Quentin discovers that there was an unusual closeness between Henry and Bon and between Henry and Judith that suggests his own complex relationship to his Harvard roommate Shreve and (by implication only, since she is nowhere mentioned within *Absalom, Absalom!* itself) to his sister Caddy: Mr. Compson envisions Henry and Judith as a ''single personality with two bodies both of which had been seduced almost simultaneously'' (92) by Charles Bon, their brother. Henry becomes Bon's closest friend and Judith becomes Bon's fiancée, and their relationship develops into what is perhaps ''the pure and perfect incest; the brother realizing that the sister's virginity must be destroyed in order to have existed at all, taking that virginity in the person of the brother-in-law, the man whom he would be if he could become, metamorphose into, the lover, the husband; by whom he would be despoiled, choose for despoiler, if he could become, metamorphose into the sister, the mistress, the bride'' (96). Henry's desires are complex, and so, indubitably, are Bon's: ''Perhaps in his fatalism he loved Henry the better of the two, seeing perhaps in the sister merely the shadow, the woman vessel with which to consummate the love whose actual object was the youth'' (108).

Mr. Compson's speculations on the matter seem almost endless at one point, as do the possible motives of the three siblings in their responses to each other. For most of the novel, Judith, Henry, and Bon are vivid only in their mutual relationships, rarely achieving real autonomy as characters.

One reason is that their interrelationships per se are of primary importance, and the qualities they evince vary from one portrayal to another. Watching the wild Negroes fight, brother and sister react differently. Judith is the ruthless and courageous Sutpen who watches eagerly, while Henry is "the Coldfield with the Coldfield cluttering of morality and rules of right and wrong" (120) who is nauseated and miserable. But once with Bon, Henry becomes heedless and instinctual, the one who "never thought. He felt, and acted immediately" (96). He stands in contrast to Bon, who remains a cerebral *élégant*, one whose dilatoriness mystifies most observers.

The knowledge a reader brings to *Absalom, Absalom!* of Quentin's problems as portrayed in *The Sound and the Fury* only serves to increase the resonance of this complex series of interrelationships, for it becomes clear that Quentin projects many of his own difficulties onto the Sutpen story and that he identifies himself with both Henry and Bon. Each represents a different facet of his personal struggle, which was undoubtedly a version of Faulkner's own. Midway in his hearing of the tale, Quentin is suddenly blocked in his ability either to listen or to comprehend. "He had something which he was unable to pass: that door," the crucial symbolic door to full understanding which has been closed by the emotional problems that interfere with his objectivity. Quentin invokes Henry, "that gaunt tragic dramatic self-hypnotized youthful face like . . . an academic Hamlet" and his fierce interchange with his "sister facing him across the wedding dress" (174) that she plans to wear, a situation identical to Quentin's own in the earlier novel. Quentin is also pictured as having a "quality of delicacy" (324) that recalls Bon's lean elegance, and Bon's effort to find the "pattern which would reveal to him at once, like a flash of light, the meaning of his whole life, past" (313) appears to be a projective result of Quentin's similar quest and much like that revealed everywhere in Faulkner's art.

Bon's anguished difficulties with his father also seem an amplification of the more subtle estrangement between Quentin and his father pictured in *The Sound and the Fury* and appear closely related to the author's own problems with Murry Falkner. As detached from his oldest son as Thomas Sutpen is shown to be, Murry had died not long before Faulkner's writing of *Absalom, Absalom!*. Thus the perpetual and frustrating estrangement between father and son was now forever irremediable. Faulkner's resulting sense of loss and hopeless waste pervades the pages portraying Bon's efforts to be reconciled with his cold father and gives them an emotional power unequaled elsewhere in the novel. Bon's yearning for "that instant of indisputable recognition" (319) by his father, "out of the shadow of whose absence my spirit's posthumeity has never escaped" (317), is overwhelmingly painful. His despondent waiting for a sign during ten days at his father's house emotionally compresses that suffered by Faulkner for thirty-five years, and Bon's efforts to put himself in Sutpen's way to achieve just the merest gesture of acknowledgment increase in their intensity and pathos:

He would just have to write 'I am your father. Burn this' and I would do it. Or if not that, a sheet, a scrap of paper with the one word 'Charles' in his hand, and I would know what he meant and he would not even have to ask me to burn it. Or a lock of hair or a paring from his finger nail and I would know them because I believe now that I have known what his hair and his finger nails would look like all my life, could choose that lock and that paring out of a thousand. And it did not come. [326]

Sutpen's refusal to respond to his son drives Bon to make a suicidal gesture, an attempted marriage involving both incest and miscegenation that is bound to arouse someone's murderous wrath. Bon's agonizing sense of defeat and desperate need for self-destruction, though extreme, are emotions with which, obviously, both Quentin and his creator can identify and sympathize.

This empathy makes the complexities of the Sutpen-Bon relationship emotionally vivid and it also vivifies the portrait of Sutpen himself. Despite Sutpen's presence in the novel primarily as an emblematic being with whom the rest of the characters grapple emotionally and ratiocinatively, he is a splendidly memorable character, one of Faulkner's strongest in this respect. In his monomania, which borders on madness, Sutpen evokes Melville's Ahab,[13] and in his dedicated pursuit of a design, he recalls Jay Gatsby, to name only two of his singleminded predecessors in American fiction. Critics have often seen Sutpen as a symbol of the Old South, courageous in action and vision, but flawed by an inhumanity which brought about its own defeat; but Sutpen also had vital personal meaning for Faulkner as a portrait of his own great-grandfather, the Old Colonel, and as one of his last statements about the dashing figure who had psychologically dominated his formative years. The writer had previously tended to romanticize his great-grandfather as the brave and glamorous Colonel Sartoris; but in his portrayal of Sutpen, Faulkner reveals a more mature sense of the deficiencies of the Old Colonel's drive to success, a realization of the folly of action unqualified by speculation or sympathy. Faulkner amplifies his portrait of Sutpen with a Conradian history of a Haitian native uprising and another melodramatic element or two, but otherwise generally adheres to the basic facts of his ancestor's life.

Sutpen is, like the first William Falkner, a "new man," a resourceful newcomer of unknown antecedents who appears in northern Mississippi in the early nineteenth century and rapidly rises from poverty to power and economic prosperity. In the process, he abandons his oldest son as not incremental to his design, even as Faulkner's great-grandfather gave up his child John to facilitate his second marriage. Sutpen is arrogant, a figure who "contrived somehow to swagger even on a horse" (16), but he is heroic in battle, with a broken plume that signifies his splendor in defeat and recalls the Old Colonel's appellation, "Knight of the Black Plume." In civilian life, Sutpen's "lust for vain magnificence" (162) drives him to exploit his slaves, to build a pretentious house, and to attempt to acquire respectability through marriage—all of which the Old Colonel did. Finally, his tendency toward violence eventually leads to his own murder and he is, like the Old Colonel himself, buried under a tombstone he had already ordered.

The manifold responses Sutpen evokes in those who knew him are related to the ambivalence Faulkner showed toward his memorable and influential ancestor. The major psychic importance of this character in Faulkner's development, however, is reflected in the manner in which his story is shaped and interpreted by the man of sensibility, the controlling artist, Quentin.[14] The thoughtless man of action is destroyed by the end of the narrative; his tale achieves its impact only through the masterful efforts of the introspective Quentin, revealing that Faulkner had finally recognized that his art was the real way to achieve meaning. His great-grandfather was also a writer, a poet and novelist, as well as a reckless man of action, yet it is only the sensitive, artistic aspect of his character that survives—through the person of Quentin-Faulkner. The author now understands the significance of his troublesome legacy from the past; mindless motion must be ordered and recorded to achieve lasting importance. There can be no history without a historian, and as artist-historian, Quentin and his author create as well as preserve events.

The "linked character" method, so dominant in *Absalom, Absalom!*, reaches its apotheosis in the duad of Quentin-Shreve and becomes at the last both embodiment of and paean to the committed working artist. The two Quentins, the one already a ghost and the one trying to free himself from the past, continue their dialogue in the narrative, as in the scene where one tells the other "that what your father was saying did not tell you anything so much as it struck, word by word, the resonant strings of remembering" (213). This is not the dissociative splitting evident in Darl Bundren during his final descent to madness, but the careful ruminative process essential to the discovery of meaning. Yet Quentin, too, finds his way to the truth partially blocked, for he lacks the irony necessary to achieve wholeness of vision. Shreve represents the deflating tendency, the other Faulknerian artistic voice always evident in his work as a counterbalance to his more passionately romantic and self-dramatizing impulses. Irony and self-pity fuse in *Absalom, Absalom!* in the figures of Shreve and Quentin, and the process by which they unite shows Faulkner to be fully cognizant of the need to present and integrate both visions.

Shreve's voice first enters the narrative after Quentin has discovered the symbolic door produced by his own tendency to project. Unable to pass through it, he reverts to his evocation of "the implacable doll-sized old woman" and her "heat-distilled old woman-flesh" until Shreve shouts, "Wait. Wait," begins his deflationary version about "this old dame, this Aunt Rosa" (176), and almost immediately proceeds to the revelation of exactly what constituted Sutpen's outrageous proposal to his young fiancée forty-three years ago. At a later point, Quentin muses on his intuitive method of acquiring knowledge "without the medium of speech somehow from having been born and living beside it" (212), yet still cannot complete his account of the trip to the old house. Again Shreve enters crying, "Wait," and jeering cynically, "Jesus, the South is fine, isn't it. . . . It's better than Ben Hur, isn't it" (217). Now the two proceed to create their final and complete version of the Sutpen story, with both past and present fully and imaginatively delineated. The intervention of the ironic Shreve and the ensuing forward movement suggest that no meaningful narrative progress can take place without integration of the differing visions.

Quentin and Shreve finally become almost as one, fused in their mutual undertaking, "the two of them not moving except to breathe, both young, both born within the same year" (258), actively imagining and creating, urging each other on to projection and disclosure. The two understand their identification with the previous "artists" of the narrative and the trickiness of the process. "Maybe we are both Father" (261), they say, aware that they are "dedicated to that best of ratiocination which after all was a good deal like Sutpen's morality and Miss Coldfield's demonizing" (280). Quentin himself moves to an increased understanding of the implications of the past: "Maybe nothing ever happens once and is finished. Maybe happen is never once but like ripples maybe on water after the pebble sinks, the ripples moving on, spreading" (261). The two young men proceed to follow these ripples to the farthest limits which they can imaginatively discover.

With their psychological and intellectual fusion complete, Quentin and Shreve now figuratively coalesce with the other linked characters of the story, the sons of Sutpen. As they relive that long-ago Christmas, they become "not two of them there and then either but four of them riding the two horses through the iron darkness" (295). The mutual identification increases to the point where "it was not even four now but compounded still further, since now both of them were Henry Sutpen and both of them were Bon" (351)—both experiencing the frustrating visit to the home of the father who refuses recognition. In their unity and mutual empathy, Quentin and Shreve transcend even the normal boundaries of their male identity and can look at one another "curious and quiet and profoundly intent . . . almost as a youth and a very young girl might out of virginity itself" (299). They have become richly sensitive to the struggles of the many characters with whom they can identify and soon engage in artistic creation on the fullest possible scale, "both thinking as one, the voice which happened to be speaking the thought only the thinking become audible, vocal; the two of them creating between them, out of the rag-tag and bob-ends of old tales and talking, people who perhaps had never existed at all anywhere" (303).[15]

In depicting the joyous quality of Quentin-Shreve's sense of discovery, Faulkner produces a virtual paean to the marvelous process of fictional creation. The two men share an experience which is so heightened that it approaches ecstasy, and the process itself becomes essentially more valuable than its product, the completed tale of Thomas Sutpen, the story of "a man who wanted a son through pride, and got too many of them and they destroyed him," as Faulkner himself described it (B, p. 854). Quentin and Shreve find that "it did not matter to either of them which one did the talking, since it was not the talking alone which did it, performed and accomplished the overpassing, but some happy marriage of speaking and hearing wherein each before the demand, the requirement, forgave condoned and forgot the faulting of the other . . . in order to overpass to love, where there might be paradox and inconsistency but nothing fault or false" (316). The "happy marriage" between speaking and hearing, and between pity and irony, reaches fulfillment at this point in the novel. Quentin and Shreve, like Faulkner himself, become the consummate artist, whose engagement in his work is so complete that the outcome is less important than the ecstatic process of creating it.

They make creative leap after creative leap with accumulating intensity, correcting the "errors" of the previous storytellers and making a number of "discoveries." They imaginatively create or re-create the counter-design of Bon's mother and her lawyer, Bon's confrontations with his father and half brother, Sutpen's offense against Rosa Coldfield, and his subsequent abuse of Wash Jones's granddaughter and retributive murder. Moreover, they find the most important missing piece in the story, the one which "explains" much of the rest of the puzzle, Charles Bon's Negro blood. Having effectively reconstructed the "dead" past with Shreve's assistance, Quentin is prepared to relive his own confrontation with the living past and thus to pass at last the obstructive door. He enters the decaying Sutpen mansion in the company of Miss Rosa. Even though she originates the psychically dangerous mission, Quentin takes over and actually confronts the living corpse that proves to be Henry Sutpen—who is, in a way, the youth's dark alter ego. In his symbolic "climbing over the sill" (368), Quentin experiences terror and acquires knowledge, even while his mentor's trip into the past proves fatal. Having faced the last of her demons and having seen the doomed house destroyed by fire, Miss Rosa understands that "it was all finished now" and takes to her bed to die. The survivor Quentin lies shivering in his cold Cambridge room remembering that other survivor, the howling black idiot Jim Bond, "the scion, the last of his race" (376), and desperately thinking about the South: *"I dont. I dont. I dont hate it! I dont hate it!"* (378).

Quentin's meeting with a living vestige of the past which haunts him does not offer a full purgation from its oppressive weight, and he still views the region and all it represents with an anguished confusion of hate and love. For the reader familiar with *The Sound and the Fury,* Quentin's failure to recollect his emotion in tranquility heralds his impending suicide. Although Quentin's final despair seems on the surface psychologically discordant, impinging as it does upon his supreme and triumphant artistic achievement of recreating the past in all its violence and splendor, the bleak ending is a vital part of Faulkner's "message." Quentin emerges from his contemplation of the satisfactions of the creative process to learn that he must now confront stressful and demanding social and personal realities. If the resolutions of art cannot always be fully carried over into life, still, art, as depicted in *Absalom, Absalom!,* offers modes of fulfillment not otherwise available to mortal man. The atmosphere of darkness and death which threatens to overwhelm Quentin at the conclusion is counterbalanced by the light of discovery and narrative order. Whatever the inadequacies of the milieu surrounding him, the committed artist intensely at work can discover the "living breath" of history and find satisfaction, even ecstasy, in the perpetually challenging and eternally fulfilling process of creation.

7

Repudiation and Catharsis:
The Unvanquished

THE EXPERIENCE OF READING Faulkner's novels progressively, in the order in which they were written, provides insights beyond those offered by the individual fiction itself, supplies, so to speak, intertextual illuminations. For the novels often carry on a dialogue among themselves as Faulkner comments implicitly and tellingly on his earlier work. The intertextual relationship of *The Sound and the Fury* and *Absalom, Absalom!* is most obvious and has already provoked much critical discussion, but such relationship exists, however subtly, throughout the whole sequence of Faulkner's novels. Viewing them consecutively, one sees the author return to the same topic or the same constellation of characters, yet with modulations in treatment or narrative development that reveal distinct alterations in Faulkner's vision of his basic materials and also, in essential ways, of himself. This modulating vision, along with its temporal components, is, of course, the basic subject of this study. Nevertheless, certain transitions from one novel to the next are particularly striking, as are the roles played by individual novels as more or less summary fictional statements on a particular theme or character. *The Unvanquished,* published in 1938, is important both transitionally and summarily.

The relationship of *The Unvanquished* to its predecessor, *Absalom, Absalom!,* is not immediately evident. The works are quite different in technique—the earlier one so richly complex that it is often regarded as Faulkner's least accessible novel, requiring multiple rereadings for full comprehension, the second so relatively straightforward in style and content that Faulkner, along with his critics, saw it as the easiest to understand. Faulkner once suggested that a new reader might begin with that work "because it's easy to read. Compared to the others, I mean" (*FIU*, p. 2). Each has, however, as its central subject matter the confrontation of a young male with a troubling and powerful father figure, a topic that both plagued and inspired Faulkner as he attempted repeatedly to come to terms with his recent and distant family past—to face, through the crucial process of fictionalization, both his father, Murry, and his great-grandfather, the Old Colonel. Charles Bon's desperate struggle with Thomas Sutpen and, by indirection, Quentin Compson's with his father, like Bayard Sartoris's confrontation with John Sartoris and all that he represents, mirror Faulkner's own need to emulate and repudiate similar figures in his own family history.

At the same time, differences between *Absalom, Absalom!* and *The Unvanquished* in both the treatment of the father figure and the psychological development of the youthful protagonist reveal that Faulkner's attitudes had undergone some changes during the brief period between them. These changes suggest that his evaluative capacity was maturing even as he became less involved with his material. *The Unvanquished* thus serves as a commentary on elements in Faulkner's previous novel; it also offers a sort of summary statement that relates it not only to *Absalom, Absalom!* but to earlier works such as *Sartoris* and *The Sound and the Fury*. It dramatizes the arrival of its protagonist at a stage of maturity not achieved by any of Faulkner's previous young males and makes a final cathartic gesture toward significant parental and surrogate-parent figures in Faulkner's past.

After *Absalom, Absalom!* made its appearance in 1936 from Faulkner's new publisher, Random House, the author felt an obligation to submit another new work at once while enthusiasm was still high. Random House had solidified its contract with him in the form of a generous advance, and Faulkner was anxious to do something substantial in repayment. He looked at a group of stories which he had recently sold to that leading organ of mass culture, the *Saturday Evening Post,* and decided that the stories had the potential for unification within the covers of a single volume. In December of 1936, Faulkner told Bennett Cerf that he had "a series of six stories about a white boy and a negro boy during the civil war" and planned to do something worthwhile with them (*L,* p. 97). Cerf was encouraging, and although Faulkner occasionally referred to these stories as "potboilers" or "trash" fit only for the average reader of magazines like the *Post,* he set about integrating them into a work that had both substance and cohesiveness.

The tales, which Faulkner often called "the Bayard-Ringo stories," have as their center Bayard Sartoris's movement from childhood to maturity during and after the Civil War, accompanied in his early adventures by his black playmate Ringo. In collecting them Faulkner intensified the focus on the moral aspects of Bayard's evolution toward manhood, a process which takes him away from the vital but flawed code of his ancestors to a personal ethic that is more humane. To the story called "Retreat," for instance, he added passages about the manner in which a child changes and matures (B, p. 959), and to the volume as a whole he added the all-important climactic tale, "An Odor of Verbena," in which Bayard completes his initiation into adulthood and becomes a man of moral stature, not only aware of the deficiencies in his father's vision, but also capable of creating his own moral code. *The Unvanquished* has often been accused of being slight, dismissed, in Cleanth Brooks's words, as "a sheaf of conventional southern Civil War stories." Certainly the work is not one of Faulkner's greatest, but Brooks, for one, praises Faulkner's refusal to romanticize Colonel Sartoris and his determination, instead, to portray that character in all his human complexity.[1]

Material from Faulkner's family history forms the basis for the stories in *The Unvanquished*. Faulkner had used this material in *Sartoris* to create the remembered heroic past which haunts young Bayard, inculcating in him a sense of personal inadequacy that drives him subconsciously to seek his own violent death in parodic emulation of ancestral glories. He used it again in *Absalom, Absalom!*, through the characterization of Thomas Sutpen, as a paradigm of the fatal flaw in southern history, which Quentin masters imaginatively by his triumphant recreation but which still drives him to despair as he ponders its legacy in the person of the howling idiot Jim Bond. In *The Unvanquished,* Faulkner takes us directly into that distant time, as if evincing a need to be, fully and experientially, there, to face once again his male ancestors directly and filially, without the complexity of the aesthetic and epistemological issues he had introduced in *Absalom, Absalom!*. Faulkner shows that past to be, though heroic in some aspects, sordid and destructive in others and hence undeserving of a romanticized response in its twentieth-century inheritors.

With this work, Faulkner completes the revisionist view of his dashing great-grandfather that he had begun in his previous novel and thus shows himself struggling almost free of the burden he had carried with such difficulty. The John Sartoris of *The Unvanquished* is more flawed than he was in *Sartoris* and less demonic than Thomas Sutpen of *Absalom, Absalom!,* who was an embodiment of the dark side of the Old Colonel. He seems to signify Faulkner's balanced and perhaps realistic final vision of the first William Falkner. After *The Unvanquished,* the Old Colonel would fictionally rise to haunt his great-grandson no more.[2] The book quite possibly represents a form of catharsis, just as *Absalom, Absalom!* represented Faulkner's last need to deal with the troubling brother-rival who had stalked the pages of his earlier fiction.

From the outset of *The Unvanquished,* John Sartoris is presented through the developing vision of his son Bayard, whose changes may be emblematic of those Faulkner himself underwent. The contrasting of childish and mature perceptions is a method Faulkner would use again. At first Bayard's outlook is romantic—he pictures war as consisting of "the cannon and the flags and the anonymous yelling" (17)[3]—but he soon discovers that war has another, less attractive and less heroic, side. He makes similar discoveries about his father during the process of his emotional development. Bayard early sees him as a heroic figure who reappears in his son's life with the awesome abruptness of a demigod, but later recognizes that he is a "little man," that "it was just the things he did . . . that made him seem big to us" (14, 10). The depiction of a heroic figure as physically small is unusual for Faulkner, who tended to equate heroism with largeness in compensation for his own smallness and correlative sense of being a military failure. Bayard gradually shows evidence of seeing through part of the romantic haze which surrounds the military hero, and in the first tale, the adult Bayard comments retrospectively on the supplanting of his childish belief that his father's odor "was the smell of powder and glory, the elected victorious" by his later realization that it represented only the less glorious "will to endure" (11).

The demythologizing of John Sartoris—and, concomitantly, of Faulkner's great-grandfather—thus begins early in the novel and reaches a climax in the final story. Sartoris is, like his real-life counterpart, the demoted former head of a regiment who raises his own unit of irregular cavalry. Sartoris's subsequent eluding of Yankee search parties, his postwar establishment of a railroad, and his election to the state legislature just prior to his murder at the hands of his estranged partner are also based on incidents in the life of Faulkner's great-grandfather, whose military exploits and rise to economic and political power during Reconstruction were the subject of frequent taletelling around the household where Faulkner spent his boyhood.

John Sartoris also has a dark side, of which Bayard quickly becomes aware. Early in the novel, the Colonel evokes Thomas Sutpen with a "Well, Miss Rosa" (10) upon his return from battle that could have been

Sutpen's postwar greeting to his future fiancée, and Sartoris's Sutpen-like qualities grow ever more evident as the narrative progresses. In "Skirmish at Sartoris," he proves a vicious antagonist to members of the Burden family, calling them carpetbaggers for their efforts to organize blacks and killing them when they persist. He perceives his action as justifiable under the terms of his code, because "I let them fire first" (238), and delusively goes on to assert that "we are working for peace through law and order" (239). His urge to preserve that for which he believes he fought in the war is possibly justifiable, but his means of implementing it are not, a deficiency which identifies him with Sutpen.

By the final story, Sartoris seems in some ways to be even less sympathetic a human being than the proprietor of Sutpen's Hundred, having helped organize the Ku Klux Klan and killed yet another man. His friends and family as well as his enemies now see him as severely flawed. George Wyatt comments on his volatility and inability to keep friends, and his son perceives his "violent and ruthless dictatorialness and will to dominate" (258). In a moment of which the more "innocent" Sutpen was incapable, Sartoris himself tacitly admits recognition of the inhumanity of his earlier actions when he announces that he is "tired of killing men" (266) and suicidally fails to draw his gun on the man who threatens his life.

Sartoris's last-minute gesture of nonviolence comes perhaps too late to fully ameliorate the criminality of his previous deeds, but it does prepare the way for his son's culminating action. For Bayard refuses to avenge his father's death in the manner required by that code, prevalent in his class and times, to which his father had adhered for most of his life. In so doing, he repudiates both the code and his father, whom he now understands to have been only superficially a "hero" and whose postwar actions he thus adjudges as villainous. "They were men. Human beings" (257), he says of his father's victims, in words that may also serve as Faulkner's judgment on the immorality of his great-grandfather's tendency to settle disputes by murder. Bayard's final repudiation signifies his entrance into the realm of moral adulthood and his creation of a personal ethic. This incident, too, came out of Faulkner's family history, for it is based on John Falkner's failure to seek vengeance upon his father's killer.

Yet Bayard is so closely identified with another character based on Faulkner himself that his arrival at a vision of his father both honest and judgmental connotes Faulkner's own arrival at a point of real maturity in his emotional responses to the past. By the late 1930s, Faulkner's heritage had become neither a "curse" nor an ideal in comparison to which he fell tragically short, but rather an important element in his personal development. By the end of *The Unvanquished*, Faulkner's family history was for him almost completely decathected. Henceforth it would appear merely as a vital component in the larger regional history with which Faulkner became increasingly concerned. The other character with whom Bayard has a revealing kinship is the Quentin Compson of both *The Sound and the Fury* and *Absalom, Absalom!*. We have already seen that Quentin seems to be largely a self-portrait of Faulkner at an earlier stage, and because Bayard Sartoris is much like the young Faulkner as the author depicted himself in the only autobiographical piece he ever published, "Mississippi," the interrelationship of Quentin, Bayard, and Faulkner is significant indeed. Whether Falkner used his own childhood as a basis for Bayard's in *The Unvanquished*, or whether he merely submitted a piece of already written fiction when asked for an autobiographical essay is unknown, but what is obvious from a comparison of "Mississippi" and the first story of *The Unvanquished* is that Faulkner imaginatively identified himself with young Bayard.

In "Mississippi" Faulkner speaks of knowing about Vicksburg before hearing of Santa Claus, and *The Unvanquished* opens with Bayard crouching before his "living map" of Vicksburg, not yet aware that the city has fallen to Union troops. In "Mississippi" Faulkner goes on to write of the black child with whom he lived in virtual twinship as a boy, the Negro boy "born in the same week with the white child and both bearing the same (the white child's grandsire's) name, suckled at the same black breast and sleeping and eating together and playing together the game,"[4] and these are very much the terms of the relationship between Bayard and his black playmate Ringo. The two are so close that "maybe he [Ringo] wasn't a nigger anymore or maybe I wasn't a white boy anymore, the two of us neither, not even people any longer" (8). The two are both physically and spiritually akin. They appear to run "as one" and when Bayard hears the words "the race gonter all be free," he excitedly believes that they apply to himself, running to tell his grandmother, "It's General Sherman and he's going to make us all free" (26). He is correct in a way, for slavery has been a thrall that binds white psyches as well as black bodies, but Bayard's glee signifies his unawareness of the racial division between himself and his black friend.

Faulkner did not include in *The Unvanquished* any scene that dealt with the painful awakening in a southern white child (such as Bayard) to the knowledge of the color differences which will make a chasm between himself and his "black twin" as they approach adulthood, although he later treated the situation poignantly in *Go Down, Moses*. The omission from the 1938 novel is perhaps unfortunate, for this "fall" into a perception of racial separation and its injustice would have increased the impact of Bayard's growth to moral awareness, racism constituting the most egregious flaw in the code which he inherits and eventually repudiates. However, in *The Unvanquished,* Faulkner chooses to concentrate on the generalized violence and potential inhumanity of the southern code as it is personified in John Sartoris. Rosa Millard is John's mother-in-law, and the inadequacy of the "code" is revealed by her actions as well as his. In the first story, she ends her absolute adherence to the belief that one must always tell the truth in order to save her grandson, lying to the angry Yankees that there are no children in her house and giving them "look for look while she lied" (35). With the Yankees safely dispatched, Rosa revives the code and washes the boys' mouths out with soap, yet this action, too, is inconsistent, for she apparently exempts herself from any like punishment.

The system has begun to break down and it soon disintegrates even further, as Rosa steals horses but asserts, "I borrowed them," and then connives with Ab Snopes in a felonious plan involving forgery and the theft of hundreds of Yankee mules. The Yankee colonel who has adhered to the code of gallantry toward women by respecting Rosa's lie and retrieving her "lost" mules and silver becomes the indirect victim of larceny on a grand scale. Rosa justifies her actions on the ground of philanthropy toward the poor of her region, "who could not help themselves" (167). Many of her actions are, of course, humanly justifiable and even admirable, but they all serve to signify the inconsistencies and incipient breakdown of the old ethic. Ironically, the ethic itself is responsible for her death, and the agents of that death come from within the southern culture. Rosa goes off to confront a gang of vicious plunderers, delusively asserting that "they won't hurt a woman" (173). But they will, and do, for in the disorder of war, as Rosa herself has shown, the old code no longer has relevance.

Although Rosa's experience serves as exemplum of the moral anarchy that now rules and of the inadequacy of the southern code, Bayard initially remains blind to its implications. When he confronts the guilty Grumby, his desire for vengeance is so strong that he shoots the man in the back and mutilates the corpse to place visible proof of his revenge on Granny's grave. "Now she can lay good and quiet" (211) says Ringo, writing finis to the undertaking. But its emotional ramifications are clearly only just beginning to manifest themselves, for both boys begin to cry and the breakdown points toward their grief and incipient remorse. The inhumanity of which man becomes capable when he follows blindly the savage principle of "an eye for an eye" is established by this incident, but so is Bayard's potential for moral regeneration. His final and crucial confrontation with the old beliefs comes when he faces the implications of the pressure to avenge his father's death.

Bayard's ultimate triumph over the forces of the past which threaten to cripple him, as they did Quentin Compson, and to drive him inexorably to kill and be killed, as they had Henry Sutpen and Charles Bon, signifies the emotional progress Faulkner himself had made since writing the earlier novels. Bayard, Quentin, and Quentin's symbolic counterparts Henry and Charles are all hampered by a difficult paternal example and troubled by an incestuous attraction, but Bayard has the strength of character to surmount these psychic obstacles, while Quentin and the other two remain trapped behind them and can envisage only death as an escape. *The Unvanquished* covers twelve years in Bayard's life and shows his evolution from a romantic, immature boy to a young man of integrity and adult individuality. By contrast, *The Sound and the Fury* focuses intensely on a single day in Quentin's late adolescence, as he hovers on the brink of suicide and makes his obsessional mental journeys perpetually backward into the past, journeys that reveal how utterly unable he is to move forward into the future, while *Absalom, Absalom!* concentrates on a few intense months previous to this moment and on the way in which Quentin's vivid recreation of the tragic story of Henry and Charles is filled with resonances and auguries of his own desperate failures. Dreams occur in Bayard's story only as a means to create suspense or to advance the action, and day and night visions are carefully distinguished, but in Quentin's tale there is no clear separation between dream and reality and his entire experience takes on the quality of a waking nightmare.

The major story in *The Unvanquished* in which the likenesses and differences between Bayard and Quentin are evoked is the final one, "An Odor of Verbena." Faulkner wrote this tale especially for the book, "to finish" the others, as he said (*L*, p. 100), and it is more serious and complex than its predecessors. The earlier physical adventures are now supplanted by a more complicated moral and psychological adventure. The story hinges on a central crisis, Bayard's decision about avenging his father's murder, much as Quentin's section of *The Sound and the Fury* and the dramatic crux of *Absalom, Absalom!* are centered on decisive moral and psychological crises engendered by a sister's wedding. Bayard is, like Quentin, Henry, and Charles before him, in college when he hears the news which promises to change the course of his life. With his father's murder, he is now *the* Sartoris, facing the attendant obligation to preserve the family's "good name." Intellectually he is aware that *"this will be my chance to find out if I am what I think I am or if I just hope"* (248), and he recalls his recent discussion with his professor, clearly an influential father-surrogate, about the Biblical injunction "Thou shalt not kill," which offers the one real chance of "hope and peace for His blind and bewildered spawn" (249).

Having made this mental commitment to what he envisages as the most important teaching of Holy Writ, Bayard carries it out in his personal actions. Though he defers to the code to the extent of confronting his father's killer, he refuses all pressure to carry a weapon or to go accompanied, and once in Redmond's office refuses to make any antagonistic gesture. Either awed or inspired by Bayard's pacifist stance, Redmond fires wide. Both men thus pay lip service to the traditional mode of behavior but put it forever behind them. The most important tributes to the rightness of Bayard's action come from those very individuals who were most insistent that he carry out the plan of vengeance, and Bayard, in affirming a new personal ethic, thus significantly affects others around him.

Bayard's espousal of a new code of nonviolence is based on his awareness of the inhumanity of his father's past violence. While Quentin Compson struggles futilely with his father's nihilistic pronouncements, and Henry and Charles are provoked by their father into a murderous duel, Bayard Sartoris successfully makes a stand against the life-denying actions of his parent. On his way to the fateful meeting with Redmond that represents his confrontation with the past, Bayard invokes all of his father's unworthy deeds of recent years and struggles free from his father's destructive example in a way that Quentin, who fulfills Mr. Compson's verbal negations with the ultimate negative act, suicide, and Henry and Charles, who are driven to a fratricidal confrontation that effectively ends both their lives, cannot. Where Quentin can only reiterate and dwell on his father's statements and Henry and Charles emulate their father's heartlessness, Bayard analyzes and judges John Sartoris's ruthless nature and destructive actions.

This same contrast between the futility of mere emotional evocation, as shown in Quentin's story, or of rash action, as shown in Henry and Charles's, and the productivity of ratiocination and moral judgment, as shown in Bayard's, is also evident in their efforts to deal with an incestuous attraction. Quentin's obsession with his sister Caddy leads him to see the announcement of her wedding as a betrayal and a virtual death sentence for himself, a sexual pathology redramatized in the complex responses of Henry and Charles to their sister and the final act of fratricide. Bayard faces the prospect of a similarly disastrous involvement with his father's wife, Drusilla,[5] who tries to seduce him on two occasions. The first time he capitulates to the degree of a brief physical embrace and then confesses to his father in a scene that recalls Quentin's similar insistence to Mr. Compson that he has committed incest and, more obliquely, Charles's attempt to force a response from Sutpen by marrying his own half sister. The fathers are essentially indifferent to the threat of incest, but where this paternal detachment is destructive for Quentin, who badly needs some moral guidelines by which to chart his way, and for Charles, who is desperate for any sort of parental recognition, Bayard is able to perceive that his father's indifference is linked to the older man's loss of the will to live. It is a perception which reveals an already internalized sense of morality and a capacity to generalize.

Moreover, Drusilla's attempted seduction of Bayard is as much ideological as it is sexual, and thus presents less of an emotional threat. In the first scene, she attempts to impose on him her idea that "there are worse things than killing men" (261). In the second, more crucial scene, sex and ideas are again associated as Drusilla tries to force Bayard to accept some pistols to use for vengeance. " 'Take them, Bayard,' she said, in the same tone in which she had said 'Kiss me' last summer." She speaks sexually of the pistols, "the two of them slender and invincible and fatal as the physical shape of love" (273). The issue here is the seductiveness of the conventional masculinity of revenge rather than sheer sexuality, and Bayard refuses totally to continue the destructive tradition of violence. He recognizes the situation for what it really is and reacts only to the ideological component, for he is both more aware than Quentin Compson, whose lack of self-knowledge spells his doom, and more rational than Charles Bon, whose anguish drives him virtually to commit suicide.

The fragrance of flowers plays a symbolic role in this story, as it did in *The Sound and the Fury,* where honeysuckle is disastrously associated for Quentin with thoughts of sex and death. Verbena, the "odor of courage" (274), is linked in Bayard's mind with Drusilla and thus with the traditional beliefs which she espouses: her placing of a sprig in Bayard's lapel functions as a command to carry out her plan of vengeance. Nonetheless, Bayard discovers a more valid form of courage in his refusal to perpetuate the code of violence. Drusilla's final recognition of this fact and her tribute to Bayard's achievement is symbolized by the sprig which she places on his pillow before departing. The odor now represents his triumph over his troubling heritage and his accession to moral manhood.

By the end of "An Odor of Verbena," Bayard has a sense of self and a balanced vision of his father that were fatally lacking in Quentin and Charles, both psychically trapped in preadult responses. Although both *The Sound and the Fury* and *Absalom, Absalom!* are unquestionably finer and more intricate works than *The Unvanquished*, the differing outcomes of the similar experiences undergone by their male protagonists suggest what sort of moral and psychological advance had been made by their creator since they were first conceived and written. As *Absalom, Absalom!* represents a vision of new possibilities for Quentin in the intellectual and creative realm not available to him in *The Sound and the Fury*, so *The Unvanquished* envisages, for its closely related protagonist, new opportunities for moral heroism. Bayard's ability to achieve a personal victory over the seductive forces of a flawed but powerful family tradition is a significant measure of how mature Faulkner's own vision had become as he depicted for one last time his personal struggle with an ambiguous heritage. The sense of the past would continue to be an important element in Faulkner's fiction, but it would henceforth be less intense, far more generalized and regional. *The Unvanquished* is Faulkner's final expression of his recurrent attempt to come to terms with his personal family history.

8

Love and Other Destructive Forces:
The Wild Palms and *The Hamlet*

TWO NOVELS PUBLISHED in fairly rapid succession in 1939 and 1940 are singular in Faulkner's canon in that their central focus is on "conventional" heterosexual relationships, which had, in his earlier work, played a minor role or been complicated by incestuous or obsessional elements. *The Wild Palms* is in some ways more intriguing than *The Hamlet,* even though the latter is generally regarded as the finer of the two, because *The Wild Palms* has greater emotional intensity and its personal revelations are more striking. Though it may not measure up artistically to *The Hamlet* or other of Faulkner's great works, *The Wild Palms* has their highly charged psychobiographical component and also shows in an unusual way the author's perpetual interest in technical experimentation with narrative forms. *The Hamlet,* though revealing the same profound ambivalence toward love and lasting liaisons as does *The Wild Palms,* has, as a result of its stylistic and topical range, its use of folk material, and its status as to some degree a compendium of previously written short stories, less the air of being an intensely subjective outpouring.

Oddly enough, *The Wild Palms,* in many ways a fascinating novel, has always received less praise and attention than its immediate successor, probably because of the latter's virtuosity, its rustic humor, and its portrayal of the alarming infiltration of the Snopeses into Sartoris terrain. The tendency to dismiss Faulkner's non-Yoknapatawpha fiction as of secondary interest may also be partly responsible for the unwarranted critical slights *The Wild Palms* has received. Artistically as well as psychological-ly, the novel is well worth careful appraisal and deserving of a wider readership and of a more sympathetic response from its commentators.[1]

Faulkner apparently used his writing of *The Wild Palms,* as he had that of *Sanctuary* and *The Sound and the Fury,* to dramatize disturbing emo-tional problems which he was experiencing even as he worked on the manuscript. In so doing, he may well have hoped to achieve mastery over as well as objectification of them. The tragic story of the romance of Harry Wilbourne and Charlotte Rittenmeyer and its comic antithesis, the "Old Man" tale of the misogynist convict, have a direct relevance to Faulkner's own life in the late 1930s and show his contradictory attitudes toward a ro-mance in which he was involved. The contrapuntal stories of the novel re-veal, strikingly, Faulkner's "two minds" about the effects of passion on his own life. Attraction and repulsion, affirmation and denial, pity and irony—all these polar states find expression in the two tales which com-prise *The Wild Palms* as Faulkner reifies his shifting responses to a prob-lematic personal situation.

The marriage between William Faulkner and Estelle Oldham Franklin, which had taken place in 1929, was rarely blissful and always turbulent. Nonetheless, the couple produced two children, one of whom survived and was well loved, albeit erratically, by her parents. Moreover, Faulkner ob-viously derived satisfaction from the masculine roles peripheral to his mar-riage—the ownership of a gracious home and his position as head of an active, burgeoning family and a staff of servants. He complained a good deal about his economic responsibilities and reiterated his longing for the days when he was a "barefoot tramp," but he luxuriated in the purchase of items ranging from airplanes and horses to handmade shoes and busily bought up all the property adjoining his own to enlarge his little estate. In addition, the psychological rewards of being a patriarchal family man were evident in his fiction, the emotional direction of which changed course shortly after his marriage and moved toward affirmation. Despite these sat-isfactions, however, the marriage itself proved difficult.

William's periodic uproarious alcoholic binges were hardly compatible with Estelle's steadier but equally destructive drinking, and their relation-ship on occasions degenerated into physical violence. Faulkner was very secretive about his private life, but a few times during the mid-1930s he is said to have been seen with painful scratches or bruises which had been in-flicted by Estelle, and at least once she appeared with bruises on her arms which may have been incurred during a marital battle (B, pp. 944–45, 956). Faulkner also told someone that his sexual relationship with Estelle had ended entirely in 1933, after their daughter was born.[2] The things that seemed to keep the couple together were their child, years of habit, and, on Faulkner's part, a sense of honor and a devotion to the idea of marriage as an indissoluble commitment.

The offers from Hollywood that began in 1932, though distasteful to Faulkner as an artist, provided a solution to some of his economic problems and a badly needed respite from his domestic wars. Thus he accepted them with some alacrity, generally going to California alone and remaining away from Mississippi for as long as six months at a stretch. Absence from home hardly offered full resolution of Faulkner's marital difficulties, but it seemed to be the only one he could contemplate at the moment. Moreover, the months of quasi bachelorhood gave him solitude in which to do his own work after hours and an opportunity to think things out.

Hollywood also exposed Faulkner to a wide array of attractive young women, many of whom were impressed by his growing literary reputation and amenable to his shy southern gallantry. Apparently only one of these young women impressed him, however, and that was Howard Hawks's secretary, a lovely blonde divorcée named Meta Carpenter who was, as Faulkner soon discovered, a fellow southerner. He became intimate with her during one of his stints in Hollywood in the mid-1930s. The Faulkner who had always been wary of women and a reluctant suitor now underwent, at least initially, a complete emotional volte-face, throwing himself passionately into this new relationship. He became the compleat romantic, telling Meta that, in the moment he arrived in Hawks's office, "When I stood in that door and saw you, I said to myself, 'There she is!,' " insisting that whatever the circumstances might have been, he knew instantly that she "was the one for him."[3]

Faulkner's ardor was magnified by gratitude, for he apparently regarded the relationship with Meta as a refuge from recent despair and from a Hollywood environment in which he was by no means entirely comfortable. He told her that she had brought him "out of a deep and bottomless pit" and that she kept him "alive and sane" amid the glossy distortions of southern California. After a period of courtship in elegant restaurants, during which Faulkner impressed Meta with his knowledge of fine wines and humorous anecdotes of Mississippi "folk," the two became lovers. The romantic quality of the affair was almost inevitably intensified by the secrecy and "self-isolation" they maintained in the early months. One weekend, at a seaside bungalow, Faulkner strewed their bed with hundreds of fragrant gardenia and jasmine petals in an extravagant gesture of passionate homage.[4]

However clear Faulkner's new self-image as an ardent lover may have been, he had a more confused conception of Meta herself. One moment he treated her as erotically and frankly as D. H. Lawrence's Mellors did Lady Chatterley, writing her letters full of candid sexuality, the next he acted as though she were a maiden, a sweet, tremulous girl for whom appropriate gifts were hair ribbons and puppy dogs.[5] Faulkner's ambivalence was pervasive, affecting not only his views of the lover but even his attitude toward the romance itself. At points he seemed fully committed to the new passion, telling Meta that he was "going to be free soon" and announcing in the Oxford newspaper, "I will not be responsible for any debt incurred or bills made, or notes or checks signed by Mrs. William Faulkner or Estelle Oldham Faulkner,"[6] which made it seem that divorce was imminent. At other times, however, Faulkner asserted that he could not leave Estelle and thus lose control of Jill, that he was "a loving father trying to protect his child,"[7] and although such statements seem somewhat undercut by the fact that he was already away from that child nearly half of the time, a comment he made later about the reason one of his characters did not divorce may well have applied to himself: "She . . . realized that every child, a young girl especially, needed the semblance of an intact home— that is, to have a mother and a father, to have the same things that the other children had," even though that home might be "tragedy ridden" (*FIU*, p. 195).

Whether from concern for his child or ambivalence about the woman he now loved, Faulkner undoubtedly felt reluctant to make his commitment complete and official. The reluctance may have been much like that he had shown in 1929, when he had had to be pressured into marriage. He later told Meta that he actually asked Estelle for a divorce but was forced to back down when she threatened to pauperize him and to drag Meta's name into court as corespondent.[8] This excuse, too, is rather unconvincing, for Faulkner already saw himself, albeit inaccurately, as a perennial pauper, and Meta had already survived the rigors of one divorce and was likely to be willing to risk being named in court if the stakes were sufficiently high.

Unable to work his problems out directly, Faulkner turned, as he had before, to writing as his means of contemplating and confronting personal difficulties. He began work on *The Wild Palms* and, in a pattern comprehensible perhaps only in and to a committed artist, started to leave the lovemaking and the woman he supposedly adored early each evening in order to go home and write about them. Art offered a means toward an "answer" which life did not, and Faulkner gradually "became obsessed with the novel'' to the detriment of his romance.[9] Not too surprisingly, Meta grew increasingly frustrated and finally relinquished her hopes altogether. In 1937 she married a young concert pianist, and Faulkner embarked on a prolonged and destructive drinking spree to assuage his grief. His destructive behavior continued, and some months later, when Meta saw Faulkner in New York for the first time after her marriage, he had incurred a terrible third-degree burn from falling when drunk against a steam pipe. It seared the flesh on his back almost to the spine and gave him a wound which bothered him for the rest of his life and produced complaints of ''nerves frayed from . . . pretty constant pain and inability to sleep'' (*L*, p. 105). The ex-lovers kept in touch for many years afterward, with Faulkner maintaining a sexual loyalty to Meta that apparently made him impotent with anyone else for a time.[10] But they never again recaptured the ardor of their first period together, settling instead for a loving but erratic friendship, while Faulkner's attention eventually became fixed on another attractive young woman.

Although it bears some striking likenesses to Ernest Hemingway's story of runaway lovers, *A Farewell to Arms*, *The Wild Palms* is fully and directly related to this passionate episode in Faulkner's life. Faulkner betrays his hesitancy by being less sympathetic to his lovers than was Hemingway, and the passion pursued in isolation proves as destructive as it is regenerative. At the same time, the piercing pain of Harry and Charlotte's portion of the novel is obviously a product of the physical and emotional pain suffered by Faulkner after the romance reached an impasse and Meta married someone else. He told a friend that it was written ''to stave off what I thought was heart-break'' and admitted to his publisher that the turmoil had seriously affected his artistic judgment, that ''I have lived for the last six months in such a peculiar state of family complications and back complications that I still am not able to tell if the novel is all right or absolute drivel'' (*L*, pp. 338, 106). His working title for the book was *If I Forget Thee, Jerusalem*, a phrase from Psalm 137 about the necessary persistence in memory of an object of loyalty, and even though he had found himself unable to make a full-scale commitment to Meta Carpenter, his anguish over their first breakup was never totally alleviated. More than ten years later, he told her that his unhappiness was still powerful: ''I know grief is the inevictable part of it, the thing that makes it cohere; that grief is the only thing you are capable of sustaining, keeping; that what is valuable is what you have lost, since then you never had the chance to wear out and so lose it shabbily.''[11] The passage offers eloquent testimony to the enduring nature of his pain, but it also discloses the way in which the memory of the romance, now past and inviolate, was somehow preferable to the relationship as an ongoing reality with discernible flaws.

Faulkner apparently was most comfortable with his women when they were at a safe distance, offering inspiration for his art and serving as recipients for his often beautifully written letters, and he was less able to deal effectively with them at firsthand. Meta Carpenter has commented on the way in which, with her, Faulkner was sometimes "restrained, remote," silent inside "the insularity that he drew over himself like a second, tougher skin," from which he "tithe[d] to her "small fragments of information." She began to feel she knew him intimately only when he started to write her letters from two thousand miles away, letters in which he poured out ideas and emotions with a warmth and openness of which he was incapable in person. "I knew more about him through his letters from Oxford than through any confidences he granted when he was in Hollywood," where he "was largely a cipher to me," she later admitted.[12]

The Wild Palms embodies Faulkner's paradoxical attitude toward the woman he loved, for Harry's passion becomes forceful and eloquent in the fullest sense only after Charlotte has died and is thus irrevocably (and perhaps safely) out of his life. The ambivalence of Faulkner's response to the affair is revealed in a number of ways in the novel, the most fundamental of which resides in the narrative technique. He presents two alternated stories about "two types of love," in which the experiences of the male protagonists represent his own two-sided reaction to his recent romance. As Faulkner described it, "one man gave up everything for love of a woman, the other gave everything up to get away from love" (*LIG*, p. 54). In a way, Faulkner himself did both. He threw himself into the affair like Harry Wilbourne, then escaped like the tall convict, though with more typically Faulknerian passivity, and finally ended up in his own self-made prison, "trapped in Oxford," as he said soon afterward.[13] Significantly, both stories, and thus both modes of response, conclude with their protagonists in prison, as though Faulkner realized that there was no possibility of escape from the dilemma with which his romance presented him.

Faulkner uses a unique method to present his dualistic vision of the difficulties, even destruction, wrought by the journey toward or away from love. There is no direct counterpart in either English or American fiction for this structure with its intertwined chapters of opposing narratives. The personal motives that led him to try this unusual experiment now seem obvious, but the manner in which he carried it out does not. In early 1939, Faulkner told an interviewer that he wrote one of the stories and then the other and interleaved the chapters "like shuffling a deck of cards" (*LIG*, p. 36). This seems far less likely an approach than sequential writing, for the chapters show an adroit mixture of likenesses and dissimilarities that substantiates the idea that they were done "in counterpoint." Faulkner said in 1955 that after he had written the first portion of "The Wild Palms," "I realized suddenly that something was missing, it needed emphasis, something to lift it like counterpoint in music. So I wrote on the 'Old Man' story until 'The Wild Palms' story rose back to pitch" (*LIG*, p. 247). That same year he went on to refute his earlier assertion that the narratives had been done separately. "I did not write these two stories and then cut one into the other. I wrote them as you read it, as the chapters," he said, and again stressed the concept of "counterpoint."[14]

What he had also probably realized after beginning his tragic tale of the doomed lovers was that the vision it presented was incomplete and thus somehow dishonest, that what was needed was a complementary vision at once more negative and more bitterly comic. Faulkner was nearly always honest in his fictional self-presentation, insofar as he dramatized both sides in one way or another, and the extraordinary narrative technique of *The Wild Palms* is only an amplification of that urge toward dramatic balance. The two stories embody the thesis and antithesis of Faulkner's inner dialectic about romantic entanglement, although the possibility of any real synthesis forever eluded him.

The story of Harry and Charlotte is clearly more important than "Old Man," despite the fact that Malcolm Cowley and others have found the latter the more effective of the two.[15] Faulkner later asserted that "The Wild Palms" was the pivotal narrative in the volume, that there "are only two stories by chance, perhaps necessity. The story is that of Charlotte and Wilbourne" (*LIG*, p. 248). "Old Man," in spite of its appeal as a piece of folk comedy with resonant overtones of myth, serves primarily as a foil to the first work, modifying and enclosing the doomed lovers' descent to death and personal purgatory.

A number of elements common to both stories give *The Wild Palms* a unity that is not always immediately obvious. There is the same configuration of characters in each—a woman, her male companion, and an observer-reverberator. The journey motif is essential to each story. Birth, either thwarted or actual, is a pivotal event, and time is the omnipresent enemy. In the background of each story is a natural force—the thrashing wild palms, the thundering river—which serves as an objective correlative of the turmoil within the protagonists and as a reminder of the primal power of nature, of which any man is a potential victim. Despite these many similarities between the two "halves," however, the differences are also crucial and underscore the way in which "The Wild Palms" is both the more human and the more personal of the two.

Charlotte Rittenmeyer, for example, is a more richly developed individual and a more realistic figure than the woman of "Old Man," with as many flaws as she has strengths. Charlotte seems to have been based on Helen Baird, the woman in whom Faulkner was interested in the mid-1920s,[16] rather than on the more ethereal Meta Carpenter, and she is well defined, both physically and emotionally. Charlotte is broad and not pretty and has a face that has been scarred by a childhood burn, but she is attractive in the heavy way "Arabian mares" are (38).[17] She is related to other Faulknerian heroines like Caddy Compson and Temple Drake, for Charlotte is the one girl in a family of brothers, one of whose roommates she married because "you cant sleep with your brother" (40). She is also rather masculine, like Joe Christmas's nemesis, Joanna Burden: she looks at Harry Wilbourne "with speculative sobriety like a man might" and takes his wrist with "a grasp simple, ruthless and firm" (39).

Although Charlotte is not conventionally attractive, Faulkner develops her into a figure both singular and compelling, more forceful in her idealism and strong-mindedness than any young woman who had appeared in his fiction up to this point. She has, unusually for a Faulknerian female, a vocation, being a working artist whose periods of nearly fanatic commitment recall Gordon of *Mosquitoes*. A sculptor, she appears admirable at times for her efforts to capture in her work "the motion, the speed" (100), although what she makes is small and rather trivial and one critic of the novel characterizes her artistry "either a complete lie or the dilettantish dabbling of a pseudo-sophisticate."[18] Whatever the value of her work, she is principled and articulate, qualities that also differentiate her from most young women in Faulkner's earlier fiction. She refuses a "back-alley" rendezvous with Harry and expounds her concept that "love and suffering are the same thing and . . . the value of love is the sum of what you have to pay for it" (46, 48), an idea she adheres to with unswerving devotion, even though it proves to have painful consequences.

Charlotte's commitment to the relationship is immediate and wholehearted, leading her to abandon her husband and children, and she develops into a figure more complex and tragic than almost any other Faulknerian heroine. She is like Thomas Sutpen in being a person whose demands on the world are too great and whose vision is powerful but flawed. Although she has a dream that is in some ways affirmative, believing utterly in her ideal that "it's got to be all honeymoon, always. Forever

and ever, until one of us dies'' (83), she is again like Sutpen in her frequent
blindness to reality, as in her belief that ''when people loved, hard, really
loved each other, they didn't have children, the seed got burned up in the
love, the passion'' (205), and in her vision's component of inhumanity: she
is all too ready to give up the children of her first marriage and to destroy
the embryonic child within her in order to achieve her romantic isolation
with Harry. She succeeds, like Sutpen, in bringing about her own destruction. But even at the moment of death she makes a last ardent testimonial to
the significance of her passion. With her fatal toxemia well advanced,
Charlotte asks her legal husband to spare Harry from punishment ''for the
sake of all the men and women who ever lived and blundered but meant the
best and all that ever will love and blunder but mean the best'' (225). Charlotte dies painfully, but the strength implicit in her efforts to make passion
a credo and a way of life remains moving and impressive. Despite its
flaws, her vision is a powerful one, and she emerges as a heroine of almost
tragic grandeur. At the same time, her stature is undermined at many
points, not only by her own harsh manner and physical unattractiveness,
but also by the jaundiced generalizations about women which issue from
Wilbourne. Looking at Charlotte, he muses on at least two occasions in uncomplimentary fashion about women's ''instinctive proficiency in and rap-
port for the mechanics of cohabitation'' (54), their ''[dis]regard for the intrinsic value of the medium which they saved or squandered,'' and their
unerring desire for ''respectability within the milieu in which they lived''
(81–82).

Although Faulkner thus makes Charlotte as distasteful as she is attractive
to both Harry and the reader and suggests at one point that she represents
''the entire female principle'' (57), he does develop her fully into an intriguing individual. The nameless woman of ''Old Man,'' on the other
hand, remains little more than an embodiment of the eternal Female, put on
earth solely to harass the misogynist convict. She first appears as a plain
country woman ''who could have been his sister if he had a sister'' (148);
but she rapidly becomes, in her pregnant state, a symbolic burden with
whom he is trapped in a runaway boat. Despite her stolid acceptance of her
plight and her triumph over the obstacles nature has placed in her way, the
woman never achieves autonomy as a character, perhaps because Faulkner
had already vividly created a similar female, Lena Grove. In ''Old Man,''
the woman exists primarily as a product of the convict's distorted vision.
He comes to see her as ''one single inert monstrous sentient womb'' (163)
and later as a ''millstone'' for whom he feels only ''savage and horrified
revulsion'' (335).

Though the females of the stories are quite different—Charlotte complexly human, the woman abstract, almost mythic—the men are essentially alike, American Adams who "fall" into entanglement with their Eves and are expelled from their monastic Edens. Harry's experience seems to be a version of that undergone by Faulkner in the mid-1930s, while that of the convict represents, in a way, Faulkner's afterthoughts on the experience. The basic likenesses between the men themselves suggest that they are meant to represent the two sides of Faulkner-in-love.[19] They are the same age, both are innocent about the ways of women, and both emerge sadder but wiser from their momentous confrontations with the Female.

Harry Wilbourne has had no time or money for women. His energy has been poured into reading his medical books and balancing his bankbooks. Though meeting Charlotte eventually catapults him into an existence at once passionate and nomadic, he is at first passive. It is Charlotte who openly acknowledges their affinity and virtually takes command of the relationship. "She held him" (92) in an action both physical and symbolic, for Charlotte supports them financially and directs their moves from place to place, until Harry admits that "she's a better man than I am" (133). He is forced at last to compromise his ideas about fulfilling work and begins writing for confession magazines, just as Faulkner had to continue the script writing he found so distasteful in order to stay with the woman he loved and to survive financially.

Harry reveals, moreover, a basic ambivalence about passion which may reflect Faulkner's own. Like many of the author's earlier male characters, Harry associates sex with death in his description of lovemaking as feeling "all your life rush out of you into the pervading immemorial blind receptive matrix, the hot fluid blind foundation—grave-womb or womb-grave, it's all one" (138). He is, however, gradually converted to a "boundless faith" (85) in Charlotte's religion of love. He becomes an active crusader for the ideal, initiating the move to Utah and to the illusory "freedom" they now both desire. But Charlotte's stronger personality still dominates him, making him capitulate to her demand for an abortion. When the abortion causes Charlotte's death, Harry becomes one of Faulkner's "crucified" heroes. Looking at Harry's pain, his doctor neighbor thinks that there must be "Limits! To . . . love and passion and tragedy which is allowed to anyone lest he become as God Who has suffered" (280). As if he has assimilated Charlotte's almost masculine strength of character and her full commitment to a dream, as if he has somehow "become" her in her absence, Harry loses his last vestige of weakness and assumes a stoic fortitude, resolutely refusing to escape either by jumping bail or by taking cyanide.

Harry thus becomes a witness, a spokesman for their passion even more eloquent than Charlotte. Alone, he asserts his need to survive because "there's got to be the old meat, the old frail eradicable meat for memory to titillate" (316). In a moving passage he affirms that "when she became not then half of memory became not and if I become not then all of remembering will cease to be.—Yes, . . . between grief and nothing I will take grief" (324). Harry's poignant last words became part of Faulkner's ardent testimony to his own lover after she had "abandoned" him, and they are perhaps his best-known lines. Passion proves a painful experience for Harry, as it had for Faulkner, but it moves him to both resoluteness and eloquence, and, by the end of the novel, to a level of tragic splendor earlier achieved only by Charlotte.

If the suffering of Harry Wilbourne represents Faulkner's romantic-tragic view of his love affair, the desperate efforts of the convict to escape the woman with whom he has been flung by fate represent Faulkner's inner repudiation of that affair. The convict has already had, before the narrative begins, a Wilbourne-like experience that has made him a woman-hater. Inspired by his reading of pulp romances and his devotion to a girl "with ripe breasts and a heavy mouth and dull eyes like ripe muscadines," he had futilely tried to rob a train. The realization that "if it had not been for her he would not actually have attempted it" (338) now coexists with his bitter memory of her decampment. Her postcard announcing "this is where were honnymonning at. Your friend (Mrs) Vernon Waldrip" (339) may be Faulkner's satiric version of Meta's announcement that she was about to marry another man. As Faulkner later said of his hapless convict-hero, "The insecurity came to him with a shock when that woman betrayed him, and he was frightened and he wanted to be where no other woman could catch him off balance and take him over the jumps again" (*FIU*, p. 175).

Prison becomes for the convict a haven from any further destructive exposure to female wiles. When fate again places him in the path of a woman, one about to give birth, he yearns only to be back in prison, to "return to that monastic existence of shotguns and shackls" (153), but his efforts to surrender are comically foiled. The woman becomes a weighty and inescapable burden, and the convict begins his enforced mock-heroic odyssey. If Wilbourne's name suggests his venture beyond the pale in pursuit of passion, the convict, too, moves into a "bourne" beyond civilization and "beyond any more amazement" (174). Relieved when he is finally recaptured, the convict surrenders his charges and summarizes his near-epic ordeal in a masterful piece of comic understatement: "Yonder's your boat, and here's the woman. But I never did find that bastard on the cottonhouse" (278).

Back in prison, the convict recounts his view of woman as an affliction from which he is delighted to be free. Despite the sexual deprivation involved in "ten more years without a woman," he spits out the judgment that becomes the last word of the novel and thus serves as Faulkner's concluding statement on the subject, "Women, shit!" (339).[20] Both the devoted tragic lover Harry Wilbourne and the woman-hating convict are doomed. They can neither escape with nor escape from women, and the novel ends with both in the penitentiary at Parchman either affirming or repudiating their entanglements with the female principle.

Charlotte's little statue called "The Bad Smell" represents the idea common to both stories that love is metaphorically like the ocean in one respect—"if you begin to make a bad smell in it, it just spews you up somewhere to die" (83), as Charlotte melodramatically expresses it. Yet the Bad Smell is an ineradicable part of terrestrial experience, as the men so painfully learn. The hunger for commitment to an ideal of romance or to a specific woman exists in both men, but the flawed nature of mankind in general and woman in particular militates against the fulfillment of that hunger. Harry is innocently laudable in his conversion to Charlotte's boundless faith in love, and the convict equally so in his desire to seem knightly to his young girlfriend, but both are defeated by the nature of the women with whom they are involved. Harry's first love is too idealistic, and the convict's is too mercenary, and both prove in some way destructive, at least in the sense that each romance ends with the man's incarceration.

The Bad Smell is a signifier of the unavoidable decay from within, the almost inevitable doom of every passion. Its message must be heeded or penalties will have to be paid. Harry and Charlotte err when they give the little statue away and thus lose the necessary reminder of their potential for failure. The convict made his error early when he was blind to the flaws of his train-robbing plan and of the woman who provoked it. Both men spend the rest of their lives paying the price for having neglected the reality that threatens any love relation, whether noble or ordinary. Passion can be destructive when it closes a man's eyes to the implications of his commitment, and women can be womb-graves, alarming in their mystery and comprehensible perhaps only at the moment of defeat and death.

The dual narrative of The Wild Palms is Faulkner's unhappy comment on the pain awaiting any man who involves himself with a woman, pain which counterbalances the pleasures of committed fulfillment and reflects the author's responses to his own love affair. Despite the tragic grandeur of "The Wild Palms," that story, as well as its comic anodyne, "Old Man," betrays Faulkner's sense that women can be death-containing as well as life-giving. His perpetual ambivalence about the female principle revealed itself subtly in his personal vacillation about the woman who awakened his ardor, and more openly in the double tragic-comic stories of his unusual novel. Harry Wilbourne discovers the richness and affirmation implicit in embracing both a woman and an enveloping vision of passion, but Harry's poignant homage to his lost love, "Between grief and nothing, I will take grief," competes with the convict's more pithy and realistic, "Women, shit." Both stories convey the message that woman are Eve-figures and that romance may end in solitary incarceration, with only the haunting pain of memory to attest I-loved, I-am.

The Hamlet, the first volume of Faulkner's trilogy about the Snopeses, seems quite different from *The Wild Palms.* Drawn from material first conceived in the 1920s, it begins a saga that is the most extended of Faulkner's fictional endeavors, depicting a large cast of characters and dramatizing a broad spectrum of private and public issues over a period of several decades. Yet *The Hamlet* continues the bleak commentary begun by Faulkner in his previous work about the penalties incurred by a commitment to passion. The novel includes a series of what one might call "love stories," a group of tales about five actual or thwarted liaisons. The first three stories are essentially comic, the fourth receives a poetic treatment, and the last has a tragic aura. Faulkner carries off this mixture of modes with great stylistic virtuosity while managing to achieve a large degree of narrative unity because the stories themselves offer a combination of likenesses and contrasts. Although *The Hamlet* is a rich work, it lacks the single focus of *The Wild Palms,* since the theme of defeated passion is complicated by the factors of economics and moralism. One sees here in its first manifestation the broadening and enrichment of the fictional canvas that was to mark much of Faulkner's late work.

Still, *The Hamlet* has important links to Faulkner's personal preoccupations at this stage of his life. The addition of unhappy love stories to the basic Snopes material, which he had had around for more than a decade,[21] suggests, for example, a continuing need to repudiate the romance for which he nearly ended his marriage. Indeed, despite its pervasive folk humor, *The Hamlet* makes an even darker statement on the topic of romance than its predecessor. The romantic liaisons pictured either are ludicrous or have been terminated by death; the only two with any poignancy are that between the idiot and his cow, which is sodomistic, and that between Houston and his wife, which is already long in the past. Even more important, the females in each are almost totally mindless, either literally or figuratively bovine. None has the strength and individuality of Charlotte Rittenmeyer of *The Wild Palms*.

Eula Varner, the woman in two of the relationships, is as inert and uninteresting as "a foetus" (96),[22] even though she suggests the sexual abundance of "old Dionysic *[sic]* times—honey in sunlight and bursting grapes, the writhen bleeding of the crushed fecundated vine beneath the hard rapacious trampling goat-hoof" (95). Houston's wife seems more "ordinarily" female, demure and devoted, but exists primarily as a being to whom Houston feels "chained" during the long years when he attempts to escape her influence. After her death, she becomes almost indeterminate, someone whose absence he grieves in "black, savage, indomitable fidelity" (205) but who herself has lost reality as an individual. Mink Snope's wife is, at least when we first meet her, a nymphomaniac whom he married out of what he characterizes as sexual "addiction" and who accepted him for pragmatic reasons, and Ike Snope's beloved is a cow. About the time *The Hamlet* was published, Faulkner made the dismissive judgment that "a woman should know only how to do three things—tell the truth, ride a horse and sign a check" *(LIG,* p. 45). His sense of having been somehow betrayed by Meta led him to increasingly bitter indictments of all females, and *The Hamlet* reveals a vision of women darker than it had been just a year or two before, a result of the author's overreaction to his failed romantic involvement.

Two other elements in the novel, the preoccupation with economics and the concern for conscience, are also related to specific events in Faulkner's personal life: he had just completed his revenge on a Snopes-figure in his own life and was himself showing a Snopes-like obsession with money, even as his conscience became awakened to general injustices. Faulkner told an interviewer shortly before this book appeared that the Snopeses crept over the town "lahk *[sic]* mold over cheese" *(LIG,* p. 39). To his readers, the Snopeses have become the symbol of the destruction of the old order by the new and of the triumph of rapacity, but Faulkner's own increasing monetary concern and some of his actions during this period seem faintly Snopesish. Faulkner's grandfather, John Wesley Thompson Falkner, had been ousted from his bank years before by a shrewd bow-tie-wearing countryman named Joe Parks,[23] and the author carried out a double-barreled symbolic revenge on Parks. Its most enduring form was Faulkner's portrayal of his grandfather's usurper as the odious Flem Snopes, but he had also, in a way, usurped the usurper in 1938 by buying Parks's farm outside Oxford with money received from the sale of one of his novels to Hollywood. Faulkner named the place, with possible intentional irony, Greenfield Farm and installed as its manager John Faulkner, describing the latter as "another indigent brother with wife and two children" whom he had just "inherited" (B, p. 1000).

Faulkner's art thus served as one form of retaliation and acted also as the pecuniary means for displacing a threatening interloper. Yet Faulkner has some likeness to Flem Snopes in his efforts to establish his relative on a recently acquired property, and the whole episode has an amusing Snopes-like tinge to it. Faulkner also became increasingly preoccupied with money, and his letters to his agent and publisher focus on little else. In a typical request, Faulkner asked Random House for a $500 advance on *The Hamlet,* admitting that "this is a nuisance to you and a damned nuisance to me. I'm going to take about six months of next year and try to write stuff that will make me a bank account for a little while"; before long he was even asking his agent for money to pay his electric bill *(L,* p. 116). Faulkner's responsibilities were large and he was at times almost criminally underpaid, but he was never quite as poor as he sounded in these letters. He made a great deal of money in Hollywood, bought several important pieces of property during the 1930s as well as large luxury items—even an airplane—kept several servants, and often exulted in being "lord of the whole damned manor."[24] While Flem Snopes was beginning his ominous rise to power, Faulkner was experiencing economic triumphs of his own that bear certain likenesses to those of his fictional villain, even though Faulkner himself was primarily motivated not by greed but by a series of heavy personal obligations.

A third important element in *The Hamlet* had its source in Faulkner's personal life, the outspoken voice of conscience makes its appearance in the character of V. K. Ratliff, the itinerant sewing maching salesman. A Ratliff-like figure had appeared briefly in Faulkner's third novel, and moral spokesmen had been central in Faulkner's great fiction of the late twenties and early thirties—figures like Dilsey, Cash Bundren, and Byron Bunch come to mind—but they had other narrative and symbolic functions as well and were intimately associated with the other characters. Their moral function was relatively subtle. Ratliff, on the other hand, is almost an allegorical figure, conscience personified. He remains outside the action for the most part, commenting on the morality or lack of it evinced in the human transactions around him. He has no family and few strong ties and wanders his four counties rather like an itinerant preacher exhorting his flock to decency and uprightness. Ratliff is an engaging figure, intelligent and given to succinct comic statements on human folly, but he is also more moralistic and less directly involved than earlier such characters. He is, relatively, a new type in Faulkner's fiction, one inspired perhaps by the author's own increasing sense of moral obligation.

At this point Faulkner's confidence in the importance of his art was being substantiated by public acceptance, and he dutifully responded with actions of conscience. Faulkner sent the manuscript of *The Hamlet* off to his publisher with the assertion that "I am the best in America, by God" (*L*, p. 113), and America, both highbrow and middlebrow, reacted with formal praise. The prestigious National Institute of Arts and Letters elected him to membership in early 1939 and almost simultaneously a popular magazine, *Time*, put his picture on its cover. Faulkner in turn showed a new sense of moral-political commitment by giving the precious manuscript of *Absalom, Absalom!* to a group which was trying to raise money for the Spanish Loyalist cause with his permission to sell it and use the proceeds as they saw fit. He spoke publicly on behalf of a cause for the first time, expressing "wish to go on record as being unalterably opposed to Franco and fascism, to all violations of the legal government and outrages against the people of Republican Spain."[25] Faulkner also made an economic commitment to a private cause when he came to the financial rescue of Phil Stone at a difficult time. Despite Stone's disparaging public comments about him, Faulkner asserted that in their lifelong friendship there was "never any question of mine and thine between us when either had it" and raised $6000 for Stone from his publisher and his own life insurance (*L*, p. 111).

Despite these contemporary resonances, the Snopes trilogy had of course evolved from an embryonic novel called "Father Abraham" which Faulkner began in late 1926. Before abandoning the project, he wrote twenty-five pages about the rise of Flem Snopes from poverty to the presidency of a bank and about the sale of the wild horses from Texas (B, pp. 528–29). That work was never published, but it contained the germ of three substantial novels. As time went on, Faulkner would increasingly turn back to early "source works" like "Father Abraham" for inspiration, and he conceived almost no fiction that was fully "new" after the early 1930s. This is a testimony to the rich suggestiveness of Faulkner's early fiction, but it also makes a poignant comment on his growing inability to find new ideas. It was primarily during those early years, when he was anxiety-ridden, celibate, and isolated in his attic room at his parents' house in Oxford or in narrow quarters in New Orleans or Paris, that Faulkner discovered the welter of ideas which would grow into a lifetime's production of major fiction.

Critical disputes have been going on for nearly two decades about whether *The Hamlet,* with its disparate narratives and tonal variations, is a fully organic structure.[26] Certainly the individual episodes have numerous interrelationships and the thematic focus on romantic and economic transactions gives them a common ground. Still, just how much more wide-ranging and less intricately woven it is than, say, *The Sound and the Fury* can be seen by comparing the four-panel structures common to both novels. Each exhibits versatility of style and mode, but the 1929 novel concentrates on one family, specifically the children in that family and their emotional responses to their parents and their crises; the children are closely interconnected psychologically and symbolically, their consciousnesses are explored fully, and the precipitating events viewed and reviewed from a variety of angles. By contrast, the very title of *The Hamlet* implies its broader focus and looser interconnections—its multiple families, its series of love stories, and its treatment of economic and communal issues that include barn burning, horse trading, usury, the acquisition of property, litigation, barter, and larcenous attempts of various sorts. Whether such amplification necessarily results in the attentuation of aesthetic coherence remains a moot point. What is clear, however, is that the delving into the darker regions of the psyche which gave previous works like *The Sound and the Fury, As I Lay Dying,* and *Absalom, Absalom!* their troubling power is almost entirely absent from *The Hamlet.* The most intriguing relationships of the novel, those between Houston and Mink Snopes and between each man and his wife, which might well have been at the center of an earlier work, are not developed with particular fullness in *The Hamlet.*

Jack Houston is a figure of emotional grandeur and Mink Snopes one of Faulkner's most memorable monomaniacs, but only a few tantalizing pages are devoted to their complex psyches. Houston, in his perpetual fury and reluctant compassion, seems to be a combination of Jewel, Cash, and Darl Bundren or of Joe Christmas, Byron Bunch, and Hightower, for he is at once violent, caring, and detached. His contempt ''for all blind flesh capable of hope and grief'' (188) allows him to impound Mink Snopes's cow in an action that ultimately causes his own death; yet his pity leads him with an oddly furious sympathy, to turn over his own cow to the love-besotted idiot Ike Snopes. Houston's psychological profile is complicated. Like Joe Christmas, he resists ''enslavement'' by a woman; he and Lucy Pate become bound in an antagonism of ''implacable constancy and invincible repudiation'' (206) from which he flees, like Joe, to refuge with a whore. Unlike Joe, Houston eventually matures and embraces his woman-fate, but he is again like Joe in causing her death: memories of his former lust for freedom lead him to buy a fierce stallion, an emblem of the "bitless masculinity which he had relinquished," and his wife fatally projects Houston's "taming" onto his horse (214–15).

Mink Snopes appears in *The Hamlet* as the agent of Houston's death, and he will later, in *The Mansion,* be more fully developed and prove the nemesis of his cousin Flem Snopes. Mink is a paranoid monomaniac who focuses first on the "wrong" he suffers when Houston impounds his cow and then on his "betrayal" by Flem, who fails to appear at his murder trial. Yet Mink also has an innocence which links him to a previous Faulkner character, Thomas Sutpen. Mink is blind to the punitive nature of society's laws in his murderous obsession with his grievance against Houston, and blind to his opportunity for plunder when he fails to remove from Houston's corpse the fifty dollars he is known to carry. Such realities never enter Mink's singleminded and somehow "innocent"—even principled— consideration of the issue, just as later, during his trial for murder, thoughts of his impending punishment never blur his focus on the desire for Flem's return. Though a killer, Mink makes claims on our sympathy which Faulkner would develop even further in *The Mansion.* In *The Hamlet,* he amplifies our response to Mink by giving him a slight aura of vulnerability and by portraying his past and present relationship with his wife. Mink's extreme smallness makes him ominous, "curious sidling deadly" (74), but also "hardly larger than a child" (332), with a child's defenselessness. He is further humanized by his ardor for his wife. After years of marriage, he still seeks her body addictively, "like drink. It's like dope to me" (221). Mink's attraction to her was strong and instantaneous, but the circumstances of their marriage relate it to the dominant economic theme of the book, in that it was occasioned by "the collapse of her father's enterprise" (238). Yet despite the pragmatic nature of their union and the occasional ensuing violence between them, the relationship is, in its way, solid, and during Mink's trial his wife is as patient and as devoted as is Ruby Lamar to Lee Goodwin in *Sanctuary.*

Both Mink and Houston are fascinating characters, and Faulkner's portrayal of their complex responses to the world and to each other could in itself have provided a powerful novel. He chose instead to concentrate the bulk of *The Hamlet* on Flem Snopes's rise to economic power in Frenchman's Bend and his concomitant acquisition of the most attractive woman in the town for a wife, and on the contrapuntal story of Ike and his cow. This portion of the novel offers comedy, social satire, and in the case of Ike and the cow, lyricism and pathos, but its central characters are both more opaque and less interesting than either Houston or Mink Snopes. Only Labove, the hapless schoolteacher whose story is a comic analogue of Houston's, has anywhere near the complex humanity of the other two men. In *The Hamlet,* Labove's tale functions much as did the convict's in *The Wild Palms*—as a humorous counterpart to a romantic tragedy. Labove and Houston both attempt to escape their female fate and then to embrace it, but both meet defeat.

Labove's story contains allusions to, and is obviously meant as a modern version of, Washington Irving's "The Legend of Sleepy Hollow,"[27] for in Irving's story romance and finance are intertwined in the same way as they are in *The Hamlet* as a whole. Labove's plight as a contemporary and equally comic Ichabod Crane, with its foreshadowing of Houston's later tragedy, plays a complicated role in *The Hamlet.* Like Ichabod Crane, Labove is a schoolteacher, and like Houston, he meets in a schoolroom the woman with whom he becomes obsessed; physically, he combines the aura of power associated with Houston with the gauntness of Crane. Labove's obsession with his young charge is far more intense than Crane's with Katrina Van Tassel—Crane seeks only comfort and appeasement of his insatiable appetite for food—but both romances are thwarted in a comic rout as Crane is dispatched by Brom Bones and Labove by the disdainful Eula herself, who says, "Stop pawing me, you old headless horseman Ichabod Crane" (122).

Although the connections of this episode with the Irving story are explicit and suggestive, Labove is singularly Faulknerian in the persistence and painful ambivalence of his obsession. Labove's monastic study of law has made him, like Harry Wilbourne of *The Wild Palms* and like the author himself, both remote from and peculiarly vulnerable to females. After Labove first sees Eula in his schoolroom, he watches her for five emotion-filled years, first with what he thinks is anger at her total inertia, but later with what he discovers is not "rage at all but terror" (117). Now school becomes "his Gethsemane" and "his Golgotha too" (118) as Labove struggles with his attraction to Eula. At last, "mad" with desire, he physicaly embraces her, only to meet with a defeat that is a comic version of the tragic ending to Houston's story of confrontation with his female "nemesis."

Labove is the first of several suitors of the beautiful Eula Varner, who remains, like the forces of nature to which she is compared, equally indifferent to all of them and as potentially destructive as a whirlpool, a "mortal natural enemy of the masculine race" (149). Faulkner's depiction of her is uncertain, as with most of his nubile women, but Eula's protean quality in *The Hamlet* is directly attributable to the fact that we see her from a series of male perspectives. Their varying judgments exalt her at points into a mythic Helen-figure and at others deride her as no more than an "unawares bitch" who exudes "too much of mammalian female meat" (130, 100). Eula is, however, splendidly attractive in her way, and it is deeply and even shockingly ironic that, after her impregnation, her father should "hire" the froglike and, as we learn in a later volume of the trilogy, impotent Flem Snopes, the man least suited by nature to match her natural splendor, to marry her. Economics rule the day in the mercenary world of Frenchman's Bend, and the physical odiousness of the financially promising clerk does not prevent his being chosen as prince consort.

Flem is a Popeye-like villain, sexually impotent and thinglike, his eyes "the color of stagnant water" and his face "as blank as a pan of uncooked dough" (22); he is also suggestive of the author himself, with his shortness and "tiny predatory nose like the beak of a small hawk" (51). Flem, like nearly all of the Snopeses, is morally as well as physically stunted, undertaking his ruthless rise to economic ascendancy like a "spider" awaiting his victims (58). Psychologically, however, Flem remains opaque throughout the entire Snopes trilogy. Though Faulkner had shown an awareness of the inadequacy of such portrayal when he added his important "epilogue" to *Sanctuary,* he repeated his mistake with Flem Snopes, who remains enigmatic, almost a symbol of pure greed, throughout the three volumes. Why Faulkner denied those psychological "explanations" to Flem is mysterious, for he created "rounded" portraits of Mink and even of Ab, the barn-burning Snopes, who proves not "naturally mean" but "just soured" (27) once his past history is explored. We are never given insight into either Flem's thoughts or his motivations, and the sources of his inhuman ambition remain puzzling. Faulkner's omission may be related to his wish to punish himself for his own Flem tendencies, his periodic preoccupation with acquisition and finance.

Flem's wife, Eula, is in this novel an equally opaque figure, and Faulkner sharply underscores her inertly bovine nature by following her story with one in which the feminine "ideal" is an actual cow. Ike's cow is never named or described, but Ike is as devoted to it as Eula's suitors are to her, and the parallels are clearly intended. Ike may be an idiot, but he is like Eula's first suitor, Labove, in his innocence of the world and his ardent focus on his desire. Ike waits for the cow to arrive, "serene and one and indivisible in joy, listening to her approach" (165), and Houston's reference to the cow as "you damn whore" (175) serves to increase the anthropomorphic nature of her emotional significance for Ike. Ike's elope-ment with his beloved is a true idyll, one that recalls Charlotte and Harry's interlude at the Wisconsin cabin away from the destructive forces of civilization.

Faulkner expends some of his most magnificent lyrical writing on Ike's "romance" with the cow—his description of Ike's experience of dawn is among the finest passages of its sort in his work—but the ugly conclusion of this episode, with the prurient villagers spying on the sexual encounters between Ike and his beloved and the brutality of their "moral" decision to kill the cow and feed it to Ike in order to "cure" him of his obsession, makes one cognizant of the misanthropy inherent in Faulkner's use of his splendid powers at their highest level to portray the futile love of an idiot for a brute. The literary "elevation" of Ike and the cow to the pantheon of great lovers exists in ironic tension with our awareness that in normal human terms they have no right to be lovers at all.

Just before this section opens, Ratliff expresses his "outrage at the waste, the useless squandering" (159) represented by Eula's marriage to Flem, and one suspects that Faulkner is subtly doing another sort of squandering to express his bleak vision of the potential for real love between ordinary human beings. Every romance meets an unfortunate end and every lover is, finally, almost as pathetic as the idiot Ike, last seen with his "devastated eyes" playing abjectly with the wooden effigy of a cow given to him as a replacement for the living animal that has been destroyed. Ike is completely a victim of "civilized" society's harsh disregard of individual human desires, but even those characters with apparent freedom and full intelligence fare little better, falling prey to their own weaknesses. Even Houston, for all his passionate acceptance of the woman with whom he is at last united, shows a complex psychology that results indirectly in his wife's death.

Despite its comedy, then, *The Hamlet* is a dark novel that exemplifies Faulkner's negative vision of the possibilities for love, and its ending extends this negativism into almost every sphere by involving the one detached moralist, Ratliff, in a sordid get-rich scheme. The theme of reversion to a primitive state is suggested on the very first page of the novel, when the Old Frenchman's place is described. Now a ruin, its "once-fertile fields had long since reverted to the cane-and-cypress jungle from which their first master had hewed them" (3). All that remains behind is "the stubborn tale of the money he [the Frenchman] buried" (4). Ratliff's moral sense is as highly developed and civilized as the land and buildings belonging to the Frenchman once were, but he proves no more impervious to the reversionary impulses of greed than the plantation does to physical decay.

Ratliff is shrewd and humorous, a purveyor of data and moral commentary who retails "from house to house the news of his four counties with the ubiquity of a newspaper" (13). He tells tall tales or explains Ab Snopes's psychic scarring by his run-in with a horse-trader with both skill and humanity, and judges the follies of his compatriots with an eye at once acrebic and amused. Though Ratliff is more detached from his surroundings than the other main characters, by virtue of his itinerancy and his freedom from romantic involvement, he is capable of the fullest possible moral engagement and readily puts his principles into action. It is Ratliff who provides the money for Ike to buy his cow, Ratliff who nails up the plank to keep the townspeople from spying on Ike's pathetic sodomy, Ratliff who gives up his room to Mink Snopes's wife so that she will have a place to stay during her husband's trial.

When the wild horses are brought to town—an event based on a similar occurrence Faulkner witnessed as a child—Ratliff is quick to judge the folly of the eager buyers' wish to own them: "I'd just as soon buy a tiger or a rattlesnake" (279). No one heeds Ratliff's caveat emptor, and all pay bitterly for their foolishness. Soon afterwards, however, Ratliff's moral sense, which is somehow all the more convincing for being based not on self-interest but on a general concern for the people of his town, is temporarily overcome; the ultimate moralist, with his concern for preserving the essential freedom that belongs inalienably to every man, becomes the ultimate dupe by falling for Flem's ploy of "salting" his land with buried money.

It is Henry Armstid, unhinged after the loss of his money, who draws Ratliff into the vortex of a plan to recover the Old Frenchman's legendary cache. Armstid descends into a trough at once literal and symbolic as he digs furiously and shouts "get outen my hole" (342) to all who threaten to encroach upon his territory; Ratliff, too, soon is sucked down into it, proving vulnerable to greed. Though Ratliff has the wisdom to escape the hole he has temporarily dug for himself, Armstid remains there, in thrall to his obsession with the putative buried treasure and surrounded by the townspeople who watch his mad digging as voyeuristically as they observed the sexual scenes between Ike and his cow.

"Couldn't nobody but Flem Snopes have fooled Ratliff" (365) says an onlooker. With this testimony to the ascendancy of the Snopeses over the hamlet and over even the seemingly incorruptible Ratliff, the novel ends. Significantly, the moral spokesman Ratliff is silent after the moment in which he comprehends how fully he has been bilked, as if guiltily aware of how meaningless will be any sort of comment now that his credibility has been undermined by his capitulation to Snopes-like greed. The last words of the novel come from Flem, who is clearly holding the reins in all ways as he spits and says to Armstid, "Come up" (366).

The several episodes of *The Hamlet,* with their interweaving of romantic and economic relationships against a background of running moral commentary by the sagacious and decent Ratliff, thus draw to a close with a man trapped in a dark hole which he has created for himself, watched avidly by his fellow men. The conclusion applies symbolically to all of the stories in the novel, for all have ended in darkness. The romances have culminated in the death, banishment, or imprisonment of one of the lovers; the one surviving marriage is the discordant union of a sex-goddess and an impotent usurer; and the one fully decent man of the novel has shown himself vulnerable to corruption. Man, Faulkner seems to be saying, too often destroys both himself and others by the hopeless quest for passion and the empty pursuit of riches.

The Hamlet's separate strands come together on the same sort of bleak note as did those of *The Wild Palms,* where both males, whether ardent or reluctant in their pursuit of the feminine ideal, end imprisoned like Armstid in cells that are the equivalent of his earthen trough. In both novels, man may appear to be merely a victim of the forces of nature or of a corrupt society, but, figuratively speaking, he almost always digs his own hole—by failing to achieve self-knowledge, by reverting to blind greed, by misusing his freedom, or by neglecting to remain alert to the ominous message of the Bad Smell that every human being and every relationship is flawed and vulnerable. For characters like Wilbourne and Houston, the discovery of passion and grief provides transfiguring moments and an affirmation of their humanity, but the rest too often, and too willingly, spend their time in darkness.

9
The End of the Major Period:
Go Down, Moses

Go Down, Moses IS THE LAST WORK of what has been called Faulkner's "great" period. Itself regarded by many critics as among the four or five greatest Faulkner novels, its publication marked the end of an era of splendid fictional achievements that began with *The Sound and the Fury*. Indeed, *Go Down, Moses* is a culminating work in many ways, manifesting important links to earlier strong works even as it introduces new fictional themes with a depth and richness almost unique in Faulkner's canon. It is also, however, a transitional work. It shows the author dramatizing new sorts of issues and introducing somewhat different types of characters. Though he treats them effectively, their presence is nonetheless faintly ominous, for he would reuse these elements again in later works with less success. The fictional methodology Faulkner employed so ably in *Go Down, Moses* would, finally, betray him.

In its transitional qualities, *Go Down, Moses* is similar to and continuous with its predecessor, *The Hamlet*. The two are alike in bringing together, daringly, but with a high degree of success, a number of disparate parts that had previously been published separately. In each case Faulkner did extensive and careful revision, amplifying much material and introducing a good deal that was wholly new, in order to integrate the variegated tales. These somewhat unusual novels, with their separately titled portions that hint at the autonomy of those parts, are thematically and, in subtle but persuasive ways, narratively unified. They are, however, less sharply focused and emotionally more diffuse than earlier works that were singly conceived and written. Faulkner's artistry was so skillful by the late 1930s that he was highly adept at making an effective whole out of fictional pieces. But the process was becoming somewhat too "conscious," and the underlying intensity that characterized his earlier works shows signs of beginning to disappear.

Go Down, Moses is like *The Hamlet* also in revealing the changing nature of the author's preoccupations. Just as in the 1940 novel Faulkner extended his portrayal of complex romances with the treatment of various economic interchanges, so in *Go Down, Moses* he shows an ever-expanding concern with issues far beyond the purely personal. Moral and sociopolitical issues in regional and national history, the problem of race relations between white, Negro, and Indian, and the question of ownership are among the new topics which make their appearance in the 1942 novel. In these two works, Faulkner began to move away from his personal obsessions and to concentrate instead on his various responses to social issues. Eventually the obsessional element would become a minor one in Faulkner's works, which increasingly seemed to verge on the hortative and sentimental.

A letter Faulkner wrote during this period shows him being explicit for the first time about his sense of moral obligation:

I have been writing all the time about honor, truth, pity, consideration, the capacity to endure well grief and misfortune and injustice and then endure again, in terms of individuals who observed and adhered to them not for reward but for virtue's own sake, not even merely because they are admirable in themselves, but in order to live with oneself and die peacefully with oneself when the time comes. [*L*, p. 142]

Faulkner's retrospective view of his fiction is mature and expansive, taking it far beyond the realm of anguished autobiography. But it also reveals a new concept of his art, one which underlay his ultimate transformation from a novelist of consciousness to one of conscience.

Faulkner's new fictional emphasis on the social rather than the strictly personal may well have stemmed from the fact that he was no longer driven by his private anxieties, not provided by them with sufficient material. As he began work on *Go Down, Moses*, he experienced for the first time in his career a severe writing block. He naturally attributed his depression and his inability to work to the war which had recently erupted in Europe. "Maybe the watching of all this coming to a head for the last year is why I cant write, dont seem to want to write that is" (*L*, p. 125). Perhaps, but psychic events rather than current events tend to produce such stoppages, and

Faulkner's difficulty may have arisen from the fact that he had, in psychoanalytic terms, "worked through" a number of his most disturbing emotional problems. With the gradual depletion of the emotional fuel that stoked his imaginative fires, Faulkner turned to more "conscious" material. He ceased to need—or, in a way, to be able to draw from—the subsonscious sources from which came his strongest art. *Go Down, Moses* is the last work in which the personal-emotional is in equilibrium with the moral-social, in which the new concerns are treated with the old fervor.

After the turbulent interlude in the late 1930s, during which Faulkner embodied and objectified his troubling involvement with extramarital passion in *The Wild Palms* and *The Hamlet,* he turned to a project he initially envisaged as being much like *The Unvanquished* in execution. He proposed to his editor that he "build onto" existing stories, "write some more, make a book like THE UNVANQUISHED," and he told Bennett Cerf that *Go Down, Moses* was "a mss. based on short stories, some published, something like the UNVANQUISHED in composition" (*L,* pp. 124, 135). Once again, the material he prepared specifically for the novel proved to be the most effective portion of the book. Faulkner's expansion of the story "Lion," which had appeared in *Harper's* in 1935, into the novella-length "The Bear" and his insertion of the all-important part 4 did for *Go Down, Moses* what "An Odor of Verbena" had done for *The Unvanquished,* providing additional resonance, complexity, and amplitude. Faulkner also arranged the stories he had gathered together in a chronology based on their narrative content in order to present, as he had in *The Unvanquished,* albeit in a rather different sense, the effect of a man's sense of the past on his evolution from childhood to maturity.

Both novels skillfully link adventure, humor, and moral comment. However, *Go Down, Moses* is a richer and more suggestive work than *The Unvanquished,* partly because Ike McCaslin's troubling heritage goes deeper into the past than that of Bayard Sartoris and because his "curse" has been confronted by several generations. Moreover, the story is amplified by the themes of race, the wilderness, and human greed, and thus attains an intricacy and profundity that is missing from the more singly focused earlier work. Faulkner had introduced the provocative subjects of interracial kinship and of the unworthiness of man's efforts to possess and control the land in *The Unvanquished,* but failed to develop them in any significant way until he began work on *Go Down, Moses.*

Faulkner's extended treatment in *Go Down, Moses* of certain themes which he had only touched upon in passing in his 1938 novel was motivated by a series of occurrences in his own life in the years between the two works. Racial relationships play a predominant role in *Go Down, Moses,* and Faulkner dedicated the book "To Mammy," his black nurse Caroline Barr, "who was born in slavery and who gave to my family a fidelity without stint or calculation of recompense and to my childhood an immeasurable devotion and love." Mammy had been with the family for almost forty years. She served first as William's nurse and surrogate mother, offering the boy the affection and attention that were not always forthcoming from his own busy and often remote mother, and then as the nurse to William's own child and stepchildren. No one knew exactly how old Mammy Callie was, but she had been a slave for many years before Emancipation and was probably well into her nineties by the time the 1930s drew to a close. Despite her advanced age and her frail, shriveled frame, Mammy remained quite independent, living in her own cabin behind Rowanoak, going for walks, doing her own sewing, and attempting in a limited way to contribute to the running of the Faulkner household. In January of 1940, however, she suffered a paralytic stroke and died.

Faulkner mourned the woman who had been an emotional mainstay in his life for many decades and assumed all responsibility for her funeral arrangements. He even preached the sermon over her coffin in the parlor at Rowanoak, paying moving tribute to the black woman who had accepted the handicaps of her lot: "I saw fidelity to a family which was not hers, devotion and love for people she had not borne." She was one of Faulkner's "earliest recollections, not only as a person, but as a fount of authority over my conduct and of security for my physical welfare, and of active and constant affection and love." He concluded, "She was born and lived and served, and died and now is mourned; if there is a heaven, she has gone there."[1]

The tiny and indomitable Mollie Beauchamp of *Go Down, Moses* is based on Caroline Barr, and Faulkner's conscientious treatment of racial injustice in the book was also evoked by his responses to Mammy Callie's death. He was sensitive enough to feel considerable guilt about the inhuman regional attitudes that made her first a slave and then the poorly paid servant of a white family and that even in death demanded she be laid to rest in the segregated portion of the Oxford cemetery set aside for blacks. In "The Fire and the Hearth," Roth Edmonds's tribute to the black woman who raised him, the "only mother he ever knew" (99–100) and the one human being "who had given him, the motherless, without stint or expectation of reward that constant and abiding devotion and love which existed nowhere else in this world for him" (117),[2] is an ardent one, clearly an extension of Faulkner's posthumous tribute to Mammy Callie Barr. The author's fictional depiction of blacks as fully human, proud, and complex was stronger in *Go Down, Moses* than it had ever been before, and the book itself serves as a form of symbolic restitution to Mammy from a member of the white society which had exploited her for nearly a hundred years.

The ownership and mistreatment of human beings in *Go Down, Moses* is related to the other major theme of the book, the possession and misuse of the land, and both have their source in human greed. The annual hunt memorialized in the novel had been a vivid part of Faulkner's own boyhood and young manhood, and he had often participated in the late fall rituals at the camp belonging to Phil Stone's father. Much of the lore in *Go Down, Moses* came from Faulkner's hunting experiences in those early years and from his listening to stories told by other hunters. But by the middle 1930s General Stone and the other old men of the hunt had begun to die out, and by 1940 the hunt had to be moved down to the Delta because timber companies had denuded the land where Stone's camp once stood (B, p. 1063). Faulkner's elegy to the vanishing wilderness of his region is coupled with an indictment of the human beings whose acquisitiveness brought it about. Yet even as he lamented the disappearance of the natural "Eden" of his younger years, he recognized that he himself was implicated in the responsibility for the loss and, moreover, that it was in some sense inevitable.

He had himself, after all, been acquiring land around Oxford at a rapid rate, had become what Ike would call a "white man fatuous enough to believe he had bought any fragment of it" (191), and by the time he began work on *Go Down, Moses,* he had purchased several lots around his house, an impressive 35-acre tract known as Bailey's Woods which was contiguous to his property, and a 320-acre farm several miles outside town. Faulkner was proud of his land acquisitions and told someone that "I own a larger parcel of it than anybody in town" (*L,* p. 128). He worked fiercely to produce saleable short stories in order to keep up his payments on these pieces of property. Thus his indictment of the acquisitive instinct in *Go Down, Moses* applies to himself as well as to mankind in general. As was often the case with Faulkner, his art revealed an honest awareness of the manifold moral and psychological implications of such undertakings not always manifested in his actions, and there is a real sense in which the book serves as both comment on and partial expiation of Faulkner's "sins" against Caroline Barr and against the land, as well as a memorial to experiences from his past.

Faulkner always referred to *Go Down, Moses* as a novel, although all of its component stories had been written separately and every one except

"Was" had been published in some form before the book appeared. It first came out with the title *Go Down, Moses and Other Stories,* which shocked Faulkner, who regarded it as a novel and asked his publisher to "call it simply GO DOWN, MOSES" (*L*, p. 285). The mistake was corrected and *and Other Stories* dropped from the title for the next printing. Nonetheless the work stands, like *The Unvanquished* and *The Hamlet,* generically somewhere between a novel and a cycle of stories. Faulkner's careful interweaving of the seemingly discrete narrative and thematic strands is not immediately apparent; the unity becomes obvious only retrospectively.

The general movement of the book is progressive and incremental. There is a slow accretion of detail about past events, about the complexity of kinship lines, both black and white, and about the intrafamily tensions over several generations. The book opens in a mood at once comic and kinetic; there is a gradual darkening of tone and slowing of movement appropriate to the increasingly serious revelations. The major themes of black-white relationships and the exploitation of land and human beings appear in every story, and the effect of the past on the present is a dominant element. There are a number of other unifying threads. Every story is in some sense a ritual hunt, as Olga Vickery has pointed out,[3] and many focus on negotiations of some sort. Black-white surrogate parent relationships are pivotal to the book and include that between the Beauchamps and Roth Edmonds and that of Sam Fathers and Ike McCaslin. Though Ike is not the central character in all the stories, he is at least mentioned in every one, and during the course of the book moves from childhood to extreme old age. His final scenes reveal the nature of his moral achievement, at once fully conscientious and yet strikingly flawed, but Faulkner avoids any full resolutions of the tensions within Ike and thus in the society around him.

Ike McCaslin is the most fully developed and complex figure in *Go Down, Moses* and is also a typically Faulknerian protagonist, with relationships to characters like Bayard Sartoris and Quentin Compson, especially in his attempts to come to terms with his family past. Ike also, in exhibiting strength in the areas of moralism, cerebration, and (at least intermittently) action, seems in some sense a "recombinant" of the linked separate characters of a work like *As I Lay Dying.* As noted in the preceding chapter, Jack Houston, a minor character in *The Hamlet,* exhibits this same reintegration of characteristics previously assigned by Faulkner to separate individuals. Such characters as Houston and Ike may signify the integration within Faulkner's own psyche of contrary impulses whose seeming incompatibility had once driven him to embody them in discrete figures. Or they may simply mark a conscious artistic departure from a generally poetic or symbolic technique. Whatever the origin, whether psychic or intentional, of a "recombinant" character like Ike McCaslin, the fusion of his characteristics in a single individual offers fewer opportunities for complex human interactions. Only in "The Old People," in Ike's interchanges with Sam Fathers, and in part 4 of "The Bear," in Ike's dialogue with Cass Edmonds—highly reminiscent as it is of that between Quentin and Shreve near the end of *Absalom, Absalom!*— does the work become effective in a psycho-symbolic way; most of its impact comes from its socio-historical dimensions.

Ike McCaslin appears to be one of Faulkner's autobiographical male protagonists. The author later displayed an ambivalence toward the character, treating Ike, as he did himself, with alternating sympathy and criticism. Faulkner spoke feelingly about him on at least one occasion, observing that "they [the things he learned from Sam Fathers] gave him serenity, they gave him what would pass for wisdom," and that Ike "was trying to teach them [children] what he knew of respect for whatever your lot in life is, that if your lot is to be a hunter, to slay animals, you slay the animals with the nearest approach you can to dignity and to decency." Yet he was elsewhere harsh in commenting on Ike's conscience-stricken denial of his tainted patrimony. He acknowledged the value of his refusal but criticized his inability to do anything more useful than figuratively "go off into a cave or climb a pillar to sit on" (*FIU*, pp. 54, 246). Faulkner also said, "I think a man ought to do more than just repudiate. He should have been more affirmative instead of just shunning people" (*LIG*, p. 225).

The passivity of Ike's repudiation is one of the more troubling elements in "The Bear," because Falkner specifically makes him a carpenter "not in mere static and hopeful emulation of the Nazarene" (309) and thus akin to his other morally engaged carpenters, Cash Bundren and Byron Bunch. But there *is* something static and merely hopeful about Ike's actions, for they never seem to take any usefully positive form. He manages to preserve into old age a "young boy's high and selfless innocence" (106), but only at the price of emotional detachment from the life which surges around him.

As *Go Down, Moses* opens, Ike is completely disengaged from close personal involvements, a storyteller who is "uncle to half a county and father to none" (3). His lack of children, particularly of a son, isolates him from the mainstream, and Faulkner may have perceived his own situation in somewhat similar terms. It is certainly likely that he felt keenly the lack of male issue in a society and in a family which so much stressed male lineage. By the 1940s, Faulkner was gentle and avuncular with his many young relatives, as he was with all children, but he seemed especially attentive to teaching the boys the proper ways of engaging in "masculine" pursuits. When his stepson Malcolm became a teenager, Faulkner taught him the principles of bird hunting and once punished him severely for shooting a bird from the nest, in betrayal of the "code" (B, p. 970). On another occasion, Faulkner presented his nephew James with a rifle and showed him how to use it "because I don't have a boy of my own."[4] To Faulkner, the instillment of the hunting code was obviously central to a father-son interchange, and both this belief and his deeply felt lack of a son are evident in *Go Down, Moses,* where relationships between fathers and foster sons focus on the inculcation of just those principles. Hunting is explicitly equated with manhood in the novel, just as aviation had been in earlier works, but it also proves to require an essential moral sense, which was irrelevant to flying. Thus Ike's initiation into manhood in the forest and his paternal "gift" from Sam Fathers are basically ethical in nature.

References to Ike as an older man appear in the first two stories to prepare us for the pivotal tales in which his own story is told, and these—"The Old People," "The Bear," and "Delta Autumn"—are, with the starkly powerful "Pantaloon in Black," the most moving sections of the book. Although Ike's spiritual father, the Indian-Negro Sam Fathers, is the central figure of "The Old People," his complex legacy to Ike portends the boy's future in important ways. Sam's mingled heritage is symbolic of Ike's own problematic background, for Sam is racially "himself his own battleground, the scene of his own vanquishment and the mausoleum of his defeat" (168), just as Ike will later be emotionally. Sam is also a brilliant storyteller, able to make "those old times and those dead and vanished men . . . become a part of the boy's present, not only as if they happened yesterday but as if they were still happening" (171), and it is Ike's similar ability to perceive the presentness of the past as a living force that will drive him to attempt to ameliorate it. Finally, when confronted with the awesome buck which looms out of the wilderness, Sam salutes its majesty and mystery, paying homage to nature's grandeur, just as Ike will later refuse to participate in puny man's efforts to own any part of that nature, to possess what he views as unpossessable.

Sam Fathers's vital tutelary role, begun in "The Old People," continues in "The Bear," in which, however, Ike fails to achieve the manhood for which Sam has so carefully prepared him. Faulkner is careful to make "The Bear" continuous with the previous tale. He complicates our view of Ike's character and his story with the resonant overtones of tragedy, elegy, and myth which amplify the moral "message." Old Ben is the apotheosis of the grandeur of the wilderness and his death portends the generalized destruction of that wilderness. In a way, Sam is an apotheosis of human grandeur, and the continuity of man and nature is so strong that Sam's death follows almost inevitably upon that of Old Ben. Thus the splendor of both the natural and the human past has been cut short, and Ike is in part responsible for the second death by failing to accomplish the first in a manly and competent way. But Sam and Old Ben are symbolically complex, and our responses to them are at once magnified and complicated by the rest of the narrative, rendering the vision of both man and nature increasingly ambiguous.

The theme of piety for all living things and for nature itself—as symbolized by those woods which are "bigger and older than any recorded document"—is central to the story. Sam and Old Ben and the dog Lion are an intimate part of that nature, and Ike refers to them as "taintless and incorruptible" (191). Yet the bear and the dog are also Melvillean symbols of natural evil, terrifying in their impersonality. Old Ben is legendary for his devouring of pigs and calves and his mangling of dogs, and his trail is "a corridor of wreckage and destruction beginning back before the boy was born" (193). Lion, named for his ferocity, displays a "cold and almost impersonal malignance" (218). Bear and dog collide with violence like the implacable natural forces they represent and both are destroyed. Though Sam Fathers is brave and decent, teaching Ike all about "loving the life he spills" (181), his participation in the pursuit and annihilation of Old Ben implicates him in the pointless destruction of the wilderness. Old Ben is, in a way, the wilderness; their time had come, but there is no real moral justification for the bear's death. Sam's complicity in the deed identifies him with other, more severely flawed, human beings and bodes his own death, while Ike's inability to recognize the inexorable reality of the changes he sees, his awareness only of their moral purposelessness, makes him unable to kill the bear according to the disciplines and the rituals he had been taught.

Our multiple responses to Old Ben, Lion, and Sam Fathers as symbols of the dying wilderness, partaking of violence and evil as well as grandeur, and to Ike's moral but unmanly failure to pull the trigger, foreshadow Ike McCaslin's complex reactions to his personal past in part 4 of "The Bear." When he pores over the dusty ledgers in the commissary on the family plantation, Ike is again driven to an action at once idealistic and useless. These books recording transactions concerning the McCaslin slaves contain in an elliptical way "not only the general and condoned injustice [of slavery] and its slow amortization but the specific tragedy" (266). In reading about his ancestors' slow manumission of their black chattels, Ike perceives "a little at least of its amelioration and its restitution" (261); but he comes to understand with horror one specific injustice and its tragic outcome, which overwhelms and negates any positive message found in the ledgers.

Their appalling tale of incest, miscegenation, and suicide, in which his grandfather is the central figure, leads Ike to believe the ledgers contain a "chronicle which was a whole land in miniature, which multiplied and compounded was the entire South" (293); overwhelmed by this dark moral burden, he feels his only possible means of restitution and escape is to relinquish the entire sullied McCaslin patrimony. Thenceforth Ike sees himself "repudiated and denied and free" (281), a propertyless carpenter like Christ, who will be an inspirational exemplar to the people of his region. Yet while Ike's action may be personally satisfying, it proves to have little effect on others. In the following story he himself appears in a morally questionable light. He shouts at the part-black woman carrying Roth Edmonds's child, "You're a nigger!" and tells her to "Get out of here" (361). Ike's anger has a life-denying quality and by the end of the story he himself appears deathlike, "the blanket once more drawn to his chin, his crossed hands once more weightless on his breast in the empty tent" (365).

Ike's vulnerability on the race issue, like his inability to take action that is useful as well as moral, proves to be the symbolic door blocking the way to real manhood, a door which he cannot pass through, much like the one that confronted Quentin Compson in *Absalom, Absalom!*. Ike's story has a number of other ties to that of Quentin. The themes of incest, miscegenation, and the unacknowledged son as they appear in a troubling family history are central to part 4 of "The Bear" just as they were to *Absalom, Absalom!*, but the similarities go even deeper. The central dialogue between Ike and his cousin Cass Edmonds in the commissary, during which they imaginatively recreate the past, is much like that between Quentin and Shreve during the latter part of the earlier novel, serving as summary and expansion of the narrative and as a metaphor of the artist creatively at work. However, the differences between the two works are also revealing. The matters that obsess Quentin are predominantly emotional and familial, regional mostly by implication, while the issues that preoccupy Ike go far beyond himself, into southern history, national history, even into the Biblical picture of Creation. Quentin remains focused on the particular, while Ike generalizes and expands; the contrast between the two is like that between Faulkner's middle and late fiction.

The cousins Ike and Cass are closer even than their blood ties signify. Cass is to Ike "his father almost" (297) and the men are separate in beliefs but somehow unified by their common past, "the two of them juxtaposed and alien now to each other against their ravaged patrimony'' (297–98). Cass serves as an interrogator of his younger cousin, gradually eliciting the entire story of the past, but he also has a function much like Shreve's, as a spokesman for realism of vision and deed and as the deflator of his companion's emotional outpourings. Ike praises blacks for their

"Endurance—" and McCaslin
"So have mules:" and he
"—and pity and tolerance and forbearance and fidelity
and love of children—" and McCaslin
"So have dogs." [295]

Cass deflates, questions, attempts to provoke Ike into justifying both his failure to shoot the bear and his repudiation of his inheritance, for the second action is foreshadowed by the first.

Thus Cass serves as a foil for Ike just as Shreve did for Quentin. Though Ike and Cass are never fully fused in psychological equilibrium in the way the two young men of *Absalom, Absalom!* were, they make some of the exuberantly creative leaps forward that were so crucial a part of the earlier work. Just as Quentin invokes the anguished rejected son—an imaginative counterpart of Quentin himself—riding alone across a winter landscape to a confrontation with a father who will not acknowledge him, so does Ike re-create, see, his grandfather's black mistress walking into the creek to drown herself because she cannot bear the knowledge that he has also impregnated their daughter. Ike's vision of Eunice's repudiation by death suggests his own repudiation by death-in-life of all the family sins; both choose total withdrawal as their mode of response. For Ike as for Quentin, the invoked past mirrors the flawed present.

Ike and Cass thus elicit, like Quentin and Shreve before them, vibrant, living history. The difference is that in *Absalom, Absalom!* the men's achievements remain predominantly imaginative, while in the later novel the protagonists' reflections lead them to attempt right action. Like Shreve, Cass is a spokesman for the sensible, realistic approach, but, unlike Shreve, he is more than a voice. Recognizing the flaws in the history of his land, "founded upon injustice and erected by ruthless rapacity," he has still managed to keep it "solvent and efficient and . . . intact" (298), fulfilling his obligation to the land and its tenants through the chaos of the Reconstruction period. Like Quentin, Ike is idealistic, but, unlike him, he tries to translate his thoughts into deeds that may be useful to others. Moved by piety for "this land this South for which He had done so much with woods for game and streams for fish and deep rich soil for seed" (283), he relinquishes his part of it to make an examplary stand against ownership of the land. Ike's gesture proves pointless, though admirable, just as Cass's actions, however effective, are based on a cynical acceptance of longstanding wrongs. Nonetheless, both men have acted in a socially committed way, whatever the flaws in their efforts. As Faulkner began to develop his own sense of moral possibilities, he dramatized that sense in his characters' dialogues and in their personal history. *Go Down, Moses's* differences from *Absalom, Absalom!* bear testimony to the author's expanding vision.

Yet, as he had in the 1936 novel, Faulkner continued to make tacit statements about the challenges and sustenance offered by creative endeavors. In part 4 of "The Bear," Ike makes pointed references to the Bible and to the family ledgers that serve to underscore the status of these works as metaphoric representatives of Faulkner's own fictional achievement. The transcribers of the Bible are said to have been "sometimes liars" because "they were human men" who "were trying to write down the heart's truth out of the heart's driving complexity, for all the complex and troubled hearts which would beat after them" (260)—much as Faulkner himself attempted to portray the manifold human acts prompted by the heart's driving complexity in works which would serve as his own message to posterity. In another important way, Faulkner's art was becoming like the McCaslin ledgers, a comprehensive record "not alone of his own flesh and blood but of all his people, not only the whites but the black one too . . . and of the land which they had all held and used" (268). The record might be one chiefly of "injustice" (261), but Faulkner's moving dramatization of those injustices, first private and then general, continued to give his work dynamic richness.

The effort to deal with the moral and personal implications of the past so pivotal to Ike McCaslin's story is equally so to Lucas Beauchamp's. Lucas is the central character in "The Fire and the Hearth," which introduces the serious themes that will be developed in "The Bear" and that are implicit in all the stories of *Go Down, Moses,* even as it provides a comic depiction of some rural confidence games and makes a parodic comment on economic transactions of any sort. Lucas is both duper and duped in humorous adventures involving a still and a gold detector, but he is also a proud man who has had to make crucial compromises in order to survive. He has learned, like many southern blacks of the period, to retreat behind a mask where his essential manhood is invisible. He becomes under duress "not Negro but nigger, not secret so much as impenetrable" (60). Faulkner himself, often estranged from his milieu, understood that sense of being a pariah and the need to mask one's true feelings with a protective persona;

he had also become capable, through his grief for Mammy Callie, of understanding from the black person's point of view the special imperatives of surviving a difficult racial situation.

Lucas, again much like the author himself, continues even in old age to relive and resuffer past indignities, particularly his misuse by a white man forty-three years before that had forced him to struggle with his dual role in the restrictive southern society. "I'm a nigger. But I'm a man too," he insists to Zack Edmonds (47), and even as he tends to idolize "the old days, the old time, and better men than these" (44), he remains painfully aware of the way in which his manhood was then violated. In a tragic cycle of repetition, Zack Edmonds's son abnegates his spiritual kinship with a black boy in an act with overtones of his father's, though it involves the physical separation of black and white rather than sexual union. Racism, the "old curse" of his ancestors, wrenches Roth from the bed of his black foster-brother, and, though he later feels grief and shame for his denial, he understands that it is "forever and forever too late" and that he must face the "bitter fruit" of his heritage (111, 112, 114). The wrongs of the distant past have been perpetuated in the recent past. The adult Roth will, to a limited degree, accept his responsibility to Lucas as a means toward restitution, but he will also later commit an even worse "sin" against a black person.

In *Go Down, Moses,* the heritage from the past is thus a complex one which involves both racial injustice and the destruction of nature, the symbolic thefts of supposedly inalienable rights. In a very powerful but somewhat anomalous story in the volume, "Pantaloon in Black," the past makes itself felt in the devastating grief suffered over the recent death of a loved one. This tale seems to have been created by Faulkner in the same heightened emotional mood in which he wrote *The Wild Palms,* and that novel is evoked directly by the line in "The Old People" to the effect that "even suffering and grieving is better than nothing" (186), which recalls Harry Wilbourne's final statement. In "Pantaloon in Black," Rider's grief at the death of his wife is physically and emotionally unbearable, driving him to prodigious feats of strength and furious defiance of fate. Rider's desperate attempt to escape his memories is futile, for he admits that "Hit look lack Ah just cant quit thinking" (159). But the tragic grandeur of his effort to overcome endows him with a stature never achieved by Harry Wilbourne. Rider's rebellious grief is almost Promethean in its power and affirms the force of his love in a singular way. Despite its preoccupation with a personal past of passionate involvement which seems to differentiate it from most of the other stories, "Pantaloon in Black" is linked to them by the blindness of the white deputy, whose comments on Rider's actions reveal his racism: "They aint human. They look like a man. . . . but when it comes to the normal human feelings and sentiments of human beings, they might just as well be a damn herd of wild buffaloes" (154). By thus decreeing that Rider's actions are based on a lack of "respect" for his dead wife, the deputy, in an abstract way, violates the emotional humanity of a black person just as, in a direct way, do the McCaslins and Edmondses of the other stories. The blacks of *Go Down, Moses* prove victims of white society in every possible respect.

The title story comes last in the volume and seems intended to pull the work together. Stevens's failure to understand the felt necessities of Mollie's situation—first, that her grandson's body must be brought home and, next, that he should not intrude on her grief—mirrors the failure of all the whites in the novel to understand the blacks. Moreover, the story's theme of loving acceptance extended even to an executed murderer and its evocation of the unifying hearth, that "ancient symbol of human coherence and solidarity" (380), links it firmly to the other tales. However, the penultimate "Delta Autumn" is more directly integrated with the previous stories, especially because it completes the portrait of Ike McCaslin and vividly opens up the chink in his moral armor suggested by part 4 of "The Bear," thus casting an ambiguous light over all of his previous rhetoric.

All the threads of the work come together in "Delta Autumn"—the elegy for the vanishing wilderness, the portrayal of the flawed McCaslin descendant who shoots the symbolic doe and thus shows himself capable of the wanton destruction of nature, and the persistent and unresolved tensions of race relations. The counterpoint of paean and irony begun with the dialogue in part 4 of "The Bear" continues with Ruth's cynical jibe at Ike's inflated speechifying, and the emptiness of Ike's repudiation becomes clear as he confronts the fact that in "saving and freeing his son, [he] lost him" (351) and will die without issue. In Ike's meeting with the young black woman who effects in him an unpleasant self-revelation of prejudice there is a significant fusion of all the motifs. Incest and miscegenation are perpetuated in the alliance of a white Edmonds and a black Beauchamp-McCaslin, Roth's efforts to "buy off" the young woman are a recapitulation of old Carothers's legacy to his black son, and Ike's sudden, conscience-stricken gift to her of Ruth's hunting horn amalgamates the themes of wilderness and race. In "Delta Autumn," the strands of *Go Down, Moses* become intertwined and Ike completes the cycle of growth from childhood to old age.

At the heart of *Go Down, Moses* is part 4 of "The Bear," with its striking similarity to the latter portion of *Absalom, Absalom!* and its comparable stress upon the creative effort to uncover the truths of the past and to act in accordance with those discoveries. In its slight dissimilarity to the earlier novel, however, that same episode subtly forecasts a significant and recurring weakness in the author's later work. Faulkner again skillfully dramatizes the quest for personal meaning, yet in broadening the terms of that quest and expanding the arena in which it can take place, he concomitantly decreases its intensity. Ike's earnest concern with the widest imaginable range of issues is a burden which finds expression in paragraphs of inflated rhetoric. That same concern would eventually constitute a similar burden for Faulkner himself. Late in his life, Faulkner came to an understanding of the fact that "when he gets involved with right and duty, [the novelist is] on the verge of becoming a propagandist, and he stops being an artist then."[5] Though he would always deal dynamically with right and duty, avoiding straight propaganda, the various testimonies of conscience began to supplant the intense dramatization of consciousness in his fiction. Thus *Go Down, Moses,* for all its power and profundity, is an unsettling harbinger of the Faulkner-to-come.

10
The Problem of Ideology and Aesthetics:
Intruder in the Dust,
Requiem for a Nun, and *A Fable*

THE EVALUATION OF FAULKNER'S works of the post–*Go Down, Moses* period presents special difficulties. Although most of them have been harshly judged since they first appeared, some Faulknerians are now pressing for reappraisal of novels like *Requiem for a Nun* and *A Fable,* based on the ambitious range of Faulkner's intentions in these works and on their thematic richness. Faulkner did certainly change the fundamental terms of his novelistic approach in the late period, a change portended by the things he was doing even in earlier works like *The Hamlet* and *Go Down, Moses,* as suggested in the previous chapter. Nonetheless, whatever criteria one uses in judging the novels that appeared after *Go Down, Moses,* it is difficult not to assess them as somewhat diminished in artistic power. Faulkner published three novels between 1948 and 1954, and though each is singular in striking ways, not only in his canon, but also by comparison with the whole body of American fiction, they must be reckoned among his lesser achievements.

In these novels, as in his earlier works, Faulkner treats serious issues—racial injustice, the complex burden (both personal and regional) of the past, and war and Christian martyrdom. But he does so with an increased element of ideation. The ideas are dramatized, to be sure, with the usual Faulknerian dynamism and unresolved tension, but their obtrusiveness still creates aesthetic problems. The characters more obviously represent moral, political, and philosophical stances than they did in earlier works, where they were, above all, complex individuals struggling to survive. Now they are more readily identified with abstract qualities and their confrontations become, in some ways, public debates on contemporary issues. Individual actions have implications that go beyond the family into the community, into the region—even, in the case of *A Fable,* into all of Western civilization.

This expansiveness is, in its way, impressive, but it is accompanied by a certain vitiation of power. Quite obviously the broad canvas does not necessitate a weakened intensity of depiction (vide *War and Peace*). The special problems in Faulkner's late work were, however, created at one level by the fact that he was not entirely comfortable with the new terms of his approach. Faulkner expressed on at least two occasions his inherent distrust of ideas. At one point he remarked "To me the New Testament is full of ideas and I don't know much about ideas. . . . I like to read the Old Testament because it's full of people, not ideas" (*FIU*, p. 167). Soon after, he again pointed out that "if one begins to write about the injustice of society, then one has stopped being primarily a novelist and has become a polemicist or a propagandist. The fiction writer is . . . telling a story, which is about people, not about the injustice or inhumanity of people but of people, with their aspirations and their struggles" (*FIU*, p. 177). No one would accuse Faulkner of being a polemicist, though there has been some tendency to read his late work as showing impulses in that direction. But the incursion of ideas, and of a trend toward allegorizing, is manifest in the fiction of this period, and while Faulkner's basic discomfort with this ideational element may be one reason why he seemed unable to bring to his late work the vitality he had shown in the previous two decades, there are also other reasons, ranging from the lessening of subjective involvement to the sheer flagging of artistic energy.

Faulkner himself insightfully commented on a number of things which contributed to his "problem," providing his own analysis of this period of decline. In 1947, for example, Faulkner told a group of Mississippi college students that "35–45 is the best age for writing novels, fire not used up, author knows more" and that "I feel I'm written out. I don't think I'll write much more. You only have so much steam and if you don't use it up in writing, it'll get off by itself." Then, in his interview with Jean Stein in the mid-1950s, he said that a man becomes "moral" and "no longer able to do" only after age forty. Before that he is "strong" (*LIG*, pp. 56, 54, 254). These retrospective comments imply that Faulkner himself regarded *Go Down, Moses,* published the year he became forty-five, as some sort of artistic watershed, and further, that he was all too aware of his own decreasing strengths. Thus the passage into middle age was, in Faulkner's eyes, one reason of itself for the change in both the nature and the power of his work.

Another, paradoxically, was his increased detachment and lessened need to be intensely "in" his fiction. Faulkner admitted, as this study has sought to demonstrate, that his early work was profoundly autobiographical, for "the young man will write about himself simply because himself is what he knows best." However, Faulkner went on, "the more you write, the more you see you have to write, the more you have learned by writing, and probably you don't have time to identify yourself with a character except at certain moments when the character is in a position to express truthfully things which you yourself believe to be true" (*FIU,* pp. 25–26). Obviously, too much identification of the author with his characters creates aesthetic problems, as Faulkner's first few novels variously revealed. He needed to "get away from himself" in order to create fiction that was fully balanced, that showed modification of the obsessional by the artistic "policeman." On the other hand, identification was for Faulkner a form of psychic investment that gave his work intensity and immediacy. When he became too detached from the work in progress, when its subjective components were minimal, there was a corresponding decrease in its vitality.

Faulkner himself attributed some of the lessening of his personal involvement with his fiction to the healing, as it were, of his psychic "wounds." As he said, "Disaster seems to be good for people. . . . If they are too successful too long, something dies, it dries up."[1] A part of the "disaster" to which Faulkner refers is the public inattention which throws the artist constantly back upon his own resources. But the "disaster" is also the personal unhappiness which provides the writer with perpetual material. Faulkner subconsciously perceived his childhood and young manhood as somehow disastrous, and his ongoing need to "write out" problems from those early years was the imaginative source from which much of his strongest fiction came. His "demons" were his muse, and when he exorcised too many of them, there was little left to inspire his writing.

Faulkner produced much less during the period after *Go Down, Moses* than previously—three novels in twelve years as compared with eleven novels in the thirteen years before that—and now he seemed to write nearly every work with a conscious goal that was somewhat impersonal in nature. He once said that when he was young, he had no concern for his audience but wrote primarily to please himself, an approach that kept him always "furiously engaged" in doing his next novel. It was only "after I got old and began to slow down that I became conscious there were people that read the books"[2] Along with this awareness came an effort to enlighten his audience, an effort that began with *Go Down, Moses,* in which he tried to make restitution to the blacks who had served his family for a hundred years by sharing with his readers his new sense of their individuality and integrity.

Moreover, some of his public comments evince hints of a new purposefulness that was, if not polemical, at least faintly doctrinaire. Faulkner asserted that he "used" evil "to try to tell some truth which you think is important; there are times when man needs to be reminded of evil, to correct it, to change it," and that he felt a writer "should not be just a 'recorder' of man—he should give man some reason to believe that man can be better than he is."[3] Though Faulkner's art never became didactic, his interest in the ameliorative impulse did lead him to create that wordy moralizer Gavin Stevens. Stevens's actions are never wholly admirable, but Faulkner lets him have his say at great length, so that his various assertions stand out, even though they are always qualified by the fictional context.

Evolution—psychological, moral, and ideational—was thus the major element of the essential change in Faulkner that manifested itself in his late work. He developed from an unhappy individual who worked in almost complete isolation and heeded only the promptings of his tormented psyche into a "smiling public man" who became a speaker, good-will ambassador, and even, abortively, a presidential advisor of sorts. By the mid-1940s, Faulkner had worked through many of his severest personal difficulties, had attained financial success and critical acceptance, and now searched conscientiously for ways to enlighten and perhaps uplift others, a process that culminated in the impassioned rhetoric of his Nobel Prize speech. However affirmative this psychic progress may have been for Faulkner as a man, it would have problematic effects on his fiction.

After the publication of *Go Down, Moses* in 1942, Faulkner entered a long fallow period during which he wrote little and published nothing. He was deeply affected by the outbreak of World War II and depressed by his unsuccessful efforts to get into uniform. Once again his two younger brothers, along with most of his other male relatives, were accepted into the service while William watched helplessly from the sidelines. In early 1942, Faulkner tried to obtain a job in the Bureau of Aeronautics "and I hope a pilot's rating to wear the wings." Rejected, he wrote plaintively to Bennett Cerf, "Do you know how he [a friend of Cerf's] managed to get into the Air Force? They turned me down on application, didn't say why, may have been age, 44. . . . I want an Air Force job if possible. I still haven't given up hope'' (*L*, pp. 149, 152).

Many of Faulkner's comments revealed how much he viewed participation in war as an affirmation of manhood. He wrote to his stepson, ''It's a strange thing how a man, no matter how intelligent, will cling to the public proof of his masculinity: his courage and endurance, his willingness to sacrifice himself for the land which shaped his ancestors'' (*L*, p. 166), and later told him, ''I envy you being young enough to have a part in it. . . . Maybe there will be a part for me, who cant do anything but use words'' (B, p. 1143). In the face of his frustrations, Faulkner's painfully achieved sense of vocation proved vulnerable. He felt himself ''still too young to be unmoved by the old insidious succubae of trumpets, too old either to make one among them or to be impervious'' (*L*, p. 181).

Near the end of the war, Faulkner was finally offered a chance to do a book on Air Force operations overseas. But he lost it by appearing for his meeting with the military officials in an alcoholic stupor. Afterward, Faulkner wired desperately to his agent about the unfortunate rendezvous: ''INCONCLUSIVE BECAUSE I WAS TIGHT. . . . CAN ANYTHING BE DONE AS I WANT THE JOB'' (*L*, p. 191). Nothing could, as it turned out, be done. This time Faulkner was the victim, not of stringent Air Force rules about height and weight, but of his own self-destructive affinity for alcohol. The situation was undoubtedly made worse by his piercing awareness that this was probably the last opportunity he would ever have to take part in large-scale military action. Moreover, Faulkner's nephew had by now distinguished himself as a pilot, and once again, as in the first war, one of Faulkner's brothers returned wounded and scarred, the bearer of physical evidence of his military involvement. Faulkner watched them with wistful envy.

During the war, Faulkner's experiences in Hollywood proved as frustrating as those with the United States military. As a result of his own error, a product of inattention and unworldliness, Faulkner became involved with an unscrupulous Hollywood agent who committed him to a disastrous and exploitative contract requiring him to work for seven years at a lower salary than he had earned on his very first Hollywood job a decade before. There were some compensations—the chance to work with Howard Hawks doing screenplays for interesting films like *The Big Sleep* and *To Have and Have Not,* and the companionship of Meta Carpenter, now divorced from her pianist husband—but Faulkner felt victimized and debased by the experience. He became depressed and, viewing the long years still to run on the contract, feared he was getting to the point ''which most artists seem to reach where they admit at last that there is no solution to life and that it is not, and perhaps never was, worth the living'' (*L*, p. 199).

To make things worse, he felt, with strong justification, that his public acceptance, never pervasive, was now extinct. "My books have never sold, are out of print; the labor (the creation of my apocryphal country) of my life, even if I have a few things yet to add to it, will never make a living for me." He declared himself desperate to do ''anything'' for ''some more or less certain revenue'' (*L*, p. 199). The length and frequency of his alcoholic binges increased, and when his daughter Jill pathetically asked him to stop, to ''think of me,'' he responded with great cruelty. "Nobody remembers Shakespeare's children'' (*B*, p. 1204). On occasion, Faulkner's own problems made him blind to the fact that in some ways he contributed to making his daughter's childhood almost as unhappy as his own. He tried at times to behave sensibly, as when he gave up flying after he had a near-accident in 1947, and he revealed another sort of positive impulse when he began going to church, but his depression was persistent. He told his agent, "I feel bad, depressed, dreadful sense of wasting time, I imagine most of the symptoms of some kind of blow-up or collapse'' (*L*, p. 199).

Faulkner attempted to deal with the gloom that engulfed him by turning to his fiction, as he had often done before, but this time the attempt was less successful. He began work on a new novel in 1944, after more than two years away from his typewriter. He drew on old movie ideas, one concerning a Christ-like young man who leads a revolt against tyranny and another about General Charles de Gaulle, then leader of the Free French, and amalgamated aspects of both movie scenarios into the germ of *A Fable*. He approached the new work with enthusiasm. He saw it for a time as his *War and Peace*, ''not just my best but perhaps the best of my time,'' but he was equally aware that the experience of writing had changed for him, that the old ''divine fury'' had vanished. "I'm doing something different now, so different that I am writing and rewriting, weighing every word, which I never did before; I used to bang it on like an apprentice paper hanger and never look back.'' He became uncertain about the work's merits and betrayed a diffidence he had not shown before: "It may not be any good and I may be wrong about it.'' Faulkner blamed his continued difficulties with the novel on his Hollywood experience: "I have realised lately how much trash and junk writing for movies corrupted into my writing.'' When the horse race portion of *A Fable* was turned down by *Partisan Review*, Faulkner raised tremulous questions about the reasons for the refusal and asked his agent for reassurance. "Did they find it dull as written? . . . What is your opinion of this section in question? Dull? Too prolix? Diffuse?'' (*L*, pp. 237, 188–89, 248, 261).

After he had worked almost three years on the new book, he felt discouraged and put it aside for a time to try something "simpler." This was a procedure he had used with considerable success in his writing of *Absalom, Absalom!*—the interlude spent on *Pylon* provided "practice" on a new approach and sent him back to the first work with renewed vigor and determination—but it worked less well with *A Fable*. There were so many fundamental problems with its conception and execution that no amount of "recess" could help Faulkner to turn it into a *magnum opus*. Moreover, he took off several years, not a few months, and by the time he finally returned to *A Fable*, it was moribund.

Unaware of the potential for failure in a method that had previously been successful, Faulkner began work on *Intruder in the Dust* in January of 1947. He based the story on an incident that had occurred in Oxford more than a decade before, when a local black killed a white man and was lynched by a large and angry mob (*B*, p. 1246). In his initial conception, Faulkner, who was an inveterate reader of detective stories, saw the novel as a "mystery story, original in that the solver is a negro, himself in jail for the murder and is about to be lynched, solves murder in self defense." But as he began work on it in the late forties, the focus changed and the work became more complicated, evolving into the tale of Chick Mallison's initiation into moral adulthood. "It started out to be a simple quick 150 page whodunit but jumped the traces, strikes me as being a pretty good study of a 16 year old boy who overnight became a man" (*L*, pp. 128, 266).

Intruder in the Dust is a generally effective story of Chick's emotional progress toward acceptance of his moral obligations to a black man who has been a sort of surrogate father to him. The work has similarities to *Great Expectations*, in Faulkner's use of the name Miss Habersham for his tutelary old woman, for instance, and in Lucas Beauchamp's interesting kinship with the convict Magwitch, which Michael Millgate points out.[4] Chick Mallison is also a typically Faulknerian protagonist of the period: like Bayard Sartoris of *The Unvanquished*, he gradually acquires a humane and individualized ethic; like Ike McCaslin of "The Bear," he tries to make personal restitution for a regional past of racial injustice.

Faulkner obviously meant the reader to make comparisons between the stories of Ike McCaslin and Chick Mallison, because the fictional contexts are much the same and the initiation experiences of the young males are essentially similar. Chick's achievement goes beyond that of Ike, however, both in the growth of perspicacity and in the capacity for right action. Where Ike believes himself "free" from the taint of racism by the renunciation of his patrimony, Chick early recognizes that his effort to be "free" of obligation to Lucas Beauchamp is delusory, that he cannot buy immunity with gifts of any sort. Ike not only fails to achieve full awareness, he fails to take positive action. Chick, on the other hand, accepts active responsibility for exculpating Lucas of the murder with which he has been wrongly charged and saves his life. Chick's journey into Beat Four to "rob a grave" is, like Ike's into the wilderness and into the commissary ledgers, a symbolic one. He travels psychically from the condition of "unwitting infant in the long tradition of his native land" to that of moral adult who can recognize the need for repudiation of what is "not a racial outrage but a human shame" (97).[5] In liberating Lucas, Chick liberates himself from the fetters of prejudice which continue to hamper Ike throughout his life.

Go Down, Moses is a more complex work, of course, than *Intruder in the Dust,* but the second serves, in a way, as an exemplum for the protagonist of the first. Chick's experience demonstrates possibilities for redemptive action that Ike has failed to see, just as, in a previous Faulknerian sequence, Bayard Sartoris of *The Unvanquished* copes more successfully with a dominant male figure than his predecessors, Charles Bon and Quentin Compson of *Absalom, Absalom!*. In returning to the same fictional situation a second time, Faulkner seems able to envisage a resolution unavailable to him the first time around. But since in each case the less resolved work is the more powerful, it may be that the struggle for an answer provided him greater inspiration than the answer itself.

Chick's evolving psychic relationship with Lucas is obviously central to *Intruder in the Dust,* and any case which can be made for the novel as a significant work is based on its status as a *Bildungsroman.* Nevertheless, it began as Faulkner's first sustained effort to write a full-length detective thriller. He had subtly used some of the conventions of the genre in *Absalom, Absalom!,* in the slow unraveling of a mysterious series of events. Now, in *Intruder in the Dust,* he employed numerous elements familiar to mystery fans, such as the wrongly accused suspect, the single-minded detective, the search for a missing body, the pivotal ballistic identification, and the final explanation of the murderer's motives and methods—and techniques like concluding a chapter with a shocking discovery that virtually "forces" the reader to go on. Other conventions he stands on their ear, for it is not the anticipated ratiocination of the "detectives" which makes them capable of important discoveries, but their antirationalism, their willingness to act while putting "all thought ratiocination contemplation forever behind them" (94). Chick, Miss Habersham, and Aleck Sander are ideally suited for their mission by their lack of interest in the ideology that becomes crippling prejudice when it dominates the adult male in the South.

Intuitive responses and readiness for pure action are the primary credentials of these "detectives." Only in *Knight's Gambit,* which Faulkner published the year after *Intruder in the Dust,* did he make use of a ratiocinative unraveler of mysteries, when he put Gavin Stevens to work on a series of challenging cases which gave the lawyer an opportunity to use his putative intellectual powers in a constructive way.

In *Intruder in the Dust,* Stevens serves primarily as a touchstone for Chick, both as a man and as a representative of certain southern racial and political stances. At first Chick's attachment to his uncle is "blind and absolute" (21), and his mind resonates with the echoes of Stevens's perpetual aphorisms. The psychic severance from his uncle so necessary to Chick's development comes when Lucas tries to enlist their help. Though Stevens refuses to hear even a description of the job at hand, Chick accepts responsibility without really being asked. Stevens is so dominated by his own assumptions on matters of race that he eventually ceases to offer much useful guidance even at the intellectual level. When Chick asks earnestly why the townspeople fled when confronted with the fact of Lucas's innocence, Stevens answers with a lengthy non sequitur about the States' Rights position which appears of little use to the boy.

A strongly implicit criticism of Stevens in *Intruder in the Dust* subtly undercuts his status as a spokesman for certain southern stances on social and political issues: he talks incessantly but fails to act. While Stevens expounds weighty moral messages about refusing to bear "injustice and outrage and dishonor and shame" (206), two boys and an old woman actually go out and exhume corpses to save Lucas Beauchamp from a lynch mob. By the end of the novel, Stevens's hands are still clean and his Phi Beta Kappa key untarnished, while the real work has been done by others. Stevens is found wanting by the activist standards fundamental to the novel: as Faulkner himself said later, "He was a good man, but he didn't succeed in living up to his ideal. But his nephew, the boy, I think he may grow up to be a better man than his uncle" (*LIG,* p. 225).

Gavin Stevens has been creating problems for critics and readers since he first appeared in *Light in August* and set forth his theory of the linkage of race and motivation in Joe Christmas. Some early critics called Stevens a Faulknerian spokesman, thus finding grounds for denouncing the fiction in which he appears as propaganda, and readers often find him irritating. Stevens, unquestionably a problematic character, seems based on the Oxford lawyer Phil Stone, whose talkativeness was an inextricable part of his personality and whose combination of proprietariness and incomprehension had become increasingly irritating to Faulkner himself over the years. Not long before Faulkner began work on *Intruder in the Dust*, Stone told Malcolm Cowley that *The Wild Palms* and *Absalom, Absalom!* were "absolutely ruined because of the fact that Faulkner apparently lacks any comprehensive sense of design" and that his style "is really not a style in the proper sense but merely a personal mannerism." Stone diagnosed Faulkner's central "trouble" as the fact "that he keeps on rewriting *Sanctuary*" (B, pp. 1181–82). Stone's statements are so wrongheaded as to be faintly comical, yet Faulkner remained loyal to him, loaned him money, and dedicated the Snopes trilogy to him in an impressive gesture of gratitude. At the same time, Stevens, who is obviously a caricature of Phil Stone and who appears ridiculous at many points, probably represents Faulkner's subtle retaliation for his garrulous friend's proprietary ways. As Stevens continued to appear in Faulkner's fiction of the 1950s, his experiences began to recapitulate those of the writer himself. Faulkner's biographer, moreover, asserts that there are elements in Stevens "that owed something to his creator as well as his creator's friend."[6] Thus Stevens becomes interesting psychobiographically, although he continues to be a difficult presence artistically.

Stevens's States' Rights stance in *Intruder in the Dust* is made questionable by the context in which it appears, yet Chick, too, evinces strong regional concern. His anger at the townspeople arises from "that fierce desire that they should be perfect because they were his and he was theirs" and a need to "excoriate them himself without mercy since they were his own and he wanted no more save to stand with them unalterable and impregnable . . . one people one heart one land" (209–10). Chick's impassioned expression of both anger at and emotional identification with his fellow Mississippians may well be Faulkner's own, for the racial problems in his state tore him apart emotionally. He had powerful ties to Mississippi and its people, but like Chick he felt driven to speak out publicly against their acceptance of racism. In *Intruder in the Dust*, as in its predecessor, Faulkner dramatized a variety of responses to past and present racial problems while making clear that the only moral and humane course was to recognize the blacks' individual integrity and their right to live with dignity. He was somewhat less clear about how that right should be implemented in a workable fashion, and his efforts to find a mediating position between the inertia of regional mores and the demands coming from the federal government caused him eventually to come under severe attack by liberals and conservatives alike and to be publicly denounced in a local newspaper by his own brother.

Lucas Beauchamp's unspoken but powerful pleas for recognition as an individual are crucial to *Intruder in the Dust*, and Faulkner, ironically, later proved deaf to the moral message of his own novel. A movie was made from the work in 1949 and much of the filming was done in Oxford. In a hospitable gesture, Faulkner and his wife invited the entire cast to Rowanoak, with the exception of Juano Hernandez, the Puerto Rican actor who played the role of Lucas (B, p. 1284). Faulkner was capable of dramatizing the need for racial equality, but incapable in his private life of always treating blacks as social equals, of withstanding the great pressure to observe racial barriers. Faulkner the novelist sensitively delineated the problems and some of the solutions, but Faulkner the man was unable to find the proper course of action. Still, he cared deeply and his conscience continued to haunt him on this subject, impelling him at a later date to set aside some of his Nobel Prize money to be used for college scholarships for worthy blacks.

The effective portrayal of Lucas Beauchamp, along with the moving story of Chick Mallison's initiation into moral adulthood and the successful intermingling of suspense and comedy, gives *Intruder in the Dust* a certain stature. But the work is marred by defects such as the narrative confusion over Crawford Guthrie's capture and suicide and the self-parodying, multi-page sentences full of confusing parenthetical comment. Faulkner's intentions appear unclear in this novel, as they did in an earlier work, *Pylon,* which he also wrote as respite from an intended masterpiece, and it seems especially significant that he becomes too explicit in his explanation of underlying emotional tensions, too overt in his connecting of parallel incidents, as though he no longer trusted his reader to do the analyzing himself.

The year after *Intruder in the Dust* appeared, Faulkner published a thematically related group of six long stories in book form. The tales of *Knight's Gambit* all contain rational exercises in mystery solving, with Gavin Stevens as the detective, a modern version of Poe's Auguste Dupin, who cleverly deduces answers from a puzzling array of facts. Perhaps the most effective of these is "Tomorrow," in which a search into the personal history of a murder trial juror ends with the poignant discovery of his long-ago devotion to a child who, as an adult, became the victim of the homicide that others see as justifiable. Much of the tale is quite moving, but Gavin Stevens pushes it over the brink into sentimentality and wordiness with his comments about "the lowly and invincible of the earth" who "endure and endure and then endure tomorrow and tomorrow and tomorrow." The title story of the volume is a weak imitation of Faulkner's own best work. It contains some major Faulknerian elements— an intense emotional relationship between a brother and sister, a family legend, a heroic horseman, and the Oedipal rivalry between a young man and his mother's fiancé—but they never coalesce into a tale of any power. *Knight's Gambit* as a whole has, in fact, little import beyond its curiosity value as Faulkner's tribute to a genre which provided much of his leisure reading.

After the completion of *Knight's Gambit,* Faulkner was still unready to return to *A Fable* and turned instead to a piece he had begun almost twenty years before. Faulkner intended *Requiem for a Nun* as a sequel to *Sanctuary* and started it soon after that novel was published, but quickly abandoned the project. He picked it up again for a number of personal reasons, few of which had much to do with the intrinsic merit of the idea. He wished to do a play for an actress friend, Ruth Ford, who had known his dead brother Dean years before at the University of Mississippi. He was also looking for a work on which he could easily engage the artistic collaboration of a young woman with whom he had recently fallen in love. Joan Williams was a twenty-one-year-old college student and aspiring writer when she met Faulkner on a literary pilgrimage to Oxford. Despite the more than thirty-years' difference in their ages, the two discovered an affinity and began a correspondence that was intimate from the very outset. Faulkner was obviously ready for an emotional involvement, for he had written Malcolm Cowley not long before, "It's a dull life here. I need some new people, above all probably a new young woman" (*L*, p. 245). Faulkner's partly facetious comment revealed an important truth, for this relationship, like his other extramarital romantic entanglements, offered him some sort of vitality and emotional regeneration which he wanted and needed.

Faulkner was rarely open with anyone, but his first letter to Joan Williams, even after an uneasy initial encounter in which he accused her of wanting to see whether he had two heads, was warm and candid and showed his readiness to become involved. She sent him some questions and he replied, "A woman must ask these of a man while they are lying in bed together . . . when they are lying at peace or at least quiet and maybe on the edge of sleep, so you'll have to wait, even to ask them." Joan was interested in a writing career, but she was also young and pretty, and Faulkner's immediate espousal of the role of mentor was not necessarily based on a principle of general support for aspiring writers. He had shown slight interest in helping his own brother Johncy to begin a similar career and had done little to encourage his daughter Jill, now in her late teens, along the same lines, although this may have been because they showed less promise than Joan. Faulkner's response to the latter, though initially disguised as that of a fellow southerner who had struggled free of his middle-class constrictions in the same way she hoped to, was obviously emotional and soon became passionate. His own concept of the relationship was a complex one, for he pictured himself variously as Pygmalion, "creating not a cold and beautiful statue, in order to fall in love with it, but Pygmalion taking his love and creating a poet out of her"; as a parent, "the father which you never had—the one who . . . desired, tried, to put always first your hopes and dreams and happiness"; and as an ardent suitor, "capable not only of imagining anything and everything, but even of hoping and believing it" (B, pp. 1299, 1303, 1484, 1313). Faulkner began traveling to Memphis and New York in order to see his new Galatea-daughter-lover. As well as advising Joan on her own writing, he enlisted her "help" on his new work, *Requiem for a Nun*.

When Faulkner had the original idea for the book in 1933, he described it as "about a nigger woman. It will be a little on the esoteric side, like AS I LAY DYING" (L, p. 75). In 1950, Joan's encouragement, along with his interest in doing something for Ruth Ford, pushed him to put a drama at the center of his work.[7] He regarded it as "an interesting experiment in form" and urged Joan to help him with the dramatized portions. He sent her the first draft and said, "Rewrite this first scene if you want to, write any of the rest of it." He next told his publisher that he intended to "see if she can lift the play scenes and condense the long speeches into a workable play script." Though Joan worked on it to some extent, she was too busy with other things to make much progress, but Faulkner was reluctant to end the collaboration. Even after it became clear that she could not be fully involved, he told her, "I still think of [it] as our play." Later, however, he conceded that he had "failed to persuade" her to help him work on it (L, pp. 299, 305, 317, 322).

When *Requiem for a Nun* was published in 1951, it was generally regarded as "didactic," as an "ambitious failure."[8] Critics were unhappy with the work's tone, and readers were put off by its unusual form as a symbolic play-cum-history-cum-novel. The dramatic portion has some similarity to *Intruder in the Dust* and *Knight's Gambit* in centering on the unraveling of motives and responsibility for a perplexing murder, and the intercalated prose essays offering regional history with a didactic overlay also recall sections of *Intruder in the Dust*. Yet the work is a startling experiment with no antecedent in Faulkner's earlier work, for it combines not only two narrative forms, the play and the essay, but two distinct styles of writing, the first unadorned, almost Hemingwayesque, the second fluid, elaborate, typically Faulknerian.[9] The slimmest of threads attach the two—the theme of guilt in both its personal and collective forms is common to the separate portions, and the essays serve as lengthy descriptions of the settings in which the ensuing dramatic action takes place. The disparity of style and mode is severe, and the novel lacks the integration of a somewhat similar work, *The Wild Palms*.[10]

Certain basic elements in the dramatic portion may well have sprung from Faulkner's complex response, in the context of his troubled marriage, now in its third decade, to his emotional involvement with Joan Williams. For the story of Temple Drake, though seemingly focused on her efforts to rescue the murderer of her child from execution, is to a large degree the story of her marriage. That marriage is, like Faulkner's, one which has survived tragedy, guilt, suffering, and infidelity, a marriage in which both members are at once responsible for the union's difficulties and committed to its survival; in their varying flaws and strengths Temple and Gowan each represent an aspect of Faulkner's complicated attitudes toward his own marriage.

Gowan is the less central figure, but his earlier decision to marry Temple because it was the gentlemanly thing to do has—like his unwillingness to leave her and his alcoholism—parallels in Faulkner's own marital history. Similarly, Temple's abortive effort to elope with another man, now secondary to her sincere effort to make her marriage survive, may reflect aspects of Faulkner's own real or imagined responses to his marriage.

Viewed in this way, the play is, oddly, both a horror fantasy about marriage and an heroic affirmation of marriage's capacity to endure. The horror arises most strikingly from the central fact that so gruesome a crime as child murder is envisioned as the penalty for the effort to abandon the marriage. Temple's punishments continue: she is allowed no opportunity to escape the implications of her past, forced back into a confrontation with her apparent complicity in her own child's murder, driven to anguished self-abasement by her interlocutor, and, finally, made to feel that her sins are an even greater cause for guilt than the actual murder of her baby. The moral disproportions so evident in Temple's suffering and guilt, like the horror of her punishment, may reflect Faulkner's guilty concern about the prolonged effects on his own family of his adulterous relationships. Yet Temple has, like the author, remained in the marriage, even though it represents a form of imprisonment and a sacrifice of the urge to seize full personal happiness. In making her gesture of forgiveness and admitting her culpability, Temple supposedly begins a ''new life'' (268).[11]

Gavin Stevens plays a disturbing role in Temple's suffering, for he is both her inquisitor and the punishing voice of her conscience. Whether Faulkner intended any parallels with Phil Stone's role in his own life is unknown, but Stone did serve as some sort of intermediary in Faulkner's love affairs, receiving mail for him and acting as an emergency contact. If the lawyer was openly critical of and inquisitive about his writer friend's adultery, he may have served as a model for the tormentor Gavin Stevens; if not, Stevens must have been patterned on the promptings of Faulkner's own conscience. Stevens believes that one's personal past is "something like a promissory note with a trick clause in it" which cannot be nullified and must be paid for (162). Though Stevens's judgment is quickly shown to be in error on major points, still his relentless quest for the "truth" of "everything" forces Temple into confessing, not only to her husband, but to the governor as the representative of the people. Temple must make her self-abasing admissions in the public sphere as well as in the private.

Presumably Stevens's intentions are good, but his means are humanly questionable, even sadistic.[12] In this he is like Nancy Mannigoe, a believer whose faith lets her arrogate to herself control over another human being's free choice. Critics have often focused on Nancy's theology, her avowals of "Just believe" and "Trust in Him" (273, 275). Cleanth Brooks calls it "sound enough" but points out, validly, that Faulkner's dramatic presentation of her faith is inadequate.[13] The real issue, though, seems to lie in the terrible acts such a faith can lead one to commit. Nancy is as desperately misguided in her blind faith as earlier believers like Doc Hines and MacEachern of *Light in August*.

Public concerns are more or less implicit in the dramatic section of *Requiem for a Nun* as it is played out in the courthouse, the governor's mansion, and the jail. Faulkner yielded to his impulse to make such things explicit in the three prose essays which he alternated with the acts of the play. The first is perhaps the finest. Folly compounds felony, as the loss of Alec Holston's lock is necessarily transmuted into the acquisition of a communal edifice. Thomas Jefferson Pettigrew, the mailrider after whom the town is named, appears to be the "hero" of the tale in his efforts to keep the town officially honest. It is tempting to see Pettigrew as a self-portrait of Faulkner in his new guise as gadfly to the public morality, for Pettigrew is small but indomitable in both his purveying of news and his actions as "a damned moralist" (26).

Faulkner had revealed a strong sense of the town as a moral and physical entity in *Intruder in the Dust*. In *Requiem for a Nun*, he looks into the past to see that it was the erection of the courthouse which created that sense of unity, for it was built in "one conjoined breath," one "compound dream-state" and gave its populace the inspiring idea that "men, all men, including themselves, were a little better, purer maybe even, than they had thought, expected, or even needed to be'' (32, 33, 42–43). "Good" comes out of "evil," and the result is affirmative even though the foundation is questionable.

The state history of the second essay reveals the same message; it is turbulent and full of human error, but like the courthouse and Temple's marriage, the state endures. The story of the jail offers perhaps the most poignant and affirmative testimony to the persistence of the past in the present, for it is full of "the old ineradicable remembering" (224) and contains a vivid trace of one individual history, the diamond-inscribed name of the jailer's daughter. The Yoknapatawpha chronicler takes the reader right up to that window to hear it speaking across time: *"Listen, stranger; this was myself: this was I"* (262). Faulkner ends his final essay by memorializing a minor character with great resonance, in a manner that serves to memorialize the entire body of his own fiction.

Shortly before *Requiem for a Nun* was published, Faulkner received a number of impressive laurels which established him in the public mind as a literary giant. Just a few years before, Faulkner's works had almost all gone out of print. Malcolm Cowley had partially rectified this depressing situation with his assembly and publication of the Viking *Portable Faulkner* in 1946, which returned the author to the public eye. By 1950, however, Faulkner had begun to accumulate honors at an awesome rate. That year his *Collected Stories* received the National Book Award; he was also given the prestigious Howells Medal by the American Academy of Arts and Letters; and in November he attained the summit of public recognition when he was named as the recipient of the Nobel Prize for Literature.

Faulkner was only the third American writer to become a Nobel laureate in the several decades since the prize had been established, and the journalists began flocking to his door to elicit staements about "how it feels." Apparently it felt troublesome, for Faulkner's immediate response was to get roaring drunk and announce that he had no intention of going to Stockholm. His family, friends, and publisher all began to apply pressure, but Faulkner was adamant until his daughter Jill said that she longed for a trip to Europe. Her father finally capitulated, but rebelliously remained in an alcoholic state of detachment while others rushed to procure plane tickets and formal dress. In his semidazed condition, Faulkner somehow managed during the trip to Sweden to write an acceptance speech which he delivered hung-over, unshaven, and in a faint voice (B, pp. 1341–68).

Ironically, the Nobel Prize speech became almost at once one of Faulkner's best-known works. Nearly everyone who is aware of the writer can quote some portion of the hopeful lines "I believe that man will not merely endure; he will prevail. He is immortal, not because he alone among creatures has an inexhaustible voice, but because he has a soul, a spirit capable of compassion and sacrifice and endurance." The writer's "privilege," Faulkner continued, is "to help man endure by lifting his heart, by reminding him of the courage and honor and hope and pride and compassion and pity and sacrifice which have been the glory of his past. The poet's voice need not merely be the record of man, it can be one of the props, the pillars to help him endure and prevail."[14] Faulkner thus affirmed both man's splendor and the tutelary role of the artist in an impassioned way; he also revealed, with an ominous self-consciousness, the ever-broadening vision which would receive its most memorable incarnation in his first post-Nobel novel.

A Fable was still unfinished after Faulkner's trip to Stockholm. In order to give himself a more congenial place in which to work on it, Faulkner used some of his growing wealth to add a study to his Oxford house, calling it an "office" in emulation of plantation owners. On two of the walls of his new office, Faulkner wrote an outline of *A Fable*, as if this unprecedented visible reminder could somehow spur him on to completion. In between bouts of back pain, caused by the fracture of several vertebrae after repeated falls from a horse, and bouts of heavy drinking, which served as his therapy for the pain, he continued to labor over the novel and finally finished it near the end of 1953.

A Fable, which Faulkner envisioned as his *magnum opus,* is an ambitious retelling of the central Christian myth in a modern context of world war. Its obvious flaws reveal Faulkner's sadly increasing inability to judge the artistic merits of his own fiction. He admitted that he could not make a final pronouncement: "It is either nothing and I am blind in my dotage, or it is the best of my time" (*L*, p. 352). He evidently cared a great deal about it and intended it to be his culminating achievement. Given these circumstances, the current impulses to critical rehabilitation of *A Fable* are understandable,[15] but while the novel certainly evinces high seriousness and an ambitious range, it remains a difficult and rather unrewarding work for both critic and reader. It reveals, even more than its immediate predecessors, Faulkner replacing the subtle yet effective coherence of his strongest work with a consciously achieved, almost schematic, unity and supplanting psychological vitality with ideological debates. Whereas in earlier works Faulkner depicted the complex responses of a series of characters to a central figure such as Caddy Compson, Addie Bundren, or Thomas Sutpen, in *A Fable* war is the central "character." The other actors are linked primarily in terms of their varying reactions to the war as both abstraction and reality; their human interactions are more limited.

What many readers find most praiseworthy in the novel is the folk tale about the legendary crippled horse, which was separately published as *Notes on a Horsethief*. But, as Hyatt Waggoner points out, the realism of the "horsethief" story exists in uneasy equilibrium with the Christian allegory of the main narrative and the novel works well at neither level.[16] Faulkner's usual rewarding complexity often degenerates here into mere inchoateness as characters prove difficult to differentiate and the narrative line becomes at points too confusing to follow. The work is frustrating to consider, for never in a Faulkner work had there been such disparity between intention and achievement. One of *A Fable's* problems is common to many of Faulkner's late works—his canvas is too large and the individual gets lost in the aggregate. Moreover, the author attempts to deal with Life instead of life and with Christ instead of an ordinary suffering human being. Tolstoy's great work, which Faulkner obviously had in mind as he wrote *A Fable,* is equally panoramic in scope. Yet *War and Peace* is filled with memorable individuals who are thoroughly alive and whose personal struggles serve as metaphoric embodiments of the larger military and political struggles raging beyond them.

Despite its flaws, *A Fable* bears some interesting psychobiographical similarities to two earlier Faulkner works, his first novel and his master-piece. With *A Fable,* Faulkner begins an earlier cycle all over again by attempting once more to deal fictionally, as he had in *Soldiers' Pay,* with his personal failure to get into military action in a world war. He also returns to a pivotal theme of *Absalom, Absalom!,* the emotional struggle between a father and an unacknowledged son which ends in the death of the younger man. This has a vital relationship both to Faulkner's own persistent difficulties with a father who refused to accept his oldest son and to Faulkner's growing awareness that he might be creating similar problems for his own child, who was becoming an adult as he worked on *A Fable.* The psychological differences between the latter and its predecessors are also significant, however. Both *Soldiers' Pay* and *A Fable* treat war and its destructive consequences for the individual caught in its midst. But the earlier work is full of self-pitying *Weltschmerz* and a romantic longing for military heroism, while the 1954 novel reveals a more sophisticated view of war as a paradigm of the generalized corruption that underlies all social systems. Faulkner had previously shown his "revisionist" view, his awareness of the potential perniciousness of the longing for military distinction, in his portrait of the vicious Percy Grimm in *Light in August*. Grimm's wish for "heroic" violence is so strong that he appoints himself killer and castrater of the murderer Joe Christmas. But Grimm and what he represents were minor elements in the 1932 novel; in *A Fable* the theme serves as the very foundation of the narrative. The novel contains no conventional war heroes who are also fully admirable, and the redemptive figure is pacifistic and self-sacrificing. The generals are first seen in a contaminated isolation "like that of three plague carriers" (15),[17] and their attempted collusion with the German leader to keep the war going at all costs betrays an almost unbelievably self-serving cynicism. The so-called perfect soldier of *A Fable* is a friendless and pastless orphan with a machinelike dedication to his role and a habit of "monotonous success" (21) who finally becomes a sacrificial scapegoat.

No glamorous Mahon-figure occupies the corrupt war theater of *A Fable,* although there is a young soldier reminiscent of Julian Lowe of *Soldiers' Pay*. David Levine, "athirst with the ringing heroic catalogue," feels that because he has missed the opportunity to join the RFC "a door had closed on glory" (88), and he has forever lost the chance to join that Valhalla of flying heroes. However, unlike Lowe, Levine acquires a realistic and appalling vision of the evil inherent in war when he witnesses the German general arriving on Allied terrain in a barrage of fake bullets and then shooting his own pilot in the face for "surrendering." The sight is fatally disillusioning for Levine, and the burning of his Sidcott coverall symbolizes the attrition of his hopes. While Lowe retains his "innocence" and loses himself in vain dreams of glory, Levine sees clearly through the romantic haze to the horrors beneath. He discovers a world he cannot accept and takes his own life, an action Faulkner himself viewed as nonconstructive, for he called Levine "the nihilistic third" of the "trinity" of man's conscience, "who in effect, to destroy evil, destroys the world too, i.e., the world which is his, himself."[18]

Levine's suicide is one of many repudiations in *A Fable,* all of which are related to an awareness of the fundamental nature of war as a symptom of man's capacity for corruption and destruction. Although Faulkner continued to be fascinated with war as an arena for human drama and was twice frustrated by his personal failure to enter that arena, by the time he came to write *A Fable* he had a much less romantic idea of military involvement than he had had in the 1920s. He portrayed the abuses of war as both more pervasive and more destructive than he had in *Soldiers' Pay*.

The struggle in *A Fable* between the Christ-like corporal and the old general who proves to be his father is central to the novel in much the same way that the crisis between Charles Bon and Thomas Sutpen was focal to *Absalom, Absalom!*. The emotional difference between these pivotal father-son tensions is significant, however, as is the difference between the fathers themselves. In the earlier novel Faulkner appears to identify himself psychologically with Bon as the rejected child looking desperately for recognition from his parent, a heartless, almost demonic figure; in *A Fable* he shows an equally strong awareness of the father, making him more complexly human a man than the father of the 1936 novel and one who, torn between his duty and his son, feels impelled to manipulate that son into a situation in which he is forced into self-sacrifice.[19] Filicide, however indirect, is an important issue in both novels, but in *A Fable* Faulkner focuses more on the parental viewpoint of the catastrophic event. Faulkner also makes the old general a far more interesting character than his son. He is an allegorical figure who partakes of both God and Satan and can be seen also as the generalized authority principle in his attempt to overcome the rebellion that threatens the ''orderly'' progression of war. The confrontations between father and son are significant scenes; though deficient in drama, they present the central philosophical tensions of the novel.

The emotional scenes between Bon and Sutpen in *Absalom, Absalom!* are evoked early in *A Fable,* as the corporal and the general exchange a glance, ''looking at each other across the fleeting instant'' (17). No sign of recognition is given, but clearly the two will face each other again. The physical and social disparities between the two men are as great and as symbolic as the differences between Bon and his father. The corporal, with his ''mountain peasant's face'' (17), is unlettered and inarticulate, while his father, frail and delicate, is the supreme general of his country, whose goal is ''the restored glory and destiny of France'' (247) and whose authority is greater than that of all other generals in the Allied Forces. The powerful father and the powerless son first meet when the latter has rebelled against the war, and hence tacitly against his father, by refusing to fight, and has been condemned to die by that same authority of which his father is the highest representative.

Faulkner's unpublished note to *A Fable* asserts that ''this is not a pacifist book. . . . If this book had any aim or moral . . . , it was to show by poetic analogy, allegory, that pacificism does not work.''[20] He thus implies that the dilemma of the general, equally with the martyrdom of the corporal, offers grounds for sympathy. The general feels pressure to reprieve the corporal, but also has a strong sense of his obligations to a larger constituency. Like Faulkner in his late work to some degree, the general is willing to sacrifice a man for the sake of Man. He must "bear the fearful burden of man's anguish and terror and at last his hope" (271). Knowing this he must keep in mind that "by destroying his life tomorrow morning, I will establish forever that he didn't even live in vain, let alone die so" (332). During the scene at the Roman citadel, as Satan tempted Christ three times, so the general urges his son at great length and with considerable persuasiveness to choose life, to "take the earth" (347), and to be rewarded with acknowledgment as his son. The corporal refuses, electing to sacrifice himself before the firing squad. His father ends the encounter with a pointed reminder of their kinship. "Good night, my child. . . . Remember whose blood it is that you defy me with" (356). Both frustration with and pride in his rebellious son are evinced by the general's parting words.

In his speech, the old general sounds as much like the Faulkner of the Nobel Prize acceptance speech as he does like God or Satan. He asserts that man "will prevail" (354), rails against cars, aircraft, and the mechanistic age beginning to overtake the old way of life, and dispenses endless paternal advice. Faulkner dedicated *A Fable* to his own child, Jill, because it was published the year she became twenty-one and "she had inherited lots of my traits. . . . This was just a gesture toward her when she became of age and was no longer under my thumb."[21] Faulkner's tendency to identify with the old general, who is trying to keep his son and everyone else in line, may account for some of the inconsistencies in his character as well as for the fact that he is more fully developed than the corporal. Moreover, the general becomes rather sympathetic in the speech that reveals his terror of death: "Nothing—not power nor glory nor wealth nor pleasure nor even freedom from pain, is as valuable as simple breathing, simply being alive even with all the regret of having to remember and the anguish of an irreparable worn-out body" (350).

Faulkner's obviously greater interest in father than in son in *A Fable,* like other changes in focus in his late fiction, reflects the new emotional and philosophical preoccupations that were altering both his approach to his work and the work itself. In another piece written at this time, Faulkner justified his altered attitudes and methods as stemming from complex motives that incorporated both personal and general goals—a "hope and desire to uplift man's heart" which is, in the last analysis, "completely selfish, completely personal. He would lift up man's heart for his own benefit because in that way he can say No to death."[22]

11
Late Middle Age:
The Town and *The Mansion*

AFTER *A Fable* WAS PUBLISHED Faulkner, prompted perhaps by his ever-increasing sense of mortality, turned to some long-unfinished fictional material. That material dated from the earliest stage of his career as a novelist, when he began the novel he then called "Father Abraham," out of which evolved the Snopes trilogy. With the publication of *The Town* and *The Mansion* in the late 1950s, Faulkner completed the most ambitious of his projects. The three Snopes novels cover several decades in the lives of Flem Snopes, his many relatives, and those with whom they come in contact, following their various triumphs and defeats as they move inexorably toward old age and death. Like Faulkner himself, few of them are willing to go gently: these works of late middle age, though less energetic than *The Hamlet,* have moments of fine comedy and piercing poignancy.

They also, however, evince some of the aestheticaly troubling qualities of Faulkner's previous three novels. A broad range of issues and human responses to them, an increasing trend toward explicitness and summary, a conscious stress on the thematic rather than the psycho-symbolic—these features which seem for Faulkner almost inevitably to cause diffuseness and attenuation are nearly as evident in *The Town* and *The Mansion* as they were in *Intruder in the Dust, Requiem for a Nun,* and *A Fable.* Yet Faulkner's decision to return to Jefferson and the struggle between Snopeses and their opponents was, on the whole, a fortunate one. These two late novels have more strengths than weaknesses, and the trilogy as a unit is an impressive achievement.

226

Both novels reveal in striking ways the presence of the aging writer, concerned with the changes for good or ill wrought by the passage of the years. He portrays the inevitable yet frustrating repetition of past errors in the present, the perpetual but futile quest for fulfillment, the need for retrospective appraisal, and the persistence of regret. These moods, thoughts, and actions, which were characteristic of Faulkner's own late middle age, appear in the stories of Gavin Stevens, Flem Snopes, Eula Varner Snopes, V. K. Ratliff, and Mink Snopes. Faulkner asserted in the preface to *The Mansion* that he had learned "more about the human heart and its dilemma than he knew thirty-four years ago," when he first began the project, and the last two volumes reveal that the part of the human "heart" with which he was now most familiar was that which confronts the implications of its own approaching death. At the same time, that heart remained endlessly susceptible to the stirrings of romance well into his late years; indeed, Faulkner's most passionate extramarital entanglements preceded his work on each volume of the Snopes trilogy, giving his most pervasive use of folk material an overlay of personal romantic experience. Even as *The Hamlet* treats, among other things, the anguish of thwarted love, its successors contain comic portrayals of a middle-aged man's ardent yet abortive involvements with an old flame and with two young women. All of these depictions grew out of Faulkner's own frustrating liaisons over a period of twenty-five years.

Faulkner continued to see the woman he had deeply cared for in the mid-1930s, Meta Carpenter, but her remarriages and his own flagging interest had virtually ended that relationship by 1950. By then, Faulkner was deeply involved emotionally with Joan Williams and was undergoing another frustrating experience. The more ardent he became, the more she felt an impulse to escape from a troubling relationship with a married man thirty-one years her senior. Faulkner offered Joan companionship and splendid advice on her first work of fiction, which eventually became a prize-winning novel under his tutelage, but she had an understandable reluctance to become fully committed. They were lovers for a brief time, but Faulkner always anticipated being dispatched. He insisted that "I am only trying to help you become an artist. You owe me nothing in return for what I try to do or succeed in doing for you" (*L*, p. 337). Almost immediately after Faulkner finished *A Fable*, the two severed their relationship. Faulkner went on a binge in Europe, where he had gone to work on a movie script for Howard Hawks, and was delivered one day, drunk and bloody, to Hawks by two policemen (B, p. 1482). Early the next year, Joan made the separation irrevocable by marrying a young writer.

Her new husband was an ex-professional athlete and a war veteran, and thus embodied certain qualities Faulkner believed to be painfully lacking in himself.

Faulkner apparently did little prolonged brooding about his replacement by the sort of troubling "real man" so frequently found in his fiction, for shortly after the break with Joan, he met and became involved with another young woman. Jean Stein was almost forty years the writer's junior, but soon after their meeting in St. Moritz, she made clear her readiness for a romantic entanglement and began traveling around Europe with him. Although Faulkner's new affair involved an enormous age difference, it obviously offered him a sense of vital possibilities which he needed. It also had a romantic, globe-trotting quality, for Jean Stein was the daughter of the wealthy founder of the Music Corporation of America and willingly traveled between New York and Rome and Paris to meet Faulkner. The relationship ended in 1957, driving Faulkner to drink and to some bitter generalizations about how women belonged only in the kitchen (B, p. 1629), but it had already produced its happiest result, the important interview, published in the *Paris Review* in 1955, in which Faulkner made what are probably the most thoughtful and thorough comments about his own work ever to appear in one place. The pattern in Faulkner's extramarital affairs was generally consistent—a brief period of intense involvement, followed by slight withdrawal on the part of one or both when it became clear the relationship would always be adulterous, after which the woman married someone else. The women were always attractive and young, and they became even younger as time went on. At some point, Faulkner must have begun to feel like Humbert Humbert, even though he was less obsessive than Nabokov's protagonist, for he exaggerates the age disparity even further in *The Town* and *The Mansion*—to the point where Gavin Stevens begins courting fourteen-year-olds.

In between his romances and his world traveling, Faulkner started writing *The Town,* which he described as an escape from the dire conditions in Mississippi. Since he was spending little time in the state, his declared motivation seems implausible, but he told his editor that "Miss. such an unhappy state to live in now, that I need something like a book to get lost in." He told Jean Stein that he felt "that perhaps I have written myself out and all that remains now is the empty craftsmanship—no fire, force, passion anymore in the words and sentences." He must have gradually overcome that sense, for he soon declared that the novel was "going splendidly" (L, pp. 390–91, 402).

Faulkner undoubtedly used *The Town,* as he soon would *The Mansion,* partly to satirize his own propensity for frustrating romantic entanglements. Sex, as much as character, is "Fate" in the town, and Faulkner tellingly portrays its victims. Especially intriguing in this respect is the way in which Gavin Stevens metamorphoses from a caricature of Phil Stone into a caricature of Faulkner himself, always eager and always thwarted. The book is dedicated to Stone, who even appears in it briefly, and Stevens has Stone's credentials—his multiple degrees from Ole Miss and an Ivy League school—and Stone's garrulousness. But he becomes involved in emotional situations much like those with which Faulkner was struggling at the time. Stevens turns his romantic attention from Eula, the woman who is his contemporary, to her teen-aged daughter Linda, just as Faulkner, after a final meeting with his old flame Meta about 1950, became involved with very young women, Joan Williams and Jean Stein. Stevens becomes the self-appointed father-protector of Linda Snopes and deludes himself that he is simply "forming her mind" by giving her the poetry of John Donne to read and that he is helping her to "escape" from her restrictive family background by arranging for her to go away to school. His role is much like that which Faulkner attempted to play in Joan Williams's life in the early fifties. The nature of Stevens's delusions is apparent to everyone—even he comments on his "delayed vicious juvenility" (89)[1]—and Faulkner himself must have been all too painfully aware of the potentially ridiculous aspects of his own predilection and regenerative need for very young women, since he satirized it trenchantly in his late fiction.

The Town deals primarily with the incursion of the Snopes clan into Jefferson and Flem's rise to economic power, opening and closing with comically terrifying anecdotes about the family. But the story of Stevens's thwarted involvements provides a vividly continuous background to the various tales of Snopeses. The novel shows Faulkner in the process of evolution as an artist and a man, yet perpetually carrying on some sort of dialogue with his earlier works and perhaps feeling again the frustrations of earlier periods as he attempted to come to terms with liaisons that created ambivalence about his masculine role. The characterization of Gavin Stevens owes much to Faulkner's preoccupations in the 1950s, yet he has significant likenesses to Faulknerian protagonists of the 1920s. He recalls Ernest Talliaferro, for example, in that he is an ineffectual creature whose impotence is revealed by his endless talk and his juxtaposition to a "real man." He similarly evokes Horace Benbow of *Sartoris,* another idealistic and sister-dominated reluctant suitor, and, especially, Quentin Compson of *The Sound and the Fury,* becoming a comic version of that earlier pivotal autobiographical character.

Gavin Stevens is Quentin Compson grown older, foolish instead of tragically doomed, but still held in thrall by the same immature attitudes that made life so difficult for Quentin. Stevens remains closely tied to his sister, "who has tried to be my mother ever since ours died and some day may succeed" (89). She, in turn, is intensely loyal to him, declaring that other women "dont deserve you!" (77). The strong brother-sister bond probably accounts for Stevens's inability to respond to women in a mature way. Again like Quentin, Stevens is a thwarted knight who adheres to an outmoded code. "Out of his depth," as Faulkner said, in "the real world" (*FIU*, p. 140), Stevens fights for a maidenly virtue that is nonexistent. He is preoccupied with ideas like "reputation" and "good name" and "innocence and virginity." Quentin is called a "half-baked Galahad" by one of his "rivals" for his sister Caddy's affection; Stevens becomes fully Quixotic and utterly ineffective as he battles for the honor of his ladies. The two novels in which these Faulknerian knights-errant appear are different in mood, for *The Sound and the Fury* is tragic, *The Town* essentially comic, but they have a close and revealing relationship.

Stevens's initial opponent in his misguided "crusade" on behalf of Eula and then her daughter is Manfred de Spain, almost a caricature of the Faulknerian "real man," a wounded and scarred war hero who has become mayor of the town. The men's first "duel" is a sophomoric one, involving the "cutout" on a roadster, a retaliatory booby trap, and a "bouquet" containing a condom; it is followed by a fist-fight and a lawsuit. Stevens loses them all, but Faulkner underscores his intended knightliness with mock-heroic language. The cycle of gallant futility begins anew in the next generation, when Stevens becomes the "champion" of Linda Snopes and begins to fight her suitors; the aging Quixote is quickly bloodied. The ludicrous nature of Stevens's derring-do and the adolescent character of his attitudes are sharply satirized in what seems clearly to be Faulkner's amused comment on his own propensities.

The story of Gavin Stevens in *The Town* is an exercise in a mock-heroic mode that serves as a humorous middle-aged counterpart to Quentin Compson's tragic tale as told in *The Sound and the Fury;* the mode itself is one which Faulkner would reuse with great success in his last novel. *The Town* is also Faulkner's one overt attempt to write a novel of manners somewhat in the vein of those written in earlier decades of the century by Ellen Glasgow and Edith Wharton. All of Faulkner's work has been treated on occasion as "social history," and with some justification; *The Town,* however, is his most explicit effort to work in the genre. It shows Faulkner deliberately recording the social dynamics of a small Mississippi town during a portion of the early twentieth century as the New South collides with the Old in the guise of Snopes v. Stevens. Gavin Stevens often confuses his vision of the town's welfare with his own need for fulfillment, and Flem Snopes is a villain both in his manipulation of the local economy and his constrictions of his wife and daughter. Town events like the Cotillion Club annual Christmas Ball and a high-school graduation form the background for important moments in the individual drama, and law offices and local drugstores provide recurrent settings. Chick Mallison serves as the generalized town sensibility, averring that "when I say 'we' and 'we thought' what I mean is Jefferson and what Jefferson thought" (3), and central characters such as Gavin Stevens and Manfred de Spain have public roles as well as private ones. The first is city attorney and the second is mayor, and their fates are intertwined with that of the community as a whole.

Faulkner here is concerned with the town almost as much as he is with individuals in it, and the social setting and local mores are portrayed with meticulous and, for Faulkner, unusual care. This new social focus is nowhere more evident than in the character of Eula, no longer a mythic fertility symbol as she was in *The Hamlet* but a bourgeois housewife surrounded with silver-plated coffee service and mass-produced furniture and concerned with her social image. Eula has become more "ordinary" but humanly more interesting. Watching the struggle between her husband and her lover for control of the bank and confronting her terrible dilemma, she recognizes that the conflicting claims of lover, husband, and child cannot be resolved in any satisfying way and elects to kill herself "in order to leave her child a mere suicide for a mother instead of a whore" (340).

Eula's emergence as a "realistic" character of human complexity gives *The Town* an additional dimension, as do Stevens's comic middle-aged re-enactment of the plight of Quentin Compson and Faulkner's reintroduction of a narrative technique reminiscent of those he had used in *The Sound and the Fury* and *As I Lay Dying*. He here establishes three different narrators—Stevens, the self-appointed guardian of the common weal; Chick Mallison, the spokesman for the general public; and V. K. Ratliff, a mediator between Stevens and the town, who understands and comments on the deficiencies in both of their outlooks. All three are participants in the ongoing story, developing among them a continuous narrative, correcting and adding to each other's versions. Whether Faulkner uses the technique successfully here is open to critical question. An early reader of *The Town* told the author he hadn't "been able to see" as well as he had in *The Sound and the Fury* "the distinct values which come from the three points of view." Faulkner responded by describing Chick as "the mirror which obliterated all except truth," Stevens as the "artificial man" impelled by a "desire to practice what he had been told was a good virtue," and Ratliff as a "man who practiced virtue from simple instinct" (*FIU*, pp. 139–40). The characters are indeed distinguishable—except for the boy, who lacks real individuality—but their narrative idioms are less distinctive than those of the three Compson siblings. They become rather more distinctive as the novel progresses, however, and Stevens at least is, by the end, in full verbal flower, endlessly summarizing, making parenthetical comments, assigning abstract qualities to other characters, and imaginatively reconstructing events ad infinitum—being, in short, utterly Stevensian.

Obviously not one of the author's major fictions, *The Town* received some poor reviews and a questioner soon asked Faulkner if perhaps he were tired of Yoknapatawpha. "I don't think that I am," he responded tentatively, "though of course the last thing any writer will admit to himself is that he has scraped the bottom of the barrel and that he should quit. . . . [T]his I have had in mind for thirty years now. So maybe it could be a little stale to me" (*FIU*, p. 107). Faulkner also spoke of fatigue and a desire to "break the pencil," saying he wanted to finish so he could "throw away the paper and rest, for I feel very tired" (*B*, p. 1680). His comments began to betray a sense of impending death: "I am afraid I shall not have time to finish the work I want to do," he said as he began on the third volume of the Snopes trilogy (*L*, p. 412).

In *The Mansion*, published in 1959, Faulkner returned once more to the problems of Gavin Stevens and the case of the people of Jefferson v. Snopes. The novel, generally regarded as stronger than its predecessor, contains some passages of superb writing, conveys a powerful sense of the passage of time, and has a wonderfully memorable character in the vicious and yet pathetic Mink Snopes. On him and on the moving dramatization of his plight, both in itself and as it mirrors that of the other characters, rests much of the value that can be claimed for *The Mansion*.

Faulkner carefully makes the work continuous with the previous two Snopes novels, despite minor inconsistencies he acknowledges in the preface. He summarizes events in *The Hamlet* and *The Town* and begins where each of the preceding novels ends, with Mink in jail and Gavin Stevens persisting in his ambiguous "protectorship" of Linda Snopes, now a deaf war widow, and in his ineffectual battle to arrest the tide of Snopesism. Drawn into an odd "platonic" romance with Linda, Stevens refuses her offer of intercourse on the ground that he wants them to be the only two "in all the world who can love each other without having to" (239).[2] His explanation is fastidiously idealistic and may have stemmed from the author's need to claim some sort of special status for his emotional relationships with much younger women.

Faulkner's awareness of his attraction to young women and theirs to him as a father-counselor is embodied in a comment by Stevens's nephew. Chick notes his uncle's tendency to "[pick] out children, or maybe he was just vulnerable to female children and they chose him" (194), and goes on cynically to assert, "The only moment of motion which caught his attention, his eye, was that one at which they entered puberty." Stevens stands always at that symbolic "door" to pubescence, watching an endless train of "adolescent leg[s]" (197) pass through with himself in eager attendance. His interest is apparently not fully sexual, for he resists various seduction attempts and contents himself with avuncular proprietorship. Perhaps in order to remove himself to a safe distance from any further involvements with pubescent females, midway through *The Mansion* Stevens marries the widow Melisandre Hariss: thus his self-delusory romantic maundering comes to an end. Stevens's action had its counterpart in the author's own life, for Faulkner had by this time more or less given up all involvements with very young women and returned emotionally to his wife.

Stevens's rather comical story is framed by the poignant and suspenseful drama of Mink Snopes's lifelong plan of revenge against the cousin who "betrayed" him by failing to appear at his murder trial. Mink is one of Faulkner's small villains who is as much lost child as he is evil monster. He is "as deadly as a small viper" (45) yet "as forlorn and defenseless as a child" (36). Though his killing of Houston is unjustifiable, its origin in economic resentment makes it almost a one-man "revolt of the proletariat" and thus understandable. Mink's anger at the man who impounds his cow and forces him to work off the fine is related to his "rage at the injustice" (13) of being temporarily indentured to a prosperous man whose black field hands live far better than Mink ever will. Mink's espousal of sentiments that could be regarded as proto-Marxist and Faulkner's amplification of his situation by the explicit introduction of communism as an impelling force both personally and socially show the author's sensitivity to some of the issues which were preoccupying America in the McCarthyite fifties. *The Mansion* is, in an indirect way, an expression of his sympathy for those former Communists whose beliefs, however misdirected, had sprung from a sincere desire for social and economic reform and who were being beleaguered by the reactionaries. Many of the major characters in the novel—Linda Snopes, Barton Kohl, and Mink Snopes—and some of the minor ones are declared or potential Marxists. Faulkner presents their views and their plights with understanding, even though he is alert to the latent destructiveness of their ideas. Linda espouses large "causes" but indirectly commits a form of patricide, while the outlook of the more sympathetic Mink is as violent as it is emotionally and ideologically conceivable.

The portrait of Mink Snopes is Faulkner's most impressive success in this direction, for Mink is at once sociopathic and humanly comprehensible. He is an underdog, painfully aware that he is "bound and chained for the rest of his life" to a "square of dirt" (90). He sees himself as implementing "a simple fundamental justice and equity in human affairs" (6) by murdering Houston. Mink's ethics are unconventional but marked by a certain integrity. Although he will murder, he will not rob. "I aint never stole," he declares. "I aint come to that and I wont never" (274).

After Mink is sentenced to life imprisonment, he commits himself to a second plan of revenge, the murder of Flem. This act also has some socio-economic justification, for Flem has displayed a lifelong commitment to an economic system marked by inequities. As a bank president, he manipulates both money and the fates of others more helpless than he. Mink's vengeful plot against his cousin proves a powerful obsessional force through the long years in prison, and in some psychological sense keeps him alive and purposeful. Mink has some of the qualities of Thomas Sutpen in the vigor of his monomania and the relentlessness of his plan of retribution against members of a society that has wronged him. Once Mink is released from prison, however, he appears as a twentieth-century Rip Van Winkle, confused and disoriented by a "new world" which he cannot comprehend, desperate to go back to "what he remembers" (106). He worries about going to the bus depot, for he has heard about new laws, "laws that a man couldn't saw boards and hammer nails unless he paid money to an association that would let him, couldn't even raise cotton on his own land unless the government said he could—might be that he would have to get on the first bus that left, no matter where it was going" (285). Mink's feet are pained by the new concrete and his psyche is pained by the inflated prices charges for everything. As a dislocated stranger in a strange land, Mink is alternately mystified and frustrated. His increasing paranoia and his fears that the plan of revenge will fail make him a sympathetic rather than terrifying figure as he returns to Jefferson on his lonely quest. Faulkner takes us inside Mink's mind and makes of him a humanly intelligible character.

Although Mink accomplishes his goal, the futility of the venture is underscored by the fact that he is defeated along with his foe. Deprived of his sustaining motivation, Mink can only return to the cellar which is all that remains of his long-ago home and crouch there waiting for death, his final reabsorption into the earth which he has always felt clutching at his body. The bleakness of the outcome is magnified because others besides Mink share a complicity in the death of Flem Snopes. Linda has requested the release from prison of the man she knows will kill her legal father. Even Stevens is implicated by the role he plays in implementing Linda's plan. The guilt is shared by everyone in the world of *The Mansion* and it is not easy to distinguish between victim and oppressor. Efforts to assign moral categories prove as pointless as the lifelong adherence to a plan of retribution.

Faulkner was over sixty when he wrote *The Mansion,* and many elements in the novel indicate that it is the work of an aging man acutely aware of the approach of death. Everyone in the work is old and seems filled with a sense of futility. Flem's accretion of "monuments" is as hollow as the house in which he passes silent evenings, and he passively awaits the death about to be visited upon him by his cousin as if aware of the emptiness of financial success in a life marked by impotence and utter estrangement. Stevens and Ratliff, too, are old men. Though the former makes a gesture to avert Mink from his violent course, he feels he has lost "not just the capacity to concentrate but to believe in it; he was too old now and the real tragedy of age is that no anguish is any longer grievous enough to demand, justify, any sacrifice" (392). His shocked recognition at the end that "I've just committed murder" (427) is accompanied by a sense of too-lateness. After the bloodshed is over, Stevens and Ratliff comment with sympathy and resignation about the pointlessness of it all. The "grabbling and snatching" of Snopesism has ended in death and Stevens feels driven to assert, "There aren't any morals. People just do the best they can." "The pore sons of bitches," answers Ratliff (428–29).

Mink Snopes is only slightly older than Faulkner, and the author sympathetically describes his patient attendance of death in a superb and moving passage. Death for Mink is a peaceful oblivion, which is perhaps how Faulkner envisaged his own, a blessed contrast to the inner and outer turbulence of his life. It involves a reintegration into the nature close to which he has spent his life and a merging with all the great and small of history in a realm without barriers of caste or economics.

He could feel the Mink Snopes that had had to spend so much of his life just having unnecessary bother and trouble, beginning to creep, seep, flow easy as sleeping . . . it was just the ground and the dirt that had to bother and worry and anguish with the passions and hopes and skeers, the justice and the injustice and the griefs, leaving the folks themselves easy now, all mixed and jumbled up comfortable and easy so wouldn't nobody even know or even care who was which any more, himself among them, equal to any, good as any, brave as any, being inextricable from, anonymous with all of them; the beautiful, the splendid, the proud and the brave, right on up to the very top itself among the shining phantoms and dreams which are the milestones of the long human recording—Helen and the bishops, the kings and the unhomed angels, the scornful and graceless seraphim. [435–36]

12
Nunc Dimittis: *The Reivers*

The Reivers, WHICH APPEARED IN 1962 shortly before Faulkner's death, brings the novelist's turbulent and variegated life and career to a fitting close. The work is gentle, filled with humor, warmth, and sentiment, and it offers a stronger vision of hopefulness than any of Faulkner's previous novels. It lacks the range and splendor of his great works, but in its own small way it is a first-rate achievement and serves as a fine valedictory. Faulkner spoke of peace as "maybe . . . only a condition in retrospect, when the subconscious has got rid of the gnats and the tacks and the broken glass in experience and has left only the peaceful pleasant things—that was peace. Maybe peace is not is, but was" (*FIU,* p. 67). Faulkner's idea of peace as an emptying-out and a sense of pastness is exemplified by his last novel: both the mood and the mode of *The Reivers* embody Faulkner's special concept of serenity, for it is in all ways a tribute to the past.

Faulkner never fully "mellowed" in the usual sense of the word. He continued much of his uproarious and occasionally self-destructive behavior up to the very end of his life. He kept riding and fox-hunting, spending almost as much time picking himself off the ground or recovering from bad falls as he did on horseback, and his alcoholic binges still recurred with some frequency. Yet there was in other ways an aura of peace about Faulkner's last years. He joined the faculty of the University of Virginia in 1957, first as writer-in-residence, then as a lecturer, and apparently enjoyed his new professorial role. He spent increasing amounts of time in Charlottesville and was negotiating to buy an impressive estate in the area just before he died. The change in milieu from the raw and isolated hills of northern

Mississippi to the lush and rolling terrain of central Virginia was somehow emblematic of all the other alterations in Faulkner's life. He became a pinks-wearing, fox-hunting Virginia gentleman and a member of the prestigious Farmington Hunt Club and thus acquired some of the trappings of elegant gentility which had been hitherto unknown to the violent Falkners of Mississippi.

Faulkner also underwent important changes in his interior life. Estelle, who had been chronically troubled by drinking problems, joined Alcoholics Anonymous about the same time her husband terminated his last major extramarital affair. The combination of her sobriety and his disentanglement from other women was felicitous. In the eyes of one young relative, the two "fell in love all over again."[1] At the very least, they declared some sort of emotional truce and managed to live their last years together in general harmony. During this period, Faulkner also grew much closer to his daughter. Jill had married a West Point graduate who went on to law school and settled in the Charlottesville area. The couple soon had three sons, one of whom Jill named William Cuthbert Faulkner Summers after her father. Faulkner spent a good deal of time playing with his grandsons and getting reacquainted with the daughter from whom he had so often been away during her formative years. With his daughter as with his wife, Faulkner discovered a new sense of closeness in his last years.

Despite his apparent new-found feeling of peace and his talk of living to be a hundred, Faulkner was sharply aware of the approach of death. It had been an omnipresent feeling since his fiftieth birthday, when he realized that "a little nearer now was the moment, instant, night: dark: sleep: when I would put it all away forever that I anguished and sweated over."[2] Now it drew even closer. People who had been crucial figures in his life were dying and his own health was deteriorating. Harold Ober, Faulkner's literary agent, who had been an unfailing source of advice, money, and dependable professional assistance, died in 1959. The following year came the death of Faulkner's mother, with whom he had always kept in close contact despite residual underlying tensions. She remained outspoken and humorously honest to the end, and her final request encouraged amusement rather than mawkishness. She demanded a simple casket and no embalming because "I want to get back to earth as fast as I can" (B, p. 1765). Despite her efforts to keep her passing free from excess sentiment, the loss of his mother was a major one for Faulkner. Whatever his subconscious ambivalence toward her might have been, he saw her every day when he was in Oxford, he admired her indomitable spirit of independence, and he found her pride in his artistic success an emotional bulwark.

The next year, Ernest Hemingway, who had always been Faulkner's chief rival in the "greatest living writer" category, killed himself. Although Faulkner later said simply that "Hemingway broke the pencil and shot himself,"[3] he was shocked and agitated by the event. The two writers were somehow indissolubly connected by their "rivalry" and opposing stylistic approaches, almost like two of Faulkner's own "linked characters," and much of Faulkner's work carried on a subtle dialogue with that of Hemingway. They were both literary "sons" of Sherwood Anderson, and Faulkner was now unhappily aware that he was the sole survivor.

As if driven by an urgency created by the deaths that foreshadowed his own, Faulkner turned to the last of his "unfinished business," a novel he had started years before. "I still have one more book I want to write," he asserted (B, p. 1729), and began it shortly after Hemingway's suicide, ignoring the pain from a recently broken collarbone. The idea for his new novel had been in Faulkner's mind for years, as was the case with all of his work after 1940. He had begun an embryonic form of *The Reivers* in 1940, referring to it then as "the Huck Finn novel," and the germ of the first chapter can be found in *Go Down, Moses*—specifically in "The Bear," where there is a reference to Boon Hogganbeck's comic shootout with a Negro, in which only a bystander gets wounded.[4] The title came from a word of Scottish origin meaning "raider" which Faulkner had used often; even in his very first novel, it appears twice. It was a subtle acknowledgment of his Scottish ancestors, the Falconers, who migrated to the United States many generations before the writer's birth, and symbolizes a return to Faulkner's earliest heritage in a way strikingly (if unconsciously) appropriate for a novel that was to mark the closing of the circle of his personal life. The novel constitutes, in fact, a retrospective gesture that encompasses all strata of the past, from his personal family history to the general literary tradition of which he was a twentieth-century inheritor.

The Reivers contains echoes of many classic literary works, mostly used by Faulkner to comic or ironic effect. Faulkner's fiction was often allusive in ways that varied from the subtle to the obvious. In *The Reivers,* the allusions are of both sorts and almost always effective. They show the author's clear awareness of the mainstream of great literature into which his own impressive oeuvre had by now unquestionably flowed, and, more important, they serve to amplify the significance of the story of Lucius Priest. In a general way, Faulkner makes use of the mock-heroic picaresque mode employed centuries before in *Don Quixote* and *Tom Jones*. The mock-heroics of *The Reivers* satirize the characters but also give them a certain stature and luminosity. The constant juxtaposition of the grandiose conception with the comic, often shoddy, reality of fact works nicely in both directions. Shortly after finishing *The Reivers,* Faulkner spoke of Don Quixote with "admiration and pity and amusement—that's what I get from him—and the reason is that he is a man trying to do the best he can in this ramshackle universe he's compelled to live in."[5] Faulkner, who kept a wooden sculpture of Quixote in his library in Oxford,[6] seems to have made his Lucius Priest a youthful Quixote who tilts at windmills, perhaps, but who also positively affects those around him in the same way as does Cervantes's hero.

Faulkner called *The Reivers* his "Huck Finn" novel when he first began it (*L,* p. 123), and shortly before returning to the work a final time he referred to Mark Twain as "the father of American literature"[7]—a phrase which recalls Hemingway's famous judgment that all modern American literature is descended from one book by Mark Twain called *Huckleberry Finn.* As critics have often noted, there are many Twainian elements in *The Reivers*—the intertwining of physical and psychological journeys in the experiences of the boy protagonist, the comradeship of white boy and black man, the earthy humor, and the maintenance of the first-person narration from a child's point of view, albeit from a grandfatherly perspective—and since Faulkner's work became increasingly like Twain's as time went on, it seems appropriate that his final novel should be a modern version of *Huckleberry Finn.*

Great works like *Huckleberry Finn, Don Quixote, Tom Jones*—even Shakespeare's valedictory play, *The Tempest*—are all implicit in *The Reivers,* and Faulkner also makes quite specific allusions to other works. Lucius sees himself as Faustus on several occasions and *The Reivers* becomes in some sense a comic version of Marlowe's Elizabethan tragedy. As Lucius unconsciously decides to go on the forbidden odyssey, he feels "suddenly that same exultant fever-flash which Faustus himself must have experienced" (53).[8] Even as he judges harshly "the clay-footed sham for which I had bartered—nay, damned—my soul" (58), he exults "in baseness" (61). Since Lucius has merely decided to go on an automobile trip, his talk of utter damnation increases the humor of the departure, even as it underscores its essential momentousness. Seriousness also lies beneath the surface comedy in Faulkner's passing evocation of *Clarissa.* The vicious sheriff who exploits the "reformed" whore, Corrie, is named Lovemaiden, and his exploitative actions are similar to those of Richardson's villain, Lovelace. Corrie, along with Lucius, is victimized by unscrupulous forces, and both woman and boy at moments seem as helpless as Clarissa. The maidenhead of Richardson's heroine represented her selfhood, which is ruthlessly violated by her rape, and when Faulkner's Lucious speaks of "losing your maidenhead" (58), he refers to his emotional deflowering, that loss of his psychic virginity which occurs on the trip to Memphis.

The references to *Clarissa* and *Faustus* are aesthetically functional and constitute Faulkner's special form of homage to the literary past. He makes another important and direct tribute to a personal connection in that past by evoking one of Sherwood Anderson's finest short stories, "I Want to Know Why."[9] The story was published in 1921 in *The Triumph of the Egg*, which Faulkner read enthusiastically and praised before he ever met the older writer. Anderson's story about the young racing enthusiast who discovers adult sexuality on a trip away from home has so many elements in common with *The Reivers* that one suspects Faulkner was quite consciously enlarging upon Anderson's tale. Both works are narrated retrospectively by their male protagonists, who attempt simultaneously to recreate the events and to "explain" their meaning. Both stories center on an odyssey from a small town to a big city and on a "fall" from innocence into a knowledge of "evil" and/or sexuality. Each boy has two adult male companions, one black and one white, who serve in some way as surrogate fathers, and each boy is knowledgeable of and affectionate toward horses. "I Want to Know Why" is probably the more psychologically complex of the two works, with a perceptible "latent content" about the boy's subconscious desire to maintain a pre-Oedipal bond with his white surrogate father and his "betrayal" by the witnessing of a "primal scene," which Simon Lesser discusses in his well-known piece on the story.[10] In *The Reivers*, Lucius's emotional bond is rather to the "motherly" whore than to his "fatherly" companions. He lashes out angrily at those who debase her and feels a mixture of "anguish, rage, outrage, grief" (258) when she relapses under pressure into the purveyance of sex.

The young males of both stories are left with a sense of change and loss. Anderson's nameless boy discovers a world where "things are different" and "the air don't taste as good or smell as good," while Faulkner's Lucius returns feeling the very scenery "should have been altered, even if only a little" (299). Anderson's story ends with the protagonist perplexed, a victim of sexual forces beyond his control, while Lucius goes on to learn a positive moral "lesson" about his own role in the events and his need to "live with" the consequences of his behavior, but the persistent wish to regain a lost innocence remains the emotional message of both tales. Faulkner's homage to his literary father is a striking one, the fictional culmination of long years of conscientious verbal acknowledgment of his indebtedness to Anderson. *The Reivers* subtly repays that debt and constitutes, in its way, a more sincere tribute to Anderson than the sum of all Faulkner's public statements.

In *The Reivers,* even as Faulkner makes gestures toward the literary tradition and toward the specific writer who influenced his career as a novelist, he also takes a nostalgic last look at his personal family past and his childhood. That family and those early years had appeared in nearly all of Faulkner's novels in one form or another, but never in a way so free from darkness and tension as in *The Reivers.* Many of the figures and elements from Faulkner's previous works appear in the novel, but they are now viewed with warmth and sentiment rather than with bitterness or despair. Moreover, Faulkner seems so comfortable with the material that he portrays it much more directly and without the distortion or "disguises" that he had used in previous works.

Two William Faulkners appear in the novel. There is the old storyteller who dedicates the work to his grandchildren, including his namesake, and who appears as "Grandfather said" on the first page and makes recurring comments about the changing landscape and the car as the "inescapable destiny of America" (94) from his 1961 vantage point. There is also the young William Faulkner of the first years of the century, the oldest of four boys, who works in his father's livery stable when he would rather play baseball and who views the first motorcars as romantic vehicles for adventure. This doubtle sensibility of Faulkner old and young is sustained throughout the novel and gives the narrative its all-important dual perspective.

Nearly all the major figures of Faulkner's childhood are also present in the novel; the work is like a family portrait album. His great-grandfather is mentioned, "the actual colonel, C.S.A.—soldier, statesman, politician, duelist," who "built his railroad in the mid-seventies" (74). Faulkner's grandfather is there, an authority figure to the young boy, a banker who owns the first automobile in town, just as did John Falkner. He is also called "Colonel," a "courtesy title acquired partly by inheritance and partly by propinquity" (74). Even Faulkner's father is present, the manager of a livery stable, called Maury instead of Murry, but portrayed in an evenhanded manner without rancor or disgust. The mother is a shadowy figure in *The Reivers*—perhaps because Maud had just died and Faulkner was still emotionally unable to deal with her—but Mammy Callie is there, toting the youngest brother as she had the baby Dean, and so are the other Faulkner family satellites, black and white, on whom Ned McCaslin and Boon Hogganbeck are based: Ned Barnett, who served as general factotum for three generations of the family, and Buster Callicoat, who worked in the livery stable run by Faulkner's father.

Faulkner seems to be dealing with all these figures from his past with affection and forgiveness, for in *The Reivers* there are no destructive individuals within the family nexus. Faulkner places the evil all without, in a telling reversal of the vision contained in an earlier novel such as *The Sound and the Fury,* in which the disruptive forces are all within the family and the only redemption comes from outside. Indeed, *The Reivers* reverses the import of other elements of that pivotal early novel. The death of a grandparent is a crucial event in both works, but in *The Sound and the Fury* it precipitates turmoil and estrangement in the children, while in *The Reivers* it is treated matter-of-factly, as a "constant familiar" in a world where people died "in the same rooms and beds they were born in" (44–45), and serves primarily as Lucius's opportunity to escape on his comic odyssey for a few days. Again, Caddy Compson, a central figure for her brother Quentin, undergoes a transformation from "mother" to "whore" which psychically destroys her brother, while Corrie, an equally important figure to Lucius, makes the affirmative change from whore to mother in the concluding action of the novel. The olfactory sense is crucial to both works, for death and sexuality can be smelled even by those who do not understand them. Yet the honeysuckle which evokes in Quentin Compson emotional turmoil is for Lucius Priest merely another element in the local scenery, whose only association is with Colonel Linscomb's wonderful office, "the best room I ever saw" (284). The complexity and interior movement of *The Sound and the Fury* become in *The Reivers* farcical complication and physical motion. *The Reivers* thus represents in several ways a more affirmative and emotionally more enervated version of Faulkner's 1929 novel.

Although *The Reivers* has a direct source in Sherwood Anderson's fine short story, it was also based on two important occurrences in Faulkner's own life. The first was his grandfather's purchase of a car, which enabled the Falkner family entourage to make motor journeys fraught with "epic" obstacles and high drama; the second, very different but equally crucial, was the occasion when Faulkner took his youngest brother—then just twelve, a year older than Lucius Priest—on a visit to a Memphis brothel. The naive boy was flattered to be introduced like an adult to the "ladies" of the house. While Faulkner vanished temporarily into the regions beyond the parlor, young Dean was sent outside to wait, undoubtedly feeling a mixture of fascination and mystification (Wells, pp. 40–41). What Faulkner's motives were for exposing the boy to the sordidly glamorous world of sex-for-sale is unknown, but the event made a strong impression on both brothers. It may have been with a real but highly belated sense of guilt, as well as with a lingering amusement, that Faulkner portrayed the occasion from the younger boy's point of view and dwelt on both the painful and the comic aspects of his premature loss of innocence. He takes Lucius Priest through the stages of his rite of passage in a way that reveals the innerness of the experience, the anguish and reluctance undergone by Lucius as he is slowly educated into the ways of the world—and also the outerness of it, the comedy inherent in our perception of the ludicrousness of Lucius "making his manners" to the brothel madam or defending the "virtue" of a whore.

In this double perspective, the adult Lucius is humorously aware of the futile contest of "odorless and tasteless virtue" against "the bright rewards of sin and pleasure" (53), even while the young Lucius periodically longs for a return to his previous state of innocence and dependency. Similarly, Lucius learns a mature sort of sympathy for all men, "the poor frail victims of being alive," yet is simultaneously "anguished with homesickness, wrenched and wrung and agonised with it: to be home. Not just to retrace but to retract, obliterate" (174–75). Maturity and a sense of loss are poignantly intermingled as he develops abruptly from a protected and uncomprehending child into an aware youth in whom sympathy and anguish vie for ascendancy.

The story has a crucial cognitive element—Lucius's changing inner vision and moral responses—and it also follows an important pattern, the archetype of the heroic journey. The psychological growth from child to individuated young adult is mirrored in the literal movement of the odyssey to Memphis—separation, "battle," and triumphal return. This journey archetype, a recurrent one in literature, and its psychological components have been commented on at length by Jung, Erich Neumann, and Joseph Campbell. Faulkner made use of the pattern in *As I Lay Dying,* in which the Bundrens' arduous forty-mile journey to Jefferson allows Cash to develop from a creature of limited sensibility into one of expanded perceptions and wide-ranging moral sympathy. The pattern is also implicit in *The Unvanquished* and "The Bear," and Faulkner once again gives it full-scale treatment in *The Reivers.* Lucius's heroism may be generally comic, but it is "real" in both the physical and the psychological sense. His engagement in various battles with emblematic "dragons" procures for him the "treasure" of incipient masculine adulthood and homage from his society.

Lucius Priest's heroic potential is early suggested by his awareness of "the knightly shapes of my male ancestors" (51) that augur his destiny.

Initially, however, Boon Hogganbeck is the "heroic" figure of the narrative, physically imposing and "tough, faithful, brave," although "completely unreliable" (19). At the outset of the "epic" journey, Lucius merely watches passively as Boon engages in his heroic efforts to surmount physical obstacles. The "trials" come in the mudholes of Hurricane Creek and Hell Creek bottom, but Boon's titanic exertions are insufficient to overcome the rigors of the latter, and the car must be "ferried" across by a Charon-like figure. Boon thereafter fades into the background as Lucius becomes the true "hero" of the odyssey. The trials of the "underworld" of nature are supplanted by the trials presented by the more complex human underworld of Memphis and demand qualities beyond the merely physical. These Lucius alone possesses.

Lucius quickly realizes that "I was smarter than Boon" (53) and soon proves in all ways his fitness for the role of hero. In the third physical trial, the challenging effort to get the stolen race horse into the boxcar, Lucius is an active participant and thus begins his transition from child-observer to youth-hero. He becomes, indeed, a chivalric figure in all ways. He engages in physical combat against disproportionate odds for the "fair maiden" of the story when he attacks the knife-wielding Otis and sustains a wound which is a badge of honor. Yet his heroism is not anarchic. Like a proper knight, Lucius retains the appropriate deference toward worthy older male authority figures like Uncle Parsham and his grandfather. He also acquires a knightly steed, the magnificent and aptly named Lightning, and realizes that upon his brave conduct rests the destiny of the horse and all the satellite figures who have somehow turned into his dependents. He does what he must both willingly and responsibly, despite his wounded hand and his sense that his heavy responsibility constitutes "a mystical condition which a boy of only eleven should not really be called to shoulder" (224).

The proper condition for the true heroic battle is isolation, and Lucius is both physically and spirtually isolated on the day of the crucial race. He is in a strange place; he is alone with his horse on the racecourse against an equine opponent, Acheron, whose name evokes the dark forces of the underworld; and he has been abandoned by his male comrades, who are missing or in jail. Lucius rises to the challenge and rides Lightning to victory in an exciting and "man-size race" (273). His active heroism is initially rewarded by the "treasure" of the prize money, which he maturely refuses out of a sense of what the true issues behind the race have been: "I wasn't doing it for money. . . . Once we were in it, I had to go on, finish it, Ned and me both even if everybody else had quit" (279). His subsequent rewards are a "triumphal return" to his home territory, where his father defers to his achievements by declining to administer the usual punishment, and his restoration of both Boon and Corrie to "virtue" by his knightly example: as Boon says, "God damn it, if you can go bare-handed against a knife defending her, why the hell cant I marry her" (299). Lucius's ultimate reward comes the following year when tribute is paid by the perpetuation of his name in the newborn child, Lucius Priest Hogganbeck.

Many of the figures whom Lucius encounters on his archetypal journey have an illustrative, faintly allegorical quality befitting their role in the narrative of a "hero." Boon is the failed knight, physically strong but spiritually inadequate, whom Lucius replaces as a true knight. Boon is also a guardian of the threshold who conducts Lucius to the nether world where his battles must be fought. Ned McCaslin is the keeper of the magic potion, the smelly sardines which spur Lucius's horse to victory. Otis is the evil Other, Lucius's dark shadow, a child whose violence and corruption must be contained and overcome by the boy hero. Corrie is both fair maiden and dark lady, for her blue eyes and dark hair mix the iconic components of both archetypes and reveal her inner struggle between virtue and vice. The former triumphs as Corrie is "redeemed" by the hero and becomes a wife and mother. Grandfather is the Theseus of this knight's tale, a repository of dignity and authority. In his absence, the Negro Uncle Parsham becomes Lucius's surrogate grandfather. He serves as both arbiter and exemplar and gives the boy the spiritual sustenance he needs. All of these characters play a role in Lucius's education and he in turn, as an emergent hero, offers them a worthy example.

By the end of *The Reivers,* Lucius has become a triumphant figure, and the gentlemanly "code" has proved vital and operable in a way never before possible in a Faulkner novel. While an earlier protagonist like Bayard Sartoris of *The Unvanquished* could only repudiate the code under which he was reared and which sanctioned killing in order to achieve moral manhood, Lucius Priest fulfills and embodies the more positive morality which had been instilled in him as a boy and of which his grandfather is the paramount representative. Lucius's actions during the adventure and his subsequent confrontation with their manifold implications bear out Grandfather's credo, which is evidently the same code by which Faulkner governed much of his personal life: "A gentleman accepts the responsibility of his actions and bears the burden of their consequences, even when he did not himself instigate them but only acquiesced to them, didn't say No though he knew he should" (302).

Lucius emerges as a "gentleman" and a hero. He also acquires the breadth of vision that makes it possible for him to understand that real intelligence is "the ability to cope with environment: which means to accept environment yet still retain at least something of personal liberty" (121). This is a conciliation toward which, at least tacitly, all of Faulkner's characters aspire but which they rarely attain. Lucius's actions prove meaningful and his understanding becomes thorough and equilibrated. His achievement—singular for a Faulkner hero—is in its way momentous, and emotionally appropriate for the novel that was to constitute Faulkner's "last word" to the ages.

Though there is no specific evidence that Faulkner expected *The Reivers* to be his final work, it is obviously the work of a man who sees the imminence of death and feels compelled to make a summary and hopeful statement. The work looks backward into Faulkner's long-vanished childhood and into literary history. It also looks forward to some form of personal immortality, as suggested by the birth of the child and namesake at the end of the novel—an echo of Faulkner's response to his newborn grandson, William Cuthbert Faulkner Summers. The novel's sentimental glow has the quality of an autumnal haze; the tale is told with very little darkness and no sense of futility. Comedy and moral lesson, past and future, black and white, man and woman, motherhood and whoredom—all polarities are reconciled by the end of the novel. It is neither weighty nor complex but is somehow the most fitting of valedictory works, with its tributes to the noble horses, temperamental motorcars, family retainers, and mock-heroics of his long-departed boyhood and its hopeful vision of unity and regeneration. The balance of self-directed irony and earnest self-dramatization has been struck in a special way. Strong tensions are absent and the past is seen purged of its injustices. Faulkner presents himself and his family without disguises and with a new compassion and acceptance, seeming to say to each and every one, so long for him a source of anguish and fury, *requiescat in pace*.

Not surprisingly, Faulkner was very fond of *The Reivers* and regarded it with the same sort of amused affection with which he treated his grandchildren and other young relatives. One of them found him at Rowanoak laughing over a book that proved to be his own, and he unabashedly told a large audience at West Point in the spring of 1962 that "it's one of the funniest books I ever read. . . . I wish I hadn't written it so I could do it again."[11] The work obviously gave Faulkner a mellow pleasure of a sort evoked by none of his earlier novels, and its epitaphic quality may actually have been intended. When he mailed out the manuscript of the novel, Faulkner told the Oxford druggist who had wrapped the bulky pages of his unpublished fiction for many years, "I been aimin' to quit this foolishness."[12] He spent most of the ensuing year in Charlottesville, as he had for the past five years, but returned to Mississippi almost as if he had a premonition that he should come home to die. He told an audience in April that "I don't like the hot summers [in Mississippi]. I have said for sixty-five years I'd never spend another summer there, and yet I am going home in June."[13]

Despite his new mellowness, traces of the old irascible and self-destructive Faulkner remained, one of which may have indirectly resulted in his death. Faulkner's irascibility appeared when he was asked by President Kennedy to a dinner at the White House and turned the invitation down unequivocally. "I'm too old to go that far to eat with strangers," he told the press. As if bent on self-destruction, he continued to ride vigorously, to jump, and perversely to choose the sort of peppery horse that would frequently throw him. A bad spill in January of 1962 left him with a bruised forehead and several broken teeth. He suffered a painful groin injury in a terrible fall in June, but immediately clambered back onto the horse, feeling he "had to conquer him" (B, pp. 1821, 1828). His body, however, was no longer capable of withstanding the perennial assaults made on it by physical trauma and alcohol. Faulkner began treating his latest injury with the usual large doses of whiskey, which in turn necessitated another sort of treatment. He was forced to take himself off to the sanitarium at Byhalia to "dry out." There, on July 6, he died of a massive heart attack.

From a medical viewpoint, it seems little short of miraculous that Faulkner physically endured as long as he did. His survival for almost sixty-five years, like his production of a body of fiction so impressive in both its quality and its quantity, is a testimony to the magnitude of the spirit which sustained and inspired him over the years. From an early age he experienced frustration and despair, perceiving himself to be rejected or ignored by his parents, physically inadequate, and inexorably burdened by his role as inheritor of a confusing family tradition of violence and self-destruction. Yet he triumphed over these psychic obstacles by making them the very foundation of his art. The pages of his fiction are filled with wounded children, despondent young men, and frustrated individuals who are in some way Faulkner himself, but who are portrayed with such sympathy and vitality that their struggles transfigure them into representative human beings, forever aspiring and forever thwarted. Faulkner's novels are all about himself, but his special balance of pity and irony, his uniquely intense and lyrical prose style, and his commanding technique move his work beyond personal document to great fictional art, capable of speaking to every man. It stands as a moving embodiment of the struggle of any human spirit to prevail over the inner and outer forces which threaten to cripple and destroy it. Faulkner's personal ordeals were those of countless other striving individuals, and his lifelong efforts to confront, to objectify, and to amplify them in his art created works whose impact is universal. His voice is often lonely and anguished, but always eloquent, and it speaks a timeless language.

Notes

INTRODUCTION

1. See list of abbreviations.

2. Malcolm Cowley, ed., *The Faulkner-Cowley File* (New York: Viking, 1968), p. 114 (hereafter cited as *Faulkner-Cowley File*).

3. William Faulkner, *Mosquitoes* (New York: Boni and Liveright, 1927), p. 251.

4. *Faulkner-Cowley File,* pp. 126, 89.

5. See Rene Wellek and Austin Warren, *Theory of Literature,* 3rd ed. (New York: Harcourt, Brace and World, 1956), p. 77.

6. *Faulkner-Cowley File,* p. 14.

7. See list of abbreviations.

8. William Faulkner, "An introduction to *The Sound and the Fury,*" in *A Faulkner Miscellany,* ed. James B. Meriwether (Jackson: University Press of Mississippi, 1974), p. 158.

9. William Faulkner, "Foreword," *The Faulkner Reader* (New York: Modern Library, 1959), p. viii.

10. See list of abbreviations.

11. *William Faulkner of Oxford,* ed. James W. Webb and A. Wigfall Green (Baton Rouge: Louisiana State University Press, 1965), p. 134 (hereafter cited as *William Faulkner of Oxford*).

12. See list of abbreviations.

13. Faulkner, *Mosquitoes,* p. 228.

14. See Edmund Wilson, *The Wound and the Bow* (Boston: Houghton Mifflin, 1941), pp. 272–95.

15. See Ernst Kris, *Psychoanalytic Explorations in Art* (New York: International Universities Press, 1952), p. 59.

16. *Faulkner at West Point,* ed. Joseph L. Fant III and Robert Ashley (New York: Random House, 1964), pp. 96, 81 (hereafter cited as *Faulkner at West Point).*

17. See Walter Slatoff, *Quest for Failure* (Ithaca: Cornell University Press, 1961).

CHAPTER 1

1. *Faulkner-Cowley File,* p. 14.

2. He later characterized the change in spelling as his means to "strike out for myself" and not "ride" on his ancestor's "coat-tails." Ibid., p. 66.

3. The most recent and seemingly most reliable biographical data may be found in Donald P. Duclos, "Son of Sorrow" (Ph.D. diss., University of Michigan, 1962). Joseph Blotner drew upon this material for the extensive presentation of the Old Colonel in his *Faulkner: A Biography* (New York: Random House, 1974).

4. Quoted in Duclos, "Son of Sorrow," p. 61.

5. Ibid., pp. 37–39, 76.

6. Quoted in ibid., p. 149.

7. Ibid., pp. 155–57.

8. Ibid., pp. 178, 197, 231, 275.

9. Ibid., p. 375.

10. Murry Falkner, *The Falkners of Mississippi* (Baton Rouge: Louisiana State University Press, 1967), p. 7 (hereafter cited as *The Falkners of Mississippi).*

11. John Faulkner, *My Brother Bill* (New York: Trident, 1963), p. 73 (hereafter cited as *My Brother Bill):* Blotner, *Faulkner,* p. 56.

12. *The Falkners of Mississippi,* p. 68.

13. Ibid., p. 47.

14. Julian B. Roebuck and Raymond G. Kessler, *The Etiology of Alcoholism* (Springfield, Ill.: Charles Thomas, 1972), pp. 180–90.

15. *My Brother Bill,* p. 11.

16. See list of abbreviations.

17. *My Brother Bill,* p. 12.

18. William Faulkner, "Elmer," typescript, Alderman Library, University of Virginia, p. 4.

19. *William Faulkner of Oxford,* p. 25.

20. *The Falkners of Mississippi,* p. 7; *My Brother Bill,* p. 70.

21. *My Brother Bill,* pp. 85, 122.

22. Faulkner, "Elmer," pp. 7, 12.

23. *The Falkners of Mississippi,* p. 34; *My Brother Bill,* p. 58.

24. *My Brother Bill,* p. 35.

25. R. D. Laing, *The Divided Self* (New York: Random House, 1960), p. 76.

26. William Faulkner, "And Now What's to Do," in *A Faulkner Miscellany,* ed. James B. Meriwether (Jackson: University Press of Mississippi, 1974), p. 146. Meriwether says that in this story Faulkner "drew upon his own life to a greater extent than he did in any piece of fiction he ever wrote," p. 145.

27. John Cullen, *Old Times in the Faulkner Country* (Chapel Hill: University of North Carolina Press, 1961), p. 10.

28. *My Brother Bill,* p. 134.

29. In John Bassett, ed., *William Faulkner: The Critical Heritage* (London: Routledge & Kegan Paul, 1975), p. 50 (hereafter cited as *The Critical Heritage*).

30. Faulkner, "Elmer," unpaginated portion of typescript.

31. Faulkner, "Foreword," *The Faulkner Reader* (New York: Modern Library, 1959), p. viii.

32. *William Faulkner's Library: A Catalogue,* comp. Joseph Blotner (Charlottesville: Bibliographical Society of Virginia, 1964), p. 24.

33. *The Falkners of Mississippi,* p. 89.

34. See Michael Millgate, "William Faulkner, Cadet," *University of Toronto Quarterly* 35 (1966): 117–32.

35. *My Brother Bill,* pp. 138–39; *The Falkners of Mississippi,* pp. 90–91.

36. *Faulkner-Cowley File,* pp. 77, 82.

37. *William Faulkner: Early Prose and Poetry,* ed. Carvel Collins (Boston: Little, Brown, 1962), pp. 44, 50.

38. See ibid. for a complete collection of these works.

39. *William Faulkner of Oxford,* p. 63.

40. *LIG,* p. 14; Stark Young, "The New Year's Craw," *New Republic* 93 (Jan. 12, 1938): 283.

CHAPTER 2

1. William Faulkner, *The Marble Faun* (Boston: Four Seas, 1924), pp. 6–8.

2. Sherwood Anderson, *Winesburg, Ohio* (New York: Modern Library, 1947), chap. 1, "The Book of the Grotesque."

3. See, for example, Thomas L. McHaney, "Anderson, Hemingway, and Faulkner's *The Wild Palms,*" *PMLA* 87 (1972): 465–74.

4. William Faulkner, *New Orleans Sketches,* ed. Carvel Collins (New Brunswick: Rutgers University Press, 1958), pp. 76–85.

5. Reprinted in *Sherwood Anderson's Notebook* (New York: Boni and Liveright, 1926), pp. 103–21.

6. Elizabeth Anderson and Gerald Kelly, *Miss Elizabeth: A Memoir* (Boston: Little Brown, 1969), pp. 40, 85.

7. Ibid., pp. 101–2.

8. James Schevill, *Sherwood Anderson: His Life and Work* (Denver: University of Denver Press, 1951), p. 195.

9. William Faulkner, "Prophets of the New Age, II: Sherwood Anderson," *Dallas Morning News,* April 26, 1925, pt. III, p. 7.

10. *Sherwood Anderson and Other Famous Creoles* (New Orleans: Pelican Bookshop, 1926).

11. Anderson and Kelly, *Miss Elizabeth,* p. 102.

12. William Faulkner, "Sherwood Anderson," in *Essays, Speeches, & Public Letters,* ed. James B. Meriwether (New York: Random House, 1965), p. 6 (hereafter cited as *Essays, Speeches, & Public Letters).*

13. William Faulkner, *Soldiers' Pay* (New York: Boni and Liveright, 1926). All subsequent page citations refer to this edition.

14. *The Critical Heritage,* pp. 55, 56, 61–62.

15. Hyatt Waggoner, *William Faulkner: From Jefferson to the World* (Lexington: University of Kentucky Press, 1966), p. 3.

16. *Faulkner at West Point,* p. 112.

17. Barbara Hand, "Faulkner's Widow Recounts Memories of College Weekends in Charlottesville," *Cavalier Daily* [University of Virginia], April 21, 1972, p. 4.

18. Albert Guerard devotes an entire chapter, "Faulkner's Misogyny," to the subject in *The Triumph of the Novel: Dickens, Dostoevsky, Faulkner* (New York: Oxford University Press, 1976).

19. Sherwood Anderson, *Letters of Sherwood Anderson,* ed. Howard Mumford Jones and Walter B. Rideout (Boston: Little, Brown, 1953), p. 155.

20. William Faulkner, *Mosquitoes* (New York: Boni and Liveright, 1927). All subsequent page citations refer to this edition.

21. *The Critical Heritage,* p. 65.

22. Olga Vickery, *The Novels of William Faulkner* (Baton Rouge: Louisiana State University Press, 1964), p. 10.

23. Henry Fielding, Preface to *Joseph Andrews* (New York: Modern Library, 1950), p. xxxvi.

24. See Panthea Reid Broughton, *William Faulkner: The Abstract and the Actual* (Baton Rouge: Louisiana State University Press, 1974), p. 29 and *passim.*

25. John T. Irwin, *Doubling and Incest / Repetition and Revenge* (Baltimore: Johns Hopkins University Press, 1975), pp. 165, 167–68.

CHAPTER 3

1. *The Critical Heritage,* p. 75.

2. *William Faulkner of Oxford,* p. 52.

3. There is some dispute on this point. Ben Wasson said at various times that it was rejected by eleven, twelve, and eighteen publishers. See Joseph Blotner, *Faulkner: A Biography* (new York: Random House, 1974), p. 570 and footnote 570.22.

4. William Faulkner, *Sartoris* (New York: Harcourt, Brace, 1929). All subsequent page citations refer to this edition.

5. T. S. Eliot, "Hamlet," in *Selected Prose of T. S. Eliot,* ed. Frank Kermode (New York: Harcourt Brace Jovanovich, 1975), pp. 48–49.

6. Sigmund Freud, *The Interpretation of Dreams,* quoted in Norman Holland, "Freud on Shakespeare," *M.I.T. Publications in the Humanities* 47 (1961): 9.

7. Ernest Jones, *Hamlet and Oedipus* (London: Victor Gollancz, 1949).

8. After the crash Faulkner kept insisting *"It is my fault."* Dean Faulkner Wells, "Dean Swift Faulkner: A Biographical Study," Master's Thesis, University of Mississippi, 1975, p. 184.

9. William Faulkner, Introduction to the Modern Library edition of *Sanctuary* (New York: Modern Library, 1932), p. vi.

10. Irving Howe, *William Faulkner: A Critical Study,* 2nd ed. (New York: Vintage, 1952), p. 50.

11. Maurice Edgar Coindreau, "Preface to *The Sound and the Fury,*" in *The Time of William Faulkner,* ed. and trans. George McMillan Reeves (Columbia: University of South Carolina Press, 1971), p. 41.

12. Faulkner's preface to the unpublished Grabhorn edition of *The Sound and the Fury,* in James B. Meriwether, "Faulkner Lost and Found," *New York Times Book Review,* November 5, 1972, p. 7.

13. Michael Millgate, *The Achievement of William Faulkner* (New York: Random House, 1966), pp. 90–91.

14. Robert A. Jelliffe, ed., *Faulkner at Nagano* (Tokyo: Kenkyusha Ltd., 1956), p. 105 (hereafter cited as *Faulkner at Nagano*).

15. See chapters five and six of this work for a fuller discussion of this technique.

16. Coindreau, "Preface to *The Sound and the Fury,*" p. 49.

17. *William Faulkner of Oxford,* p. 108.

18. *Faulkner at Nagano,* pp. 103–4.

19. John Cullen, *Old Times in the Faulkner Country* (Chapel Hill: University of North Carolina Press, 1961), pp. 79–80.

20. As John Irwin notes, *Doubling and Incest / Repetition and Revenge* (Baltimore: Johns Hopkins University Press, 1975), p. 52.

21. William Faulkner, *The Sound and the Fury* (New York: Cape and Smith, 1929). All subsequent page citations refer to this edition.

22. Andre Bleikasten, *The Most Splendid Failure* (Bloomington: University of Indiana Press, 1976), p. 78.

23. Cleanth Brooks, *William Faulkner: The Yoknapatawpha County* (New Haven: Yale University Press, 1963), p. 326.

24. See Charles D. Peavy, "If I'd Just Had a Mother," *Literature and Psychology* 23 (1973): 114–21.

25. Otto Rank, *Art and Artist,* trans. Charles Atkinson (New York: Alfred A. Knopf, 1943), p. 145.

26. Faulkner, "An Introduction to *The Sound and the Fury,*" in *A Faulkner Miscellany,* ed. James B. Meriwether (Jackson: University Press of Mississippi, 1974), p. 159.

27. Andre Bleikasten points out that the revolver, like Herbert Head's cigar, is a phallic symbol and that Quentin's refusal of it is equivalent to a denial of male

sexuality, in which his impotence originates. *The Most Splendid Failure*, p. 255, n. 25.

28. James Dahl, "A Faulkner Reminiscence: Conversations with Mrs. Maud Falkner," *Journal of Modern Literature* 3 (1974); 1028.

29. William Faulkner, Appendix to *The Sound and the Fury* (New York: Modern Library, 1946), p. 17.

30. Maud Falkner said later, "And of course Dilsey in that story is Mammy Callie." Dahl, "A Faulkner Reminiscence," p. 1028.

31. *The Critical Heritage*, p. 87.

32. Evelyn Scott, *On William Faulkner's "The Sound and the Fury,"* (New York: Cape and Smith, 1929), p. 6.

CHAPTER 4

1. *Faulkner at Nagano*, p. 9.

2. William Faulkner, *Sanctuary* (New York: Modern Library, 1932), pp. v–vi.

3. George Marion O'Donnell, "Falkner's Mythology," in *Faulkner*, ed. Robert Penn Warren (Englewood Cliffs, N.J.: Prentice-Hall, 1966), pp. 23–33.

4. Irving Howe, *William Faulkner: A Critical Study*, 2nd ed. (New York: Vintage, 1952), pp. 56, 58.

5. Olga Vickery, *The Novels of William Faulkner* (Baton Rouge: Louisiana State University Press, 1964), chap. 7.

6. Wyndham Lewis, cited in *The Critical Heritage*, p. 15.

7. Lawrence S. Kubie, "William Faulkner's *Sanctuary*," in *Faulkner*, ed. Robert Penn Warren, pp. 140, 144.

8. Maurice Edgar Coindreau, "Preface to *The Sound and the Fury*," in *The Time of William Faulkner*, ed. and trans. George McMillan Reeves (Columbia; University of South Carolina Press, 1971), p. 49.

9. *William Faulkner of Oxford*, p. 52.

10. William Faulkner, *Sanctuary* (New York: Random House, 1958). All subsequent page citations refer to this edition.

11. See Linton Massey, "Notes on the Unrevised Galleys of Faulkner's *Sanctuary*," *Studies in Bibliography* 8 (1956): 195–208, and Gerald Langford, *Faulkner's Revision of Sanctuary* (Austin: University of Texas Press, 1972), for a thorough collation of the unrevised galleys and the published book.

12. See James R. Cypher, "The Tangled Sexuality of Temple Drake," *American Imago* 19 (1962): 243–52, for a fuller discussion of this topic.

13. Cypher suggests this analogy, ibid.

CHAPTER 5

1. *Faulkner at Nagano*, p. 162.

2. As John Irwin notes in *Doubling and Incest / Repetition and Revenge* (Baltimore: Johns Hopkins University Press, 1975), p. 53.

3. William Faulkner, *As I Lay Dying* (New York: Random House, 1964). All subsequent page citations refer to this edition.

4. Irwin, *Doubling and Incest*, p. 54.

5. James B. Meriwether, "Faulkner Lost and Found," *New York Times Book Review*, November 5, 1972, p. 7.

6. "Faulkner's Correspondence with the *Post*," *Mississippi Quarterly* 30 (1977): 474.

7. *My Brother Bill*, p. 222.

8. William Faulkner, *Light in August* (New York: Modern Library, 1950). All subsequent page citations refer to this edition.

9. John Cullen, *Old Times in the Faulkner Country* (Chapel Hill: University of North Carolina Press, 1961), pp. 89–92, recounts the incident in detail.

10. Olga Vickery, *The Novels of William Faulkner* (Baton Rouge: Louisiana State University Press, 1964), p. 82.

CHAPTER 6

1. *Sanctuary,* which is here treated as a "single" work, had a sequel which Faulkner began to conceive shortly after he finished, and *Sartoris* and *The Sound and the Fury* are closely related in essential thematic and characterological ways.

2. Michael Millgate comments on the poetic technique common to both in *The Achievement of William Faulkner* (New York: Random House, 1966), p. 149.

3. *Oxford Eagle,* August 11, 1932.

4. See Millgate, *The Achievement of William Faulkner,* pp. 139–41, for an elaboration of specific incidents in the opening of the airport that Faulkner used.

5. Carvel Collins, Introduction to William Faulkner, *New Orleans Sketches,* ed. Carvel Collins (New Brunswick: Rutgers University Press, 1958), p. 26.

6. William Faulkner, *Pylon* (New York: Smith and Haas, 1935). All subsequent page citations refer to this edition.

7. See Cleanth Brooks, *William Faulkner: Toward Yoknapatawpha and Beyond* (New Haven: Yale University Press, 1978), pp. 190–91, 194–95, for a discussion of the reporter's likeness to Horace Benbow in this respect.

8. As Olga Vickery notes in *The Novels of William Faulkner* (Baton Rouge: Louisiana State University Press, 1964), p. 145.

9. Irving Howe, *William Faulkner: A Critical Study,* 2nd ed. (New York: Vintage, 1952), p. 218.

10. John Irwin, *Doubling and Incest / Repetition and Revenge* (Baltimore: Johns Hopkins University Press, 1975); Estella Schoenberg, *Old Tales and Talking* (Jackson: University Press of Mississippi, 1977).

11. William Faulkner, *Absalom, Absalom!* (New York: Modern Library, 1951), All subsequent page citations refer to this edition.

12. See chapter five of this work.

13. Faulkner had always been drawn to the mad sea captain. He kept a picture of Ahab hanging in his library, and a few years before beginning *Absalom, Absalom!*

he cited *Moby Dick* as the book he would have most liked to write, because of "the Greek-like simplicity of it: a man of forceful character driven by his sombre nature and his bleak heritage, bent on his own destruction and dragging his immediate world down with him with a despotic and utter disregard of them as individuals." *Essays, Speeches, & Public Letters,* p. 197.

14. See Louis Rubin, "William Faulkner: The Discovery of a Man's Vocation," in *Faulkner: Fifty Years After The Marble Faun,* ed. George H. Wolfe (University, Ala.: University of Alabama Press, 1976), pp. 43–68.

15. Critics before me have discussed *Absalom, Absalom!* as a study of the fictionalizing process. See Cleanth Brooks, *William Faulkner: The Yoknapatawpha County* (New Haven: Yale University Press, 1963), chap. 14, and Schoenberg, *Old Tales and Talking,* pp. 70, 80, 134–35.

CHAPTER 7

1. Cleanth Brooks, *William Faulkner: The Yoknapatawpha County* (New Haven: Yale University Press, 1963), pp. 75, 76, 79.

2. Save for the brief synopsis of his career which appears in several late novels.

3. William Faulkner, *The Unvanquished* (New York: Random House, 1938). All subsequent page citations refer to this edition.

4. *Essays, Speeches, & Public Letters,* p. 17.

5. Faulkner may have named this character with derogatory intention after a car which belonged to Phil Stone in 1921–22. *William Faulkner of Oxford,* p. 50.

CHAPTER 8

1. The sort of faint praise which the novel elicits is exemplified by Hyatt Waggoner's judgment of the work as "a failure," though Waggoner goes on to say that "this failure is more interesting, more alive, more rewarding in the whole complex experience we get from works of art, than most ordinary successes." *William Faulkner: From Jefferson to the World* (Lexington: University of Kentucky Press, 1966), p. 145. Thomas L. McHaney has begun the necessary critical correctives with his thorough critique of the novel, *William Faulkner's The Wild Palms: A Study* (Jackson: University Press of Mississippi, 1975).

2. Meta Carpenter Wilde, *A Loving Gentleman* (New York: Simon & Schuster, 1976), p. 52.

3. Ibid., pp. 22, 24.

4. Ibid., pp. 57, 47, 67, 79.

5. Ibid., pp. 77–78.

6. Ibid., p. 104; Joseph Blotner, *Faulkner: A Biography* (New York: Random House, 1974), p. 938.

7. Wilde, *A Loving Gentleman,* p. 165.

8. Ibid., p. 184.

9. Ibid., p. 140.

10. Ibid., p. 244. Faulkner wrote her that he was unable to be with another woman, that "I simply won't rise."

11. Ibid., p. 317.

12. Ibid., pp. 62, 50, 181, 101.

13. Ibid., p. 264.

14. *Faulkner at Nagano,* p. 80.

15. Such as Michael Millgate, in *The Achievement of William Faulkner* (New York: Random House, 1966), p. 175.

16. McHaney also finds in her a likeness to Sherwood Anderson's second wife, Tennessee Mitchell. *William Faulkner's The Wild Palms,* pp. 11–12.

17. William Faulkner, *The Wild Palms* (New York: Random House, 1939). All subsequent page citations refer to this edition.

18. McHaney, *William Faulkner's The Wild Palms,* p. 72.

19. The phrase used by Malcolm Cowley in his review of Meta Wilde's book, *New York Times Book Review,* December 19, 1976, p. 12.

20. I have taken the liberty of restoring the letters excised by Faulkner's publishers from his typescript of the novel.

21. Millgate, *The Achievement of William Faulkner,* p. 187.

22. William Faulkner, *The Hamlet* (New York: Random House, 1940). All subsequent page citations refer to this edition.

23. John Cullen, *Old Times in the Faulkner Country* (Chapel Hill: University of North Carolina Press, 1961), p. 104.

24. His self-description quoted in Wilde, *A Loving Gentleman,* p. 293.

25. *Essays, Speeches, & Public Letters,* p. 198.

26. Millgate, for example, in *The Achievement of William Faulkner,* asserts that it is "carefully organized and wholly organic," and refutes Peter Swiggart's and Lawrance Thompson's assertion that it is not, pp. 185–86.

27. See Edward Stone, *A Certain Mobidness* (Carbondale: Southern Illinois University Press, 1969), pp. 100–120.

CHAPTER 9

1. *Essays, Speeches, & Public Letters,* pp. 117–18.

2. William Faulkner, *Go Down, Moses* (New York: Modern Library, 1955). All subsequent page citations refer to this edition.

3. Olga Vickery, *The Novels of William Faulkner* (Baton Rouge: Louisiana State University Press, 1964), p. 124.

4. Talk, James Faulkner, University of Mississippi, August, 1976.

5. *Faulkner at West Point,* p. 57.

CHAPTER 10

1. *Faulkner at Nagano,* p. 37.

2. Ibid., p. 68.

3. Ibid., pp. 13, 14.

4. Michael Millgate, *The Achievement of William Faulkner* (New York: Random House, 1966), p. 219.

5. William Faulkner, *Intruder in the Dust* (New York: Random House, 1948). All subsequent page citations refer to this edition.

6. Joseph Blotner, "Sole Owner and Proprietor," in *Faulkner: Fifty Years After The Marble Faun,* ed. George H. Wolfe (Tuscaloosa, Ala.: University of Alabama Press, 1976), p. 12.

7. Letter from Joan Williams, July, 1978.

8. See Noel Polk, "A Textual and Critical Study of William Faulkner's *Requiem for a Nun*" (Ph.D. diss., University of South Carolina, 1971), pp. 2–3.

9. As Hyatt Waggoner points out in *William Faulkner: From Jefferson to the World* (Lexington: University of Kentucky Press, 1966), p. 220.

10. For an opposing view see Polk, "A Study of *Requiem for a Nun*," p. 3. Polk asserts the novel is "nearly flawless."

11. William Faulkner, *Requiem for a Nun* (New York: Random House, 1951). All subsequent page citations refer to this edition.

12. As Polk points out, "A Study of *Requiem for a Nun*," p. 111 and *passim*.

13. Cleanth Brooks, *William Faulkner: The Yoknapatawpha County* (New Haven: Yale University Press, 1963), p. 146.

14. *Essays, Speeches, & Public letters,* pp. 119–20.

15. See, for example, Abner Keen Butterworth, "A Critical and Textual Study of William Faulkner's *A Fable*" (Ph.D. diss., University of South Carolina, 1970), p. 166. He asserts that it is "the richest of all Faulkner's novels in its complexities."

16. Waggoner, *William Faulkner,* p. 230.

17. William Faulkner, *A Fable* (New York: Random House, 1954). All subsequent page citations refer to this edition.

18. William Faulkner, "A Note on *A Fable*," *Mississippi Quarterly* 26 (1973): 417.

19. John Irwin, *Doubling and Incest / Repetition and Revenge* (Baltimore: Johns Hopkins University Press, 1975), p. 141.

20. Faulkner, "A Note on *A Fable*," p. 416.

21. *Faulkner at Nagano,* p. 130.

22. *Essays, Speeches, & Public Letters,* p. 181.

CHAPTER 11

1. William Faulkner, *The Town* (New York: Random House, 1957). All subsequent page citations refer to this edition.

2. William Faulkner, *The Mansion* (New York: Random House, 1959). All subsequent page citations refer to this edition.

CHAPTER 12

1. Victoria Black, Interview, August, 1976.
2. *Faulkner-Cowley File*, p. 141.
3. *Faulkner at West Point*, p. 78.
4. See William Faulkner, *Go Down, Moses* (New York: Modern Library, 1955), pp. 235–36.
5. *Faulkner at West Point*, p. 94.
6. William Styron, "As He Lay Dead, a Bitter Grief," *Life* 53 (July 20, 1962): 41.
7. *Faulkner at Nagano*, p. 88.
8. William Faulkner, *The Reivers* (New York: Random House, 1962). All subsequent page citations refer to this edition.
9. As Richard P. Adams points out in "The Apprenticeship of William Faulkner," *Tulane Studies in English* 12 (1962): 124.
10. See Simon Lesser, *Fiction and the Unconscious* (Chicago: University of Chicago Press, 1975), chap. 9.
11. Victoria Black, Interview, August, 1976; *Faulkner at West Point*, p. 68.
12. *William Faulkner of Oxford*, p. 187.
13. *Faulkner at West Point*, p. 115.

Index

261